None past the post

MANCHESTER
1824

Manchester University Press

None past the post

Britain at the polls, 2017

Edited by Nicholas Allen and John Bartle

Manchester University Press

Published by Manchester University Press
Altrincham Street, Manchester M1 7JA
www.manchesteruniversitypress.co.uk

British Library Cataloguing-in-Publication Data
A catalogue record for this book is available from the British Library

ISBN 978 1 5261 3006 8 paperback
ISBN 978 1 5261 3328 1 hardback

First published 2018

Typeset by Out of House Publishing
Printed in Great Britain
by CPI Group (UK) Ltd, Croydon, CR0 4YY

Dedicated to the memory of Anthony King

Contents

Illustrations

Figures

Tables

Contributors

NICHOLAS ALLEN is Reader in Politics at Royal Holloway, University of London

JOHN BARTLE is Professor of Government at the University of Essex

SARAH BIRCH is Professor of Political Science at King's College London

ROSIE CAMPBELL is Professor of Politics at Birkbeck, University of London

HAROLD D. CLARKE is Ashbel Smith Professor at the University of Texas at Dallas

JOHN CURTICE is Professor of Politics at the University of Strathclyde

MATTHEW GOODWIN is Professor of Politics at the University of Kent

ROBERT JOHNS is Professor of Politics at the University of Essex

MERYL KENNY is Lecturer in Gender and Politics at the University of Edinburgh

THOMAS QUINN is Senior Lecturer in Government at the University of Essex

PAUL WHITELEY is Professor of Government at the University of Essex

Preface

There was a time in the early 2000s when British general elections were remarkably predictable. Most people expected the then prime minister Tony Blair to call an election in the spring of 2001, and almost everyone expected a rerun of Labour's 1997 victory over the Conservatives. No one was surprised, therefore, when Blair called an election to coincide with the May 2001 local elections or when Labour secured another thumping win. (The only surprise was the one-month postponement of polling day because of an outbreak of foot-and-mouth disease.) Similarly, almost everyone thought Blair would call a general election in the spring of 2005, and almost everyone thought Labour would triumph for a third time. Once again, expectations were fulfilled.

Needless to say, such predictability led to two very dull contests. They were still hugely important, of course – general elections determine which party and group of politicians get to govern in Britain's power-hoarding political system. The two elections were also fascinating for students of British party politics. They confirmed the centre-left Labour Party's unprecedented 13-year period of electoral supremacy over the centre-right Conservative Party, prompted much discussion of ideological convergence, and saw the further fragmentation of Britain's party system and the erosion of the two major parties' electoral duopoly. Yet, their long-term significance could not disguise their short-term monotony. It was no coincidence that turnout in both 2001 and 2005 was historically low.

The 2010 general election broke the run of predictable contests. To be sure, it was a good bet that polling day would occur in May 2010 once Gordon Brown, Blair's successor as prime minister, decided not to call an election in the autumn of 2007. Also to be sure, most people expected Labour to be ejected from office and for the Conservatives to return to power under their new leader, David Cameron. Nevertheless, it was unclear whether or not the Tories would win an overall majority, and, if not, form a minority government by themselves or go into coalition with another party, most likely Nick Clegg's Liberal Democrats. The campaign was further enlivened by the novelty of televised leaders' debates. The outcome – a hung parliament and the formation of the Conservative–Liberal

Democrat coalition, Britain's first peacetime coalition government since before the Second World War – was itself hugely exciting.

The run of uncertainty and excitement continued in 2015. Once again, the date of the election took no one by surprise, this time because of the Fixed-term Parliaments Act 2011, a law introduced to underpin the coalition's survival. But while pre-election opinion polls suggested the likelihood of another hung parliament and coalition government, it was by no means clear if Cameron's Conservatives or Ed Miliband's Labour Party would emerge as the largest parliamentary party. The coalition's spending cuts – Britain's own variant of 'austerity' – were beginning to bite, and many voters had had enough of the fiscal retrenchment. The final result – a narrow House of Commons majority for the Tories and their first outright victory in a general election since 1992 – came as a shock. It also meant, of course, that the Conservatives would now have to make good on their promise to hold an in–out referendum on Britain's member-ship of the European Union (EU).

The twists and turns of the following two years – the period between the 2015 and 2017 general elections – made many yearn for the certainty of the early 2000s. During that time, voters took part in only the country's third ever national referendum and voted, by a narrow margin, in favour of Brexit and Britain's withdrawal from the EU. The same period also witnessed Cameron's resignation as prime minister, making him the first occupant of 10 Downing Street to quit as a result of calling and then losing a referendum, and his replace-ment by Theresa May, who became Britain's second female prime minister. It saw Labour's apparent abandonment of moderation and the election of Jeremy Corbyn, its most left-wing leader in generations. And it ended with a snap election that took everyone by surprise and an even more shocking result: the unexpected loss of the Conservatives' majority and May's return at the head of a minority Tory government.

Indeed, there was almost nothing about the 2017 general election that followed the expected script. Over the course of seven weeks, British democ-racy experienced probably the most dramatic reversal in political fortunes since 1945, when voters decided to eject Winston Churchill from Downing Street in favour of Clement Attlee. The campaign witnessed a remarkable implosion in Theresa May's standing, an equally remarkable improvement in Corbyn's and Labour's fortunes, the apparent collapse of the United Kingdom Independence Party (UKIP), the resurrection of the Scottish Tories as a significant electoral force, and the Liberal Democrats' failure to harness the support of the '48 per cent' who had voted against Brexit. By the end, and despite the formation of a minority government, British politics even seemed to be reverting to its trad-itional two-party character, but with the two main protagonists ideologically further apart than they had been since the 1980s.

This book tells the story of the unexpected 2017 general election and its equally unexpected outcome. *None past the post: Britain at the polls, 2017* is the tenth book in the *Britain at the Polls* series, which has been published after every general election since February 1974, with the exception of the 1987 and 2015 elections. Its main purpose, as with all previous volumes, is to provide general readers, professional political scientists and students alike with a series of interpretations of the election. It does not seek to provide a blow-by-blow account of the campaign, nor does it seek to provide a detailed survey-based account of voting behaviour. Instead, and in keeping with the spirit of the series, the volume offers readers a broader analysis of recent political, economic and social developments and assesses their impact on the election outcome. It also addresses broader questions about the state of the political parties and the party system in the wake of the election, and reflects on the future of British electoral and party politics.

British general elections are some of the best documented in the democratic world. In addition to *Britain at the Polls*, there are a number of other established book series, including *The Times Guides to the House of Commons*, which are standard works of reference, and the 'Nuffield Studies', formerly associated with David Butler and now with Philip Cowley and Dennis Kavanagh, which provide detailed accounts of the campaigns. Since 1979, these books have been supplemented by the *Political Communications* series, which tends to focus on aspects of the parties' campaign, communication and media strategies, and, since 1992, the *Britain Votes* series, which is based on a special issue of the journal *Parliamentary Affairs*. Lastly, but certainly by no means least, there are the outputs of the British Election Study, which provide sophisticated analyses of individual-level survey data.

Theresa May's decision to call an early election caught almost everyone unawares. Most election books take some planning, with the groundwork usually being laid over many months before polling day. The suddenness of the 2017 general election meant there was virtually no time to lay the usual groundwork. Other work had to be set aside, decisions swiftly taken, and outlines prepared. If that was not enough, the dramatic reversal in the political parties' fortunes obliged almost all editors and authors to question their prior assumptions and set aside their plans. Interpreting and explaining events that confirm existing theories and beliefs is relatively straightforward. Interpreting and explaining the unexpected requires additional reserves of intellectual energy. In the specific context of the 2017 election, it did not help that so many political scientists felt already overloaded with trying to make sense of the political turbulence of recent years.

Whereas some books try to offer a comprehensive treatment of every issue and aspect of an election, *Britain at the Polls* has traditionally taken a more selective approach, offering readers a smaller number of longer essays. The precise content of each volume has thus varied. The essays have always been selected on the basis of the key developments, the election outcome and what the editors judge to be important. Thus readers of the present volume will find a chapter on Scotland, since electoral developments north of the border have had a significant impact on the course of recent British politics and the outcome of the 2017 election, but no chapter on Wales, where developments have been far less impactful. We would like to have covered more, but limited space required us to make difficult choices.

In keeping with previous volumes, the first chapter focuses on the record of the governing party. In Chapter 1 Nicholas Allen tells the story of the Conservatives in power and how the Brexit referendum was intended but failed to end their bitter divisions arising from Britain's membership of the European Union. It also examines the records of the Cameron and May governments and how their two leaders both came to gamble their fortunes on the electorate – and lose. Thomas Quinn in Chapter 2 describes the eventful journey of the opposition Labour Party after 2015 and how its left wing finally took control of the leadership. It explores the resulting tumult and how Jeremy Corbyn defied expectations by not leading the party to a catastrophic defeat and instead dramatically increasing its vote share.

Chapters 3 and 4 then examine the mixed fortunes of two other national parties in British politics, the Liberal Democrats and UKIP. In Chapter 3, John Curtice examines how the Liberal Democrats under their new leader, Tim Farron, struggled to recover from their membership of the coalition and subsequent drubbing in 2015. The Brexit referendum was an enormous opportunity for the traditionally pro-European Liberal Democrats to reach out to all those who had voted Remain, and yet their message failed to have much of an impact. The party increased its presence at Westminster, thanks to the vagaries of the voting system, but experienced a decline in its vote share. In Chapter 4, Paul Whiteley, Matthew Goodwin and Harold Clarke chart the rise and fall of UKIP. For a party that only ever won two seats in the House of Commons, its impact on British politics has been enormous. The surge in its support after 2010 was a major factor in David Cameron's fateful decision to promise a referendum on Britain's membership of the EU. But this surge was also driven by other factors, including economic conditions and concerns about both immigration and national identity. With the Brexit vote won, UKIP's job was essentially done, and its decline created a space that both the Tories and Labour sought in different ways to fill.

Robert Johns in Chapter 5 narrows the geographic focus to explore developments in Scotland. The Scottish National Party (SNP) had been gaining support ever since the creation of a Scottish Parliament in 1999, and, off the back of the 2014 independence referendum, dramatically ended Labour's traditional predominance north of the border by winning 56 of Scotland's 59 Westminster seats in 2015. The surprise event of the 2017 election in Scotland was not so much that the SNP lost ground – it was almost inevitable given their previous high – but that the Scottish Tories beat Labour to take second place with 13 MPs. This shift in fortunes was partly down to the Conservatives' success in positioning themselves as the champions of Scottish unionism, and partly down to Scottish voters focusing on the implications of an anticipated Tory landslide in Westminster.

The next two chapters take a step back to consider two longer-term issues in British electoral politics. Meryl Kenny in Chapter 6 considers the place of women in UK politics, a topic last covered in a volume of *Britain at the Polls* in 1979, after Margaret Thatcher became the country's first female prime minister. Theresa May's election as Conservative leader and re-election as Britain's second female prime minister provides an opportune moment to consider both how far women have come since 1979 – and how far there is left to go in terms of achieving gender equality at Westminster. Sarah Birch in Chapter 7 examines the integrity of British electoral politics, an issue that was relatively salient in 2017 thanks, in part, to a number of party-funding scandals, but also thanks to the rise of 'fake news' and concerns about 'post-truth' politics. While British elections, including the 2017 general election, were comparatively clean, the rise of new technologies and changing behaviour around social media raise important questions about their long-term integrity.

In Chapter 8, John Bartle seeks to answer the all-important question of why the Conservatives lost their majority in 2017 – but still won the election. While the contest was supposed to be all about Brexit, voters were also concerned with more conventional issues, including the economy and the state of the public services. As a result of long-term forces and voters' responses to seven years of austerity and cuts to public services, the electorate had also shifted leftwards, making it more receptive to the arguments now being articulated by a Jeremy Corbyn-led Labour Party. The Tories also gambled on targeting former UKIP voters who had voted Leave in the referendum, thereby reducing their ability to appeal to Remain voters. These developments, coupled with a Conservative campaign that highlighted Theresa May's inability to conform to her own promise of providing 'strong and stable' leadership cost the party dear. In the last chapter, Rosie Campbell takes stock of the post-election landscape to consider the question of: what next? She describes how the Conservatives cobbled together a deal with Northern Ireland's Democratic Unionist Party (DUP) and considers the twin challenges posed by austerity and Brexit. She also examines the instability of the party system and the choices now facing each of the major parties.

Acknowledgements

We would like to thank Tony Mason and Rob Byron of Manchester University Press for their enthusiastic support for this volume. We would also like to thank Gail Welsh for her careful copy-editing of the text and Rebecca Willford for guiding the book through its production.

Above all, we would like to take this opportunity to acknowledge our immeasurable debt of gratitude, admiration and respect for the man to whom this book is dedicated. Most students of British politics will be aware that this is the first volume in the *Britain at the Polls* series to be published since the death of Anthony King, who passed away in January 2017. Tony had been associated with the series from the start, and had edited or co-edited the 1992, 1997, 2001 and 2005 volumes. A stylish writer and distinguished scholar, he always demanded the highest standards from contributors. He also possessed an uncanny ability to interpret an election and communicate his interpretation to a reading or watching audience. Like so many others, we learnt a very great deal about elections from Tony. We can only wonder at what he would have made of the remarkable 2017 general election.

1

Gambling with the electorate

The Conservatives in government

Nicholas Allen

On 23 June 2016, by a narrow majority of 51.9 per cent, Britain voted to leave the European Union (EU). The Brexit referendum was a defining juncture in British politics and the pivotal moment of the short 2015 parliament.[1] Just a year earlier, after five years of heading a coalition government, David Cameron had led the Conservatives to their first outright general election victory since 1992. With his authority as prime minister bolstered, he now sought to resolve an issue that had divided his party for over four decades: Britain's membership of the EU. The immediate point of contention had changed over the years, from the initial terms of entry, through the provisions of the Maastricht Treaty and potential adoption of the European single currency, to the ratification of the Lisbon Treaty; but the underlying issue had always been the question of national sovereignty.[2] Past battles had been fought between Europhiles and Eurosceptics. Now the Tories were split between 'soft' Eurosceptics, who wanted no further integration, and 'hard' Eurosceptics, who simply wanted out.[3] Calculating that a referendum was inevitable and that the best chance of remaining inside the EU would be for him to lead the debate, Cameron hoped that a popular vote would confirm British membership and silence the hard Eurosceptics. His gamble failed. The referendum cost him his job and precipitated Britain's exit from the EU. It also left his party as divided as ever, this time over the form Brexit should take.

It was left to Theresa May, Cameron's successor as Conservative leader and Britain's second female prime minister, to heal the party's divisions and lead the government in its hugely complex task of extricating Britain from the EU. It was with an eye on these goals that she called a snap election less than ten months after taking office. May hoped that going to the country early would increase her parliamentary majority and strengthen her position. Yet her gamble with the electorate, like Cameron's a year before, failed. The Conservatives lost their overall majority and May returned as a greatly diminished prime minister at the head of a divided minority government. This chapter tells the story of what went wrong.

Returning to power

The Conservatives' surprise victory in the 2015 general election was David Cameron's crowning achievement as party leader. First elected to the post in December 2005, he had inherited a party reeling from its third successive election defeat at the hands of Tony Blair and New Labour, riven by internal battles, especially over Britain's EU membership, and unable to move on from its past triumphs.[4] The party, moreover, had trouble appealing to voters outside of England: as Robert Johns details in Chapter 5, Scotland, in particular, was virtually a no-go area for Conservatives. Nationally, the Tories' reputation for economic competence was still tarnished by memories of 'Black Wednesday', the day in September 1992 when John Major's government had spent billions of pounds in a vain attempt to maintain the value of sterling and keep Britain's currency inside the European Exchange Rate Mechanism (ERM). And if all that was not enough, the Conservatives were distrusted to manage the National Health Service (NHS) and other public services, and were also widely perceived to be out of touch with modern Britain. In the wake of the 2005 defeat, an influential report by the party donor, Lord Ashcroft, suggested that around six-tenths of voters disagreed that the Tories shared their values, were competent and capable, or cared about ordinary people's problems.[5]

Cameron had been elected leader in part because he offered the Tories a clear sense of how to return to power. The Conservatives needed to detoxify their brand and show voters they resembled contemporary British society. They needed to 'modernise'. Once elected leader, Cameron swiftly abandoned Thatcherite policies on health and education, and vociferously asserted his commitment to the NHS, which would be 'safe' in his hands.[6] He embraced environmental issues and projected his social liberalism by, among other things, apologising for Section 28 of the 1988 Local Government Act, which the Tories had introduced and which prohibited the promotion of homosexuality. He downplayed talk of tax cuts and, before the 2007–08 financial crisis, promised to match Labour's spending plans for the NHS and schools. He also sought to increase diversity in the party and encouraged local constituency associations to select female and/or ethnic-minority candidates from an 'A List' of preferred individuals. He even told his party to 'stop banging on about Europe'.

Partly because of his 'modernisation' agenda, Cameron had always been more tolerated than loved by his party. He was tolerated because his strategy appeared (or promised) to be successful. He was unloved because many MPs and party members did not share his values. Some still wanted to bang on about Europe, as well as core issues like tax cuts, immigration and law and order. There was also widespread mistrust of Cameron's operating style and his exclusive inner circle, disparagingly referred to as 'the Notting Hill set'.

As the 2010 general election approached, many Tory MPs anticipated a return to power after 13 years in opposition. In the event, expectations were only partially met. The Conservatives won the popular vote (36.1 per cent) and the most MPs (306 out of 650) but fell short of an overall majority. Cameron chose to strike a deal with Nick Clegg's Liberal Democrats (who had won 23.0 per cent of the vote and 57 MPs) to form Britain's first post-war coalition government.[7] Coalition was better than opposition, but the outcome did little to change many Tories' ambivalence towards their leader.

Now prime minister, Cameron continued his modernising agenda. Barely a month after taking office, he made the remarkable step for a Conservative leader of apologising for the 1972 'Bloody Sunday' killings, when British soldiers opened fire on a group of marchers in Northern Ireland. He promoted his vision of the 'Big Society', a nebulous term that embraced various initiatives to empower communities and encourage civic voluntarism.[8] More concretely, he committed the government to spending at least 0.7 per cent of gross national income on international aid, a promise subsequently enshrined in law but one that was frequently attacked in some sections of the right-wing press. And in an act of great symbolic importance, he backed the right of same-sex couples in England and Wales to marry. When the House of Commons first voted on the matter in February 2013, Cameron joined a minority of Tory MPs, but a majority of all MPs, in supporting what became the Marriage (Same Sex Couples) Act.[9]

There were limits to Cameron's embrace of social liberalism. Responding to pressure from within his party and the electoral success of the United Kingdom Independence Party (UKIP), which was starting to gain support on the issue, the 2010 Tory manifesto had committed the party to reducing annual levels of net-migration to below 100,000.[10] It was not universally popular with his modernising allies, who recognised the economic arguments for immigration. So long as Britain remained inside the EU and accepted the principle of free movement of labour, it was also wholly unrealistic. Nevertheless, Cameron persisted with the commitment.

Contrary to some initial expectations, the coalition survived for a full five-year term.[11] Contrary to almost all expectations, the Conservatives went on to win the 2015 election with 36.8 per cent of the vote and 330 MPs, thereby securing an overall majority.[12] They had done so in apparent defiance of the 'costs of ruling', the tendency for governments to lose votes by virtue of being in power.[13] Their coalition partners were less fortunate. The Liberal Democrats' vote share collapsed to just 7.9 per cent, and the party was left with just eight MPs. There was more than a grain of truth to former Tory mayor of London Boris Johnson's description of Clegg as a 'prophylactic protection device for all the difficult things David Cameron has to do'.[14]

Cameron and the referendum: from hero to zero

David Cameron could now bask in the sunshine of being the first Conservative leader since John Major in April 1992 to win an overall majority in the House of Commons. There were, however, two clouds on the horizon. The first was the knowledge that Cameron would not go on to lead the party into the next election. In March 2015, he had said in a BBC television interview: 'Terms are like Shredded Wheat – two are wonderful but three might just be too many.'[15] The admission did not immediately make him a lame-duck prime minister, but it was only a matter of time before his colleagues' thoughts turned to the future and the succession and inevitable leadership contest.

The second and more ominous cloud was a promised referendum on Britain's membership of the EU, which the Conservative manifesto pledged to hold 'before the end of 2017'. Promising this referendum had been Cameron's option of last resort for resolving the deep divisions in his party and the deep hostility that many hard Eurosceptics felt towards European integration. He had previously sought to appease them by withdrawing the Tories from the mainstream centre-right grouping in the European Parliament and by enacting a 'sovereignty lock' that required any new EU treaty to be approved in a referendum. But nothing he could do would ever be enough to satisfy the hardest Eurosceptics, whose conviction had been emboldened by the aftermath of the 2007–08 financial crisis and the resulting Eurozone crisis, and by UKIP's growing popularity. As Paul Whiteley, Matthew Goodwin and Harold Clarke describe in Chapter 4, UKIP had finished second in the 2009 European Parliament elections and would go on to top the poll in the 2014 European elections. Many Tories saw them as a major threat to their grip on the centre-right of British politics. For some in the party, accommodating UKIP's agenda was vital for ensuring their future success.

Demand for an in–out referendum on Britain's membership of the EU had been brewing for some time. Back in October 2011, no fewer than 81 Tory MPs had defied the government and supported a House of Commons motion calling for such a vote. With support surging for UKIP and pressure building from within his own party, Cameron bowed to the hard Eurosceptics' demands in January 2013. Taking his cue from Harold Wilson, who had dealt with divisions in the Labour Party by 'renegotiating' Britain's relationship with the Common Market, as it was then known, and holding a referendum in 1975, Cameron now promised to do the same.[16] He would negotiate a new 'settlement' with the EU and then put Britain's membership to the people.

It was unclear whether Cameron thought he would have to fulfil his pledge; after all, most people had expected another hung parliament in 2015, and the prime minister might have thought the pledge would be sacrificed as part of a coalition deal. Whatever his private thoughts, however, the surprise outcome of the election meant that the Tories were compelled to keep their promise. UKIP had followed up their success in the 2014 European Parliament elections by winning 12.6 per cent of the vote in the general election, and it would have been politically impossible for Cameron not to honour his commitment.

Accordingly, the prime minister's attention now shifted to negotiating a new settlement with the EU.[17] In November that year he sent a letter to Donald Tusk, president of the European Council, setting out his four main goals: to reform economic governance in the EU by securing rights and protections for non-Eurozone members, like Britain; to improve competitiveness through targets for cutting EU regulations; to protect Britain's sovereignty by allowing it to opt out from the commitment to pursue 'ever closer union' and by empowering national parliaments; and to address immigration by revisiting the rules on free movement of people for future members and by restricting EU migrants' access to some benefits. Intense lobbying and negotiations followed, and a deal was struck with EU leaders in February 2016. Cameron could claim some concessions but there was no fundamental change in Britain's relationship with the EU, and there was certainly no dilution of the principle of free movement of labour.[18] Nevertheless, the prime minister now promised to campaign for continuing UK membership in a referendum to be held on 23 June. As he told MPs, 'I believe Britain will be stronger, safer and better off by remaining in a reformed European Union'.[19]

In many respects, the terms of Cameron's deal were irrelevant. The hard Eurosceptics in his party and in the press were never going to be satisfied. But the deal potentially mattered for its effect on senior figures less certain of their position. In the event, five cabinet-level ministers – Michael Gove, Chris Grayling, Priti Patel, Theresa Villiers and John Whittingdale – announced that they would campaign for Brexit. Like Harold Wilson before him, Cameron freed them from the constraints of collective responsibility on this one issue. The five ministers were joined by a further 133 Tory MPs, including former leader Iain Duncan Smith, who had resigned from the government in March 2016, and the outgoing mayor of London, Boris Johnson.[20] Gove's and Johnson's support for Brexit was particularly galling for Cameron. Gove had been one of his closest modernising allies and political friends. Johnson, too, had been part of Cameron's modernising project, if less of a friend, and was an extremely effective campaigner.

The referendum campaign formally began on 15 April. It was ill-tempered, unedifying and, for Labour MP Jo Cox, who was murdered in her constituency by a right-wing fanatic, lethal. The officially designated campaign group for the Remain side was the cross-party organisation 'Britain Stronger in Europe'; its pro-Brexit counterpart was the simply named 'Vote Leave'. In practice, the Remain campaign was dominated in strategy and personality by Cameron and his chancellor of the exchequer George Osborne. Partly because they were constrained by years of soft Eurosceptic rhetoric, and partly because it had seemingly produced the desired 'No' vote in the 2014 Scottish independence referendum, their strategy appealed to voters' risk-aversion by highlighting the dangers of leaving the EU. Theirs was not a campaign built on Europhile sentiment. In June, as the polls narrowed, Osborne even went so far as to threaten a punitive emergency budget should voters opt for Brexit. The threat backfired spectacularly.

The official Leave campaign, meanwhile, promised a future of economic growth outside of the EU and invited voters to 'take back control' of their country. Vote Leave was given credibility by the prominence of Gove and Johnson. It was further helped by at least three other factors. First, while the opposition Labour Party was ostensibly pro-European, its leader Jeremy Corbyn refused to share a platform with Cameron, and many Labour supporters were left unsure of the party's position. Second, UKIP's leader Nigel Farage headed what was effectively a parallel Leave campaign, Leave.EU, which focused less on economic issues and more on the sensitive issue of immigration. At one point, he was accused of inciting racial hatred after unveiling a poster that showed a line of mostly Syrian refugees with the slogan: 'Breaking point: The EU has failed us all.' Vote Leave immediately distanced itself from the stunt but simultaneously benefited from the sentiments it aroused. Finally, Vote Leave was in the position of offering the only positive message of the campaign thanks to the Remain side's risk-aversion strategy. Indeed, by emphasising the dangers of leaving the EU, Cameron and Osborne allowed themselves to be branded as proponents of 'Project Fear'.

The result of the referendum became clear in the early hours of Friday 24 June. Across the United Kingdom as a whole, a narrow majority of voters – 51.9 per cent – discounted the risks and accepted Vote Leave's invitation to take back control. Among the four nations that comprise the UK, England and Wales voted Leave – by 53.4 per cent and 52.5 per cent, respectively – whereas Scotland and Northern Ireland voted Remain – by 62.0 per cent and 55.8 per cent, respectively. Urban metropolitan areas were generally more likely to vote Remain than rural areas – nearly six-tenths of Londoners backed EU membership – while education was also a significant correlate of support.[21] Although Leave voters were motivated by a range of considerations, the outcome was, in many respects, a victory for those, especially white working-class men, who felt or were materially 'left behind' by the economic and social transformations associated with globalisation.[22]

Further evidence in support of this interpretation comes from individual-level survey data. The polling company Ipsos MORI, for instance, aggregated its various campaign polls to estimate which groups voted which way.[23] Table 1.1 draws on some of these estimates. It shows a slight gender gap – men (55 per cent) were more likely than women (49 per cent) to vote Leave – but an even bigger age gap: a quarter of 18–24-year-olds backed Leave whereas around two-thirds of pensioners did so. Older voters were also more likely to vote. Similarly, those in social-class grades C2 and DE were much more likely to back Leave, but less likely to vote, compared with AB and C1 voters. Education also mattered: 70 per cent of those without any qualifications voted for withdrawal, while nearly the same proportion of those with degree-level qualifications (and 80 per cent of current students, not shown) backed Remain. Non-white (BAME) voters were also far more likely to back Remain compared with white voters but much less likely to vote. Lastly, prior vote choice was also associated with voting behaviour in the referendum. Among those who said they voted Conservative in the 2015 general election, 59 per cent voted Leave.

Table 1.1 How Britain voted in the 2016 EU referendum, Ipsos MORI

	Voted Remain (%)	Voted Leave (%)	Turnout (%)
Gender			
Male	45	55	67
Female	51	49	64
Age			
18–24	75	25	53
25–34	60	40	54
35–44	55	45	64
45–54	44	56	69
55–64	39	61	76
65–74	34	66	78
75+	37	63	66
Social class			
AB	59	41	74
C1	52	48	68
C2	38	62	62
DE	36	64	57
Education			
No qualifications	30	70	64
Other qualifications	44	56	64
Degree or higher	68	32	71
Ethnicity			
White	46	54	68
BAME	69	31	47
2015 vote			
Conservative	41	59	82
Labour	64	36	73
Liberal Democrat	69	31	80
UKIP	1	99	86
Did not vote	42	58	30

Source: Ipsos MORI. Turnout is estimated among the total population.

In contrast, around two-thirds of Labour and Liberal Democrat voters backed Remain. The Leave campaign was also successful in appealing to those who had not voted in the 2015 general election, a further sign that it had enthused those who felt left behind.

It would be up to the parties and politicians to interpret the results and respond accordingly. What mattered for the very immediate future, however, was that Cameron had called and then lost the referendum. With little choice, he promptly resigned. It was an earlier and very different kind of departure from Downing Street than he had anticipated.

The Conservatives in power

David Cameron's resignation brought an end to a remarkable and at times turbulent premiership. From the start of his six years in office, he and his party had been committed to transforming large swathes of domestic policy. Conscious that their time in office would be limited, they had hit the ground running. At times Cameron's ministers resembled a group of middle-aged men and women in a hurry. There were many rushed proposals, frequent objections from Tory MPs, and numerous U-turns.[24] But despite the U-turns, the party changed much in a relatively short space of time.

Healthcare was one policy area that saw radical change. Cameron had once attacked New Labour's hyper-activism in this area and promised 'No more pointless reorganisations' of the NHS in England. 'Pointless' was the crucial qualifier, however, for the Tories would go on to introduce what David Nicholson, then chief executive of the NHS, described as a package of reforms so massive 'you could probably see it from space'.[25] The then health secretary, Andrew Lansley, was the driving force behind the reforms. Under his plans, healthcare would remain largely free at the point of delivery, but new commissioning rules and major restructuring sought to increase competition, productivity and patient choice. It was hoped the resulting efficiency savings would reconcile the spiralling cost of healthcare and the government's tight fiscal constraints. Opposition to the plans would later cost Lansley his job, but there was no altering course. There were further reforms and controversy after the 2015 election, when Jeremy Hunt, Lansley's successor as health secretary, pressed on with plans to 'deliver a truly 7-day NHS'. Junior doctors responded angrily to proposed changes to their contracts and took part in a series of strikes. For a public sceptical about the Tories' commitment to the public services, these were further reasons to doubt Cameron's insistence that the NHS was safe in his hands.

Education was another area to witness change. Driven by a Thatcherite wish to 'roll back the frontiers of the state', Cameron's first education secretary, Michael Gove, expanded New Labour's 'academies' programme by encouraging more state-funded schools to secede from local-authority control and by promoting the creation of similarly autonomous new 'free schools'. In 2015 Gove's successor, Nicky Morgan, even floated plans to force all schools in England to become academies. She was forced to back down after opposition from MPs and several Tory-controlled local authorities. Nevertheless, by the beginning of 2016, nearly two-thirds of secondary-school pupils and one-fifth of children in primary education were attending academies.[26]

Other reforms targeted universities. In 2010 the coalition raised the maximum cost of undergraduate tuition fees from £3,000 to £9,000, with students funding their degrees through a new system of loans. Further reforms followed after 2015, including a new Teaching Excellence Framework and the linking of universities' ability to raise fees to the quality of their teaching. These changes were partly about increasing competition, but they were also about raising standards to satisfy the demands of students who wanted more for taking on the burden of debt.

Welfare payments were a third area of domestic policy to witness significant change. The driving force in this instance was Iain Duncan Smith, a former Tory leader and now the secretary of state for work and pensions. His goals were to reduce inefficiencies in the system and to end the welfare-dependency culture by prompting more people to look for work. The centre-piece of his efforts was the Welfare Reform Act 2012, which introduced, among other things, a new Universal Credit scheme and a Personal Independence Payment benefit to encourage more disabled people to seek employment. The same legislation also introduced caps on the total amount of benefits that recipients could claim and a new under-occupancy penalty – the so-called 'bedroom tax' – for housing-benefit recipients who lived in social housing. For Duncan Smith, the measures were meant to advance the cause of social justice and save money for hard-working taxpayers. For critics, the measures were portrayed as a typical Tory assault on the most vulnerable in society. The left-wing film-maker Ken Loach would go on to scoop the Palme d'Or at the 2016 Cannes film festival for *I, Daniel Blake*, his polemical attack against the cuts.

Underpinning almost all domestic policy was the party's long-term economic plan, known colloquially as 'austerity'. The genesis of this plan lay in the financial crisis of 2007–08 and the subsequent spike in public sector net borrowing, the shortfall between what the government earns and what it spends (see Figure 1.1). All parties had accepted the need for some retrenchment in the wake of the crisis. Sensing that a policy of fiscal rectitude could re-establish the Tories' reputation for economic competence, Cameron and his then shadow chancellor George Osborne championed the need to cut the deficit more quickly than Labour were promising to do. Indeed, they promised to eliminate the structural deficit before 2015.

All governments have two basic ways of reducing budget deficits: they can increase revenue or reduce spending. Predictably, given voters' dislike of tax rises and the Tories' ideological commitment to tax cuts, the assault against the deficit would come primarily through savings in public expenditure and the fruits of hoped-for economic growth. Now in coalition, the Conservatives initially found the Liberal Democrats to be willing partners in this strategy. As the Coalition Agreement made clear, the two parties would 'significantly accelerate the reduction of the structural deficit over the course of a Parliament, with the main burden of deficit reduction borne by reduced spending rather than increased taxes'.[27] There would be no cuts to the NHS, schools and overseas-aid budgets, however; these areas would be protected, meaning that cuts elsewhere would be greater still.

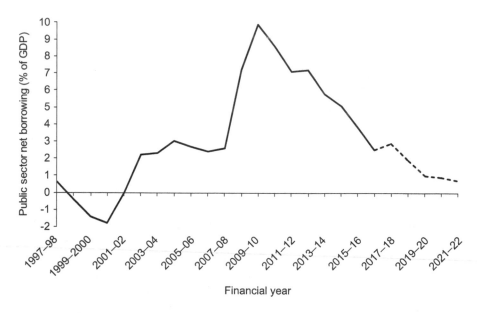

Figure 1.1 The UK deficit: public sector net borrowing as a percentage of GDP, 1997–2022
Source: Office for Budget Responsibility. The dashed line represents forecast figures.

Politics and economic realities required frequent tinkering with the deficit-reduction schedule. By 2013, a weaker-than-expected economy obliged Osborne, now chancellor, to move his initial commitment to eliminate the deficit to some point after 2015. After Labour claimed that cuts to public spending outlined in November 2014 would reduce the size of the state to pre-war levels, Osborne further amended his targets in his March 2015 budget so that spending would fall no lower than the level it had been under New Labour in 1999–2000.

Deficit reduction remained central to the party's agenda after the 2015 election, subject, again, to political and economic realities. Thus a manifesto pledge to cut public spending by 1 per cent per year in real terms was sweetened by promised increases in spending on the NHS of £8 billion per year. Osborne also relaxed the speed and scale of planned cuts in his July 2015 budget. He even found an extra £4 billion for the NHS in November 2015 after a spate of damaging stories about the plight of healthcare. In the wake of the Brexit referendum, Osborne abandoned altogether his goal of generating a budget surplus by the end of 2020.

Despite the practical flexibility in the Tories' financial plans, the cuts were real. As Figure 1.2 shows, government spending, especially as a proportion of gross domestic product (GDP), fell precipitously after 2010. The cuts affected most areas of public policy. In his October 2010 spending review, Osborne announced that government departments would, on average, suffer a 19 per

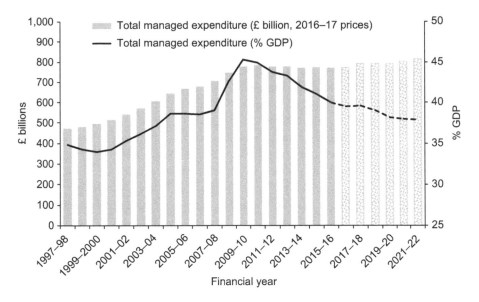

Figure 1.2 Government expenditure, 1997–2022

Source: Office for Budget Responsibility. The dashed line and patterned columns represent forecast figures.

cent cut in their budgets over four years. He also announced cuts to the police and welfare budgets and the loss of nearly half-a-million public sector jobs. In his June 2013 spending review, he announced further savings, with affected departments subjected to an average 8 per cent cut in their 2015–16 budgets and public sector pay rises capped at 1 per cent. In November 2015, after that year's election, Osborne outlined yet more cuts to departmental budgets, as well as further savings on welfare payments. Ahead of the 2017 election, the Office for Budget Responsibility predicted expenditure would fall to just under 38 per cent of GDP by 2021–22.

When first outlining his programme of cuts, Osborne had insisted that the burden would be shared by all in society: 'We are all in this together', he had said. Yet, protestations of solidarity were sometimes hard to reconcile with Osborne's decision to reduce the top rate of income tax from 50 to 45 per cent in 2012. They were also hard to reconcile with the Conservatives' commitment to protecting above-inflation increases in the state pension and certain universal benefits, like free bus passes, for all pensioners. It was easy for cynics to note that older voters were more likely to vote, and to vote Tory. It was also clear that the cuts hit many of those worst off in society the hardest. Local authorities saw their budgets slashed, which in turn affected those who relied on their services. By 2015, English local government had experienced cuts twice as great as those made to public spending as a whole.[28] Welfare-benefit recipients were also directly affected by the cuts, in particular by the introduction and subsequent extension of caps on the total amount of money households could claim.

Opposition to the cuts came from all quarters, from Labour and other parties, from trade unions, from charities, from left-leaning journalists and from some sections of the public. In October 2015, there was even a mini constitutional crisis when the House of Lords – which ordinarily respected the House of Commons' primacy in fiscal matters – voted to delay £4.4 billion worth of cuts to tax credits and to require the government to compensate those affected. In the event, an improving economic forecast enabled Osborne to perform a U-turn. There was even opposition to the cuts from within the Conservative Party. In 2016, Iain Duncan Smith, the author of earlier savings, quixotically resigned from the government in protest at cuts – subsequently shelved – to disability benefits.

Among the wider public, austerity was perceived to be a bitter but generally necessary medicine. Since June 2010, the polling organisation YouGov had regularly fielded a battery of questions about the way the government was cutting spending in order to reduce the deficit.[29] From 2011 through to 2017, most respondents consistently said the cuts were being done 'unfairly', but most respondents also consistently said the cuts were 'necessary'.

Whether or not austerity helped the wider economy is another matter. Since 2010, the Conservatives had presided over a period of relative economic calm but sluggish growth. GDP saw modest quarterly increases, as shown in Table 1.2, but productivity remained low, and it took until 2014 for overall levels of GDP to reach those achieved before the 2007–08 financial crisis. Inflation and interest rates remained low and stable – the latter had first been set at 0.5 per cent as long ago as March 2009 – while levels of unemployment, which had spiked after the crisis, began to fall. Yet, falling unemployment masked the precarious reality of work in the 'gig economy'. More and more people were nominally self-employed, personified by the growing number of Uber drivers. A growing proportion of workers were also employed on zero-hours contracts with no certainty of income. By the spring of 2017 nearly one million workers had such contracts.[30] The improving employment figures also masked a long-term decline in 'real wages', that is, the amount people earned after controlling for inflation. In many areas, younger workers in particular found themselves unable to get onto the property ladder. According to a 2016 report by the Trades Union Congress, British workers had seen their wages fall by 10.4 per cent on average since the financial crisis, a decline matched only by Greece among the members of the Organisation for Economic Cooperation and Development (OECD).[31]

For many economists, the sluggish growth was a direct consequence of Conservative austerity, particularly as it was implemented in the first years of the coalition.[32] Spending cuts, it was argued, had been too severe and had stifled the economic recovery. In turn, lower-than-expected tax receipts further undermined the Tories' attempts to cut the deficit. Nevertheless, what

Table 1.2 Objective economic indicators, 2010–17

		GDP quarterly growth (%)	Inflation (%)	Unemployment (%)	Interest rates (%)
2010	Q2	1.0	1.8	8.0	0.5
	Q3	0.6	1.5	7.9	0.5
	Q4	0.1	1.7	8.0	0.5
2011	Q1	0.6	2.5	8.0	0.5
	Q2	0.1	2.9	8.1	0.5
	Q3	0.4	3.2	8.5	0.5
	Q4	0.2	3.2	8.5	0.5
2012	Q1	0.4	3.5	8.4	0.5
	Q2	−0.1	2.7	8.2	0.5
	Q3	1.1	2.4	8.0	0.5
	Q4	−0.2	2.7	8.0	0.5
2013	Q1	0.6	2.8	8.0	0.5
	Q2	0.5	2.8	7.9	0.5
	Q3	0.8	2.9	7.8	0.5
	Q4	0.5	2.2	7.4	0.5
2014	Q1	0.8	1.8	6.9	0.5
	Q2	0.9	1.8	6.4	0.5
	Q3	0.8	1.5	6.1	0.5
	Q4	0.8	0.9	5.9	0.5
2015	Q1	0.3	−0.2	5.7	0.5
	Q2	0.5	−0.1	5.7	0.5
	Q3	0.3	−0.1	5.4	0.5
	Q4	0.7	−0.1	5.2	0.5
2016	Q1	0.2	0.3	5.2	0.5
	Q2	0.6	0.2	5.0	0.5
	Q3	0.5	0.6	4.9	0.25
	Q4	0.7	1.1	4.9	0.25
2017	Q1	0.3	2.0	4.7	0.25

Source: Office for National Statistics and Bank of England. Growth is shown as the percentage increase in gross domestic product (GDP) at market prices compared with the previous quarter. The inflation measure is the Consumer Price Index annual percentage change. Unemployment is shown as the ILO rate, including all adults (16+) to retirement age. Interest rates are the Bank of England's official rate at the end of each quarter.

mattered most politically was the framing of the economy. In this respect, Osborne had created a powerful narrative to justify the cuts.[33] The 2015 Conservative manifesto had heralded the success of the party's 'long-term economic plan' and Britain's 'strong economy'. Ahead of the Brexit referendum, Osborne had warned against jeopardising the economy and 'all the hard work' that the British people had done. Many voters were sympathetic to the narrative. As the 2017 general election approached, the Conservatives continued to enjoy a large lead over Labour as the best party to handle the economy in general (see Table 1.3 below).

Choosing Cameron's successor

In Britain's parliamentary system, the resignation or death of a prime minister midway through a parliament does not necessitate a general election. The choice of successor is solely a matter for the governing party. The Conservatives' rules for electing a leader – and thus David Cameron's successor as prime minister – had been used twice before, to elect Iain Duncan Smith in 2001 and Cameron himself in 2005. The rules entailed a two-stage process, one involving MPs, the other extending to all party members. In the first stage, all nominated candidates – who had to be MPs – took part in a series of eliminative ballots among fellow MPs until just two remained. In the second stage, party members voted on the top two candidates in a simple run-off. The rules thus made it possible for a leader to have the backing of the membership but not of a majority of MPs, a situation that could make their tenure a difficult one. The Tories had experienced exactly this problem after 2001: Duncan Smith had been the members' choice but never enjoyed the support of his parliamentary party. He was subsequently deposed by Tory MPs in 2003.

Although Cameron's resignation in the referendum's aftermath triggered the contest proper, likely candidates had been jostling for position ever since he had let slip his intention of serving for only two terms. There were initially three frontrunners to succeed him: Boris Johnson, George Osborne and Theresa May.[34] Johnson was an ambitious, bombastic and charismatic figure, who had served for two terms as London's mayor between 2008 and 2016. Ahead of the Brexit referendum, he had caused dismay in Downing Street by backing Leave. It was unclear whether his decision was prompted by genuine principle, or by an expedient wish to boost his future leadership prospects by making himself the champion of the Eurosceptic cause. The uncertainty continued after it later emerged that he had written two newspaper articles, one explaining why he opposed Brexit, which he did not publish, and one explaining why he supported Brexit, which he did. Osborne, the chancellor of the exchequer, was more cerebral. Close to Cameron, he was the party's chief strategist and a prominent Remainer. Yet, his personal stock had collapsed in the months before the leadership contest, thanks to several clumsy policy U-turns, his role in the pre-referendum EU re-negotiations and his threatened punitive emergency budget during the campaign.

The third likely candidate, May, was more enigmatic. She was a former party chairman who had promoted modernisation before Cameron and had warned the Tories of their reputation as 'the nasty party'. But she had developed a more authoritarian persona after becoming home secretary in 2010, especially in her pursuit of reducing immigration. She had opposed Brexit ahead of the referendum, but her contributions to the Remain campaign were infrequent and largely under the radar. She had also swiftly accepted the result. In the suspicious world of Conservative politics, cynics suggested hers was the optimal strategy for a would-be unifying leader.[35]

Of the three initial frontrunners, only May ended up contesting the leadership. Obsorne, recognising his lack of support, chose not to participate. Johnson was set to run but suddenly withdrew after his campaign manager, Michael Gove, now the justice secretary and a prominent Leaver, publicly denounced his suitability for high office. Four other MPs now joined May in the contest: Gove himself; Liam Fox, a former defence secretary and also a Leaver; Andrea Leadsom, a junior minister and yet another Leaver whose participation in the referendum campaign had given her a sudden boost of celebrity; and Stephen Crabb, the work and pensions secretary and a Remainer.

In the first round of voting among Tory MPs on 5 July, May emerged as the clear favourite, with 165 out of the 329 votes cast. Leadsom was second (66 votes), ahead of Gove (48 votes), Crabb (34 votes) and Fox (16 votes).[36] Fox was duly eliminated, and Crabb withdrew. May extended her lead in the second round of voting on 7 July, this time securing 199 votes or 60 per cent of the total. Leadsom (84 votes) comfortably beat Gove (46 votes) and secured her place in the membership ballot. May and Leadsom now prepared for a two-month campaign ahead of the final vote planned for 9 September. Within days, however, Leadsom's campaign had collapsed. Showing her inexperience in frontline politics, she contrasted her own experience of motherhood with May's childlessness in a newspaper interview and suggested that this gave her 'more of a stake' in the future. Uncomfortable with the backlash and aware of her very limited support among Tory MPs, she withdrew. May was duly declared the winner. She replaced Cameron as Tory leader on 11 July and as prime minister two days later.

Three factors help to explain May's victory. The first was simply the ineptitude of her rivals. Johnson's campaign was so disorganised it never got going, whereas Leadsom demonstrated her weaknesses at the first opportunity. The second factor was May's ability to appeal to all sides of her party. On Brexit, she had been a conditional Remainer but was now committed to implementing the result. She thereby succeeded in appealing to a number of Leavers, helped by the fact that her leadership campaign manager, the cabinet minister Chris Grayling, had actively campaigned for Brexit.[37] On social values, meanwhile, she was not associated with Cameron's modernising 'Notting Hill set' but had been a proto-moderniser and had supported same-sex marriage. She was a candidate for all tastes. Leadsom, in contrast, appealed to just one side on both these issues: she was an ardent Leaver, and she had opposed same-sex marriage.

The third factor was May's relative experience and perceived competence. It is often suggested that, when choosing leaders, MPs prioritise a candidate's acceptability to all parts of the party ahead of his or her wider electoral appeal, and the latter ahead of governmental competence.[38] The underlying logic is that party unity is a necessary condition for electoral victory, which in turn is a necessary condition for implementing policy. May was the unity candidate in 2016. But in the chaotic aftermath of the Brexit referendum, considerations of experience and effectiveness were amplified. The Leavers had pledged to 'take back control', but Cameron's resignation had seemingly left no one in control. In addition to being a candidate for all tastes, May was widely perceived to be the safest pair of hands among those in the race.[39]

May's easy win had two important consequences, both largely unnoticed at the time. The first was that she had not actually proven herself as a national campaigner. The curtailment of the leadership contest meant she was never subjected to the intense and sustained media scrutiny that prime ministers have to contend with, especially during general elections. The second was the absence of any serious debate about the party's ideological direction. May hinted at offering something different to Cameron's economic and social liberalism, as we shall see, but the absence of Osborne and Johnson from the contest meant there was no heavyweight rival to challenge her ideas. Instead, the contest was dominated by Brexit and the question of who could best deliver it. Questions about the party's broader programme and future played second fiddle.

May's vision and campaigning abilities were thus untested in the crucible of a leadership contest. Anyone wishing to know the risks of selecting a leader in such circumstances had only to look back at the effectively unchallenged coronation of Gordon Brown as Labour leader and Tony Blair's successor in 2007. Brown's easy win had masked profound deficiencies. His subsequent performance in office was an unhappy precedent.[40]

A different leader

While Theresa May was something of an enigma, it was already clear that she was a very different kind of politician to David Cameron. Nick Clegg, the former Liberal Democrat deputy prime minister, had called her the 'Ice Queen', while his colleague David Laws described her as being 'instinctively secretive and very rigid'.[41] She lacked a close circle of supporters in the parliamentary party, akin to the 'Notting Hill set', and made a virtue of her reluctance to go drinking in Westminster's bars. In terms of style, she was a less polished performer than her predecessor and seemed less comfortable in the public spotlight. She had no apparent wish to project a likable persona, and she certainly did not court the old or new media in the way Cameron had done. As she put it at the start of her leadership campaign: 'I know I'm not a showy politician. I don't tour the television studios.' If the line was a moment of self-awareness, it was also an intentional effort to contrast herself with her predecessor.

May was also less of a 'big tent politician' than Cameron. She seemed to relish in the former Tory chancellor Ken Clarke's description of her as a 'bloody difficult woman', not least because it drew parallels with Margaret Thatcher and suggested strong leadership.[42] Cameron's ability to work with others had been exemplified in his approach to working with the Liberal Democrats in coalition, but he had also been happy to appoint as ministers Tories who had different views to his own. Cameron, moreover, took a relaxed approach to leadership, trusting his ministers to get on with their briefs. May, in contrast, seemed set on making enemies when forming her government. She unceremoniously sacked George Osborne, reportedly telling him to 'get to know the party better', and appointed Philip Hammond as chancellor of the exchequer in his place. She also dismissed a number of other modernisers, most notably Michael Gove, with whom she had previously clashed. Lastly, the new prime minister transplanted into Downing Street the team that had surrounded her in the Home Office, including her former special advisers Nick Timothy and Fiona Hill, now elevated to co-chiefs of staff. In keeping with her reputation for being 'very closed, very controlling, very untrusting', she seemed intent on limiting her ministers' autonomy.[43] Policy reportedly had to go through her, and she was not averse to contradicting her ministers in public.

The new prime minister may not have changed her operating style, but she certainly talked of change more generally. During her leadership campaign and immediately after taking office, May had sketched out an agenda for re-orientating party policy and taking the Conservatives in a more interventionist direction. Accepting that Brexit meant Brexit, she sought to define Britain's departure from the EU as an opportunity to create a more meritocratic society. Drawing on her party's 'one-nation' traditions, and in a calculated bid to distance herself further from the Eton-educated and privately wealthy Cameron, she promised her government would not be driven 'by the interests of the privileged few' but would 'make Britain a country that works for everyone'.[44] Any future tax cuts would be aimed at those who were 'just managing', and there was a new emphasis on reaching out to working-class voters. She wanted employees to be represented on company boards, and she wanted shareholders' votes on corporate pay to be binding. She also promised a 'proper industrial strategy', something anathema to Thatcherites and their dogmatic worship of the free market, and further promised to invest in house building and infrastructure. She wanted to protect workers' rights, control immigration, and crack down on individuals and firms who avoided or evaded taxes. Such rhetoric not only helped to differentiate her from her predecessor; it also suggested a potentially canny strategy to win over working-class voters who felt left behind by globalisation and mainstream parties.

Dealing with Brexit

Brexit was the new prime minister's immediate concern, however. Vote Leave had won the referendum, and the Tories' 2015 manifesto had committed them to implementing the result. Thus even though Theresa May, a majority of ministers and most Tory MPs had backed Remain, they were bound, politic-ally if not legally, to deliver Brexit. Doing so would mean overcoming arguably the greatest challenge facing any British government since May 1940. For this reason, a very great deal of the party's attention was fixed on Brexit.

The first element of the challenge facing the government is easily stated: the Tories were utterly divided. On the surface, there were soothing platitudes about coming together. Beneath the surface it was very different. Looking back, a bad-tempered referendum campaign had featured many 'blue on blue' clashes, an apt military term for when armed forces fire on their own side. There was also lingering resentment over the way David Cameron had been forced from office. Looking forward, there was no consensus about what sort of Brexit the govern-ment should now pursue. Two broad positions emerged in the party and in the country: 'hard' Brexit and 'soft' Brexit. The former was generally occupied by the erstwhile Leavers and supported a clean break with the EU and the reasser-tion of sovereignty. In practice, this meant taking back control over borders and immigration, ceasing payments to the EU and removing Britain from the jurisdiction of the European Court of Justice (ECJ). The latter position was gen-erally occupied by former Remainers and prioritised economic considerations. In practice, this meant looking to maximise access to the EU single market, and perhaps maintaining membership of the EU's customs union. If, as a corollary, Britain remained subject to the ECJ and continued to pay into the EU budget, so be it: after all, nearly half of Britain's trade in goods and services was with the EU.

Responding to these divisions required a careful balancing of personnel and policy. May appointed mostly former Remainers to her new cabinet, including Philip Hammond as chancellor and Amber Rudd as home secretary, but she also appointed prominent Leavers to the key portfolios for delivering Brexit. These included Boris Johnson as foreign secretary, David Davis as the head of a new Department for Exiting the European Union, and Liam Fox in the new position of secretary of state for international trade.[45] May also frequently insisted that 'Brexit means Brexit' without saying what form it would take. It was only in January 2017 in a speech at London's Lancaster House that she finally came down in favour of a harder Brexit.[46] Expedience and principle were both factors. On the one hand, hard Eurosceptics among her MPs, and in the Tory press, were better organised than supporters of a softer Brexit. May probably thought they posed the greatest threat to her leadership and needed placating. On the other hand, the referendum was at least in part a vote for 'taking back control' and reclaiming sovereignty. May thought it ought to be respected.

The second element of the challenge facing May is less easily stated, since it comprised the many practical difficulties of actually delivering Brexit. For a start, the referendum was not self-executing. The government still had to notify the EU of its intention to leave under the provisions of Article 50 of the Lisbon Treaty, but the legislation allowing for the referendum had not authorised the government to do this. While May's government initially insisted that it could trigger Article 50 through prerogative powers, Gina Miller, a wealthy businesswoman, initiated a legal challenge to contest this. The Supreme Court subsequently ruled that the government had no such powers, and that acting in this way would be contrary to the constitutional principle of parliamentary sovereignty.[47] EU membership was underpinned by statute, specifically the European Communities Act 1972 Act, and only legislation could empower a government effectively to seek its repeal. The government duly introduced and secured passage of the European Union (Notification of Withdrawal) Act in March 2017. Within days May notified the EU of Britain's intention to leave the EU.

Another practical difficulty would be negotiating the terms of Britain's withdrawal from the EU. As with any divorce settlement, the shared assets and liabilities, such as outstanding budget and pension contributions, needed to be apportioned. As with any divorce negotiations, emotions would run high. On the EU side, attention came to focus on the terms of the financial settlement, the rights of EU citizens living in Britain and the Irish government's concern about its border with Northern Ireland. Such attention was reciprocated on the British side, to be sure, but the primary concern was always on negotiating a new long-term trading relationship with the EU. It was not clear if these two sets of negotiations would proceed concurrently, as the British government wanted, or consecutively, as the EU insisted. Timing mattered because, according to Article 50 of the Lisbon Treaty, the negotiations had to be completed within two years. If there was no deal after that time, Britain could find itself trading with the EU on less favourable terms stipulated by the World Trade Organization (WTO). Given the difficulties in negotiating and implementing a long-term deal in two years, it was generally thought that Britain would also need to negotiate some kind of transitional arrangement with the EU.

A third practical difficulty would be negotiating trade deals with other countries. Britain's non-EU trading relationships were presently defined through EU membership; they would need to be redefined. These negotiations would be essential for the long-term economic health of the country. Unfortunately, they could not formally begin until Britain had left the EU. Even more unfortunately, the government lacked the capacity and expertise to conduct so many trade deals.

The magnitude of the challenge confronting May was further compounded by a number of domestic policy considerations. The public services and especially the NHS, issues on which the Conservatives remained vulnerable, depended on EU workers. Any sudden exodus or restriction in future recruitment could create havoc. Moreover, EU membership affected many areas of public policy: agriculture and food, for example, were defined almost entirely by the EU's Common Agricultural and Common Fisheries Policies, while most commercial activity was governed by the regulations and rules that underpinned the single market. Britain would now need to make its own policies in these areas. The government would also need to ensure that Britain was not left effectively lawless upon withdrawal from the EU. The solution was a promised 'Great Repeal Bill', which, to the ears of hard Eurosceptics, echoed the promise of the 1832 Great Reform Act. The proposed legislation would transplant all EU law into British law at the moment of departure. It would then be up to successive governments gradually to replace EU-derived laws with new British laws.

A final element of the challenge confronting the government was also domestic: maintaining the integrity of the United Kingdom. If the referendum had split the Tory party, it had also split the country. Majorities in England and Wales had voted for Brexit; majorities in Scotland and Northern Ireland had voted against. In the case of Scotland, Brexit risked inflaming nationalist sentiment. The successful 'No' campaign during the 2014 independence referendum had argued that Scotland's continued membership of the EU rested on its remaining part of the United Kingdom. The Brexit referendum turned this argument on its head: now remaining part of the United Kingdom guaranteed Scotland's withdrawal from the EU. The Scottish National Party, which was in government in Holyrood and had won all but three of Scotland's 59 Westminster seats in 2015, could now turn Brexit into another anti-London grievance. Almost inevitably, Nicola Sturgeon, Scotland's first minister, suggested there should be a second independence referendum. In the case of Northern Ireland, Brexit threatened the peace process that had brought an end to 'the Troubles' that had blighted the region. The post-1998 power-sharing settlement was built, in part, on an open border between the North and the Republic, and this open border rested, in turn, on British and Irish membership of the EU. A hard border would hurt the Northern Irish economy and potentially fuel political instability.

A snap election

One of the many remarkable features of the 2017 general election was the fact that there was an election in 2017. There was certainly no constitutional requirement for one, in the sense that Theresa May needed a mandate of her own. Even more importantly, the Fixed-term Parliaments Act 2011 had set the date of the next election for 7 May 2020. Previously, British prime ministers had enjoyed the right to call an election at the time of their choosing – or, more accurately, British monarchs had enjoyed the right to dissolve Parliament at the time of their choosing on the advice of their prime ministers. The Fixed-term Parliaments Act, a consequence of the 2010 coalition negotiations, had removed this right. It allowed for an early election in only two circumstances: if at least two-thirds of all MPs approved a specific motion authorising one; or if the government lost a vote of confidence in the House of Commons and no new government was able to win a similar vote within two weeks.[48]

It was generally accepted that the deprivation of the prime minister's right to call an early election was a serious impediment to there being one.[49] May, moreover, did everything in her power to lower expectations of an early election. She had inherited a small but viable parliamentary majority of 16, and was absolutely clear from the outset that it would suffice. As she said when launching her leadership campaign in June 2016, 'there should be no general election until 2020'. Three months later, during an interview with the BBC's Andrew Marr, she was again emphatic: 'I'm not going to be calling a snap election.'[50] In March 2017, as speculation mounted and pressure grew within Conservative circles for an early poll, Downing Street sources were adamant that there would be no election.[51]

It is impossible to know how sincere May's pronouncements were, but her approach was probably wise. For the time being, and certainly until parliamentary authorisation had been secured to trigger Article 50, an early election would have been a huge distraction. Permitting speculation would also have been destabilising. Gordon Brown's reputation and standing as prime minister had never recovered after he had stoked rumours of an early election in the autumn of 2007, and then baulked at the idea.[52] May had to be emphatic if her denials were to be credible. She could always reconsider her options if or when circumstances changed.

If May's approach was wise, it was also effective. By April 2017, the conventional wisdom at Westminster, and around the cabinet table, was that there would be no early election.[53] As a result, there was complete surprise when, on the morning of 18 April, the prime minister suddenly announced that she would go to the country on 8 June. No less surprising was the ease with which the government secured the necessary two-thirds vote in the Commons on the following day. Only 13 MPs voted against the motion.[54] Support for the principle of fixed-term parliaments proved to be as narrow as it was shallow.

May's decision to seek an early election reflected several factors beyond the obvious point that all prime ministers like to win elections. The first and most important of these factors was her party's clear lead in the opinion polls, as shown

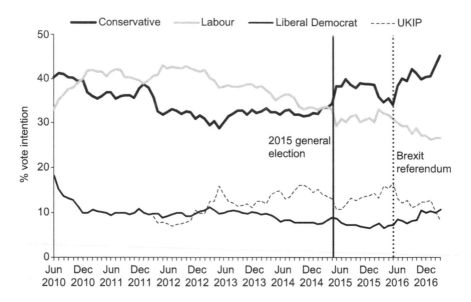

Figure 1.3 Voting intentions, 2010–17

Source: UK Polling Report. Average findings by calendar month of all polls published between the 2010 and 2017 general elections.

in Figure 1.3. Behind Labour for much of the 2010 parliament, the Tories had been ahead ever since the 2015 election (the first vertical line). Their advantage had only grown after the Brexit referendum (the second vertical line). Indeed, the Conservatives now also anticipated benefiting from the sudden collapse in UKIP's support that had occurred after the referendum vote, and which had continued apace into the New Year. UKIP's anti-European *raison d'être* had been largely fulfilled with the Brexit vote, and former Tories who had defected to them now seemed to be drifting back. The Liberal Democrats, meanwhile, continued to languish in the polls, notwithstanding their victory in the highly unusual Richmond Park by-election in December 2016 (see John Curtice in Chapter 3). There were, moreover, strong reasons for thinking the opinion polls were accurate. In February 2017, the Tories had won the Copeland constituency from Labour, the first time that a governing party had gained a seat in a by-election since 1982. The Tories now looked set to gain many more seats in an early election. Such an outcome would, in turn, bolster May's position and ability to pursue a hard Brexit. It would also provide a mandate for her wider agenda.

Underpinning the Tories' lead over Labour was their perceived relative competence in most areas of public policy. The polling company YouGov, for instance, had regularly asked respondents which party would best handle selected problems.[55] Table 1.3 reports the average responses to these questions from the beginning of January 2017 to mid-April, when May

Table 1.3 Conservative advantage as 'best party' on selected problems, January–April 2017

	% saying Conservatives	Conservative lead over Labour
Law and order	34	+21
Economy in general	35	+21
Britain's exit from the EU	29	+19
Asylum and immigration	26	+13
Taxation	28	+9
Unemployment	27	+5
Education and schools	25	+3
Housing	20	−3
National Health Service	21	−8

Source: YouGov. Respondents were presented with the following question: 'Here is a list of problems facing the country. Could you say for each of them which political party you think would handle the problem best?' The numbers are the averages of responses up to 13 April.

called the election. As can be seen, many more people consistently said the Conservatives were the best party to handle law and order, the economy, Brexit and immigration than said Labour. Only on housing and the NHS was Labour regarded as the better party to handle the problem, and only then by relatively small margins.

Also underpinning the Tories' lead over Labour, and a distinct factor in May's calculations, was her personal advantage over Jeremy Corbyn, the Labour leader. Corbyn had been elected to the post in September 2015 (see Thomas Quinn in Chapter 2). He was from the old left of the party, a prominent opponent of the 2003 Iraq War and the most rebellious MP when Labour had last been in government. Like the former Tory leader Iain Duncan Smith, Corbyn had been elected by party members against the wishes of most of his own MPs. In the wake of the Brexit referendum, nearly three-quarters of Labour MPs had expressed no confidence in his leadership in a non-binding vote. Corbyn refused to budge. He could count on the enthusiastic support of Labour trade unionists and members, especially its newer members. Most voters, however, shared the misgivings of Labour MPs. Between July 2016 and April 2017, whenever YouGov asked respondents who would make the best prime minister, nearly three times as many said May as said Corbyn (see Figure 1.4).[56] According to the current orthodoxy among students of voting behaviour, perceptions of leaders and their competence are thought to be especially important drivers of vote choice.[57] May's lead over Corbyn thus reinforced confidence in the Tories' lead in the opinion polls.

Another distinct factor in May's calculation was timing. In March 2017, as seen, the prime minister had formally notified the EU of Britain's intention to withdraw, triggering the two-year process set out in Article 50. There was now a small window before negotiations began. These were likely to fuel divisions in her party. The hard Eurosceptics on her backbenches were

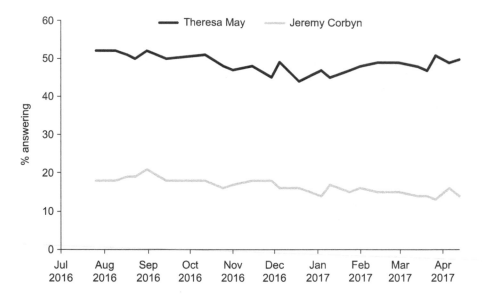

Figure 1.4 The 'best prime minister', July 2016–April 2017

Source: YouGov. Respondents were presented with the following question: 'Which of the following do you think would make the best Prime Minister?'

already organised and ready to create mischief if there was any backtracking on Brexit. The former Remainers in the party could become more organised and create mischief in a bid to soften the economic impact of Brexit. Moreover, the next election was scheduled for just a year after the conclusion of the process. There would be almost no time for the government to recover from any adverse deal. More generally, of course, the government would also almost certainly be buffeted by what former the prime minister, Harold Macmillan, called 'events, dear boy, events'. In April 2017, the prospects for victory thus looked good, and there was every chance they would not look so good by May 2020.

A final factor, which overlapped with the others, was the growing demand for an election from within the Tory party itself. In early March, former party leader William Hague publicly called for an early election.[58] Later that month, newspapers reported pressure from MPs for an early poll.[59] There was also pressure from within the cabinet. All these voices were responding to the same polling data. If May had any doubts, such demands would almost certainly have assuaged them.

Ultimately, however, it was May's call. The polls looked promising but much could change. Former prime ministers would have sympathised with her predicament. As Harold Wilson once observed, 'if things go wrong [a prime minister] is as likely to be criticised for missing a favourable tide as for plunging in too early'.[60] For May, the tide must have seemed highly favourable.

An eggs-in-one-basket campaign

Electioneering began the moment Theresa May announced her intention of going to the country. At first, everything appeared to go according to plan. The Tories re-signed Lynton Crosby, the Australian campaign strategist who had directed their successful 2015 campaign, and Jim Messina, his American counterpart who had helped the party target key voters in 2015. A fortnight after May's announcement, there was every reason to suppose that it had been an inspired call. On 4 May, separate and long-planned elections were held for 35 local authorities in England, six new regional combined-authority mayors, and all local councils in Scotland and Wales. The Conservatives did extremely well, gaining 500 councillors, taking control of 11 additional councils and winning the mayoral contests in the West Midlands, West of England, Cambridgeshire and Peterborough and the Tees Valley. With Labour haemorrhaging support, projections from the results suggested that the Tories were on course to win a parliamentary majority in excess of 100 MPs. May insisted that she was 'not taking anything for granted', but at this point almost everyone else was.

The Conservative strategy had three elements. First, it was about leadership. Capitalising on May's relative advantage over Jeremy Corbyn, the Tories relentlessly attacked the latter's suitability to be prime minister. They did so through carefully targeted messages and with the assistance of the partisan right-wing press. The party also shone a spotlight on May and her promise of 'strong and stable' leadership. Some of the campaign literature referred to 'Theresa May's candidates'.[61] Voters had to look carefully to see the words 'Conservative Party' on promotional material.

Second, the Tory campaign sought to focus on Brexit. More specifically, it sought to highlight May's ability, as a strong and stable leader, to deliver on her vision of a hard Brexit. As she put it when first calling the election, her vision was

> in the national interest, but the other political parties oppose it … I am not prepared to let them endanger the security of millions of working people across the country because what they are doing jeopardises the work we must do to prepare for Brexit at home and it weakens the Government's negotiating position in Europe.[62]

Third, the campaign was about targeting those parts of the country that had voted for Brexit, especially traditional Labour heartlands with high proportions of disenchanted 'left-behind' voters, where UKIP had previously fared well. The Conservatives would make good on May's earlier promise 'to make Britain a country that works for everyone'. In this spirit, the prime minister's first campaign speech was in Bolton in the North West of England, and she launched her party's manifesto in Halifax, Yorkshire. Campaigning in Tynemouth, she attacked Labour and Corbyn for deserting 'working-class people in towns and cities across Britain'.[63] Overall, she visited more Labour-held seats than

Table 1.4 The most important issues facing Britain today, 2010–17

	Cameron's first term (2010–15)	Cameron's second term (2015–16)	May's first term (2016–17)
Health	24	36	41
Europe	6	18	39
Immigration	30	49	39
Economy	49	26	24
Housing	9	16	18
Education	15	16	17
Unemployment	29	16	15
Poverty	12	16	14
Defence/foreign affairs	11	17	12
Crime	17	11	11
Low pay	8	11	8
Pensions	10	10	7

Source: Ipsos MORI. Respondents were presented with the following question: 'What would you say is the most important issue facing Britain today? What do you see as other important issues facing Britain today?'

Conservative constituencies, taking in places like Bridgend in the Welsh valleys where previous Conservative leaders had feared to tread.[64] It was a bold move that suggested the Tory leadership was more interested in taking the battle to Labour than in shoring up existing support.

The problem with the Tory strategy was that emphasising May's leadership and Brexit risked alienating former Remain supporters without any guarantee of taking votes from Labour. It was an eggs-in-one-basket campaign. The risks should have been apparent to anyone who looked at responses to polling companies' 'most important issue' questions. Table 1.4 draws on Ipsos MORI data and offers a sense of the policy agenda after 2015, how it changed after the referendum, and how it compared with David Cameron's first term as prime minister.[65] To be sure, Europe became more important during Cameron's brief second term, and especially after May assumed the premiership. But it was never voters' sole preoccupation. Instead, voters were increasingly concerned about health and housing, as well as about immigration, the economy and education. To a large extent, these concerns mirrored those about the effects of Conservative austerity. The other big story from Table 1.4 concerned the economy. Its importance between 2010 and 2015, and the party's advantage over Labour on this issue, was an important factor in the Tories' victory in the 2015 election.[66] The issue's diminished importance after 2015 would almost certainly reduce the net impact of the Tories' advantage on this issue.

Flaws in the Tory campaign became clear in the days after the local elections. A pledge to cap the prices charged by energy companies, a policy that had appeared in Labour's 2015 manifesto, was criticised by economic liberals. Almost everyone opposed to fox hunting expressed outrage at May's support for the practice and promise to allow a free vote among MPs to overturn the existing ban. The party's manifesto, meanwhile, outlined policies almost designed to alienate traditional, especially older, Conservative voters. These policies included the introduction of means-testing for the winter fuel allowance, the downgrading of the 'triple lock' that protected state pensions, and the abandonment of past pledges not to raise income tax or national insurance contributions. Back in March 2017, chancellor Philip Hammond had been forced to make an embarrassing U-turn after initially proposing to increase self-employed workers' national insurance contributions. The manifesto reminded voters of the episode and disappointed those who wanted lower taxes. Most damagingly of all, the manifesto proposed raising the threshold for free domiciliary social care – care received in people's own homes – by bringing it into line with the threshold for free residential care. The proposal, which had been little discussed by ministers, was labelled a 'dementia tax'. It elicited an apparent U-turn just days later. The costs of domiciliary care would now be capped. During one press conference, an exasperated May insisted that nothing had changed. No one believed her.

If events highlighted problems with the Conservatives' message, they also highlighted problems with the messenger. May's selling point was supposed to be her strong and stable leadership. Policy U-turns exploded such notions. More generally, the seven-week campaign accentuated May's apparent discomfort at being in the limelight. She seemed 'robotic' in interviews, while journalists expressed frustration at the excessive control over her media appearances. May's spell as home secretary and record on security also came under greater scrutiny after terror atrocities in Manchester, which claimed 22 lives, and London's Borough Market, which claimed eight. May was further criticised for failing to participate in either of the televised head-to-head leaders' debates planned for the election campaign. Her absence from the ITV debate was masked by Corbyn's decision also not to participate. Her absence from the subsequent BBC debate was underlined by his sudden decision to take part. Rarely had a prime minister appeared less able to provide strong and stable leadership. The Tories' decision to build their campaign around the figure of their leader without any proof that she actually was a good campaigner backfired enormously.

As Figure 1.5 illustrates, the Tories' poll lead began to slide from almost the moment the prime minister called the election. The slide had less to do with any sudden catastrophic implosion in Conservative vote intentions, although these did fall away especially after the bungled manifesto launch on 18 May, and more to do with a sharper and sustained increase in support for Labour. There was nothing the Tories could do to stop Labour gaining ground. Nevertheless, most commentators still expected the Tories to win an overall majority, even if not a landslide. When the broadcasters released their exit poll after voting

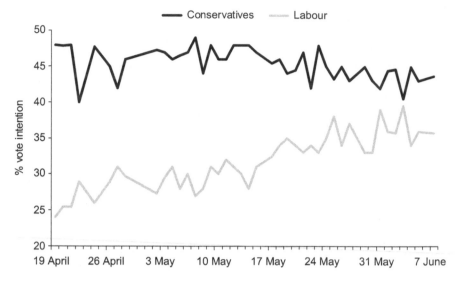

Figure 1.5 The 2017 campaign polls
Source: UK Polling Report.

closed on 8 June and predicted a hung parliament, the shock was palpable. In the event, the Conservatives increased their vote share to 42.3 per cent across the country and gained a dozen seats in Scotland, where they had their best showing in over three decades. However, they also lost more seats in England than they gained. They were still comfortably the largest party with 317 MPs in total, but May had squandered Cameron's surprise majority, not to mention her personal authority. Another prime minister's gamble had failed. Electoral lightning, it seemed, had struck twice.

Conclusion

Just as the outcome of the 2015 general election had been a welcome surprise for the Conservatives, so the outcome of the 2017 election was a nasty shock. The brief interlude of single-party majority government had been difficult, divisive and dominated by Britain's decision to leave the EU. For these reasons, the 2015 parliament was largely a coda to the preceding five-year period of coalition government. One important electoral consequence was that, while most Tory politicians were utterly fixated with Brexit ahead of the 2017 election, a majority of voters were not: they were also mindful of the Conservatives' broader legacy, especially austerity, student debt and the state of Britain's public services. The apparent mismatch between elite and mass preoccupations was almost certainly a factor in the weakness of the Tory campaign.

Viewed from a longer-term perspective, the 2015 parliament was also the culmination of a story arc in the Conservatives' history dating back to the 1960s, when Harold Macmillan first sought to join the Common Market, as the EU was then known. Since then, official party policy had been to seek or maintain membership. For some Tories, however, opposition to this policy had transcended all other considerations, including the party's unity and electoral appeal. At times the hard Eurospectics' zeal recalled that which had influenced some Conservatives' opposition to Irish home rule and to free trade at the start of the twentieth century. As a result of David Cameron's decision to call a referendum, they had fulfilled their ambition. But if the referendum caused a U-turn in the Conservatives' policy towards the EU, it did little to heal the party's divisions over Europe.

This last point brings us to a final irony of the 2015 parliament. Theresa May had called an early election in the hope of bolstering her authority and reuniting the party. The outcome was not an outright defeat for her in the same way the referendum had been for Cameron, but it only exacerbated the Tories' divisions. Internal tensions over Brexit and social values were now compounded by anger over the result and disagreement about how to proceed. They were further compounded by the almost inevitable speculation over who eventually would replace a gravely weakened May.

Notes

1   Among post-war parliaments, only those elected in 1950, 1964 and February 1974 were shorter. They were certainly less eventful.

2   Good general accounts of Britain's relationship with Europe are provided in Stephen George, *An Awkward Partner: Britain in the European Community*, 3rd edn (Oxford: Oxford University Press, 1998); Hugo Young, *This Blessed Plot: Britain and Europe from Churchill to Blair* (London: Macmillan, 1998); and David McKay, 'The reluctant European: Europe as an issue in British politics', in John Bartle and Anthony King (eds), *Britain at the Polls 2005* (Washington, DC.: CQ Press, 2006), pp. 78–96. For a specific account of how the issues has divided the Tories, see N.J. Crowson, *The Conservative Party and European Integration since 1945: At the Heart of Europe?* (London: Routledge, 2007).

3   The distinction between 'hard' and 'soft' Euroscepticism was developed by Aleks Szczerbiak and Paul Taggart. See, for instance, Paul Taggart and Aleks Szczerbiak, 'Contemporary Euroscepticism in the party systems of the European Union candidate states of Central and Eastern Europe', *European Journal of Political Research*, 43 (2004), 1–27. The difficulties of managing this divide is discussed in Philip Lynch and Richard Whitaker, 'Where there is discord, can they bring harmony? Managing intra-party dissent on European integration in the Conservative party', *British Journal of Politics and International Relations*, 15 (2013), 317–339.

4   The story of the Conservatives' recent travails is told in Tim Bale, *The Conservative Party: From Thatcher to Cameron* (Cambridge: Polity, 2010).

5   See Michael Ashcroft, *Smell the Coffee: A Wake-up Call for the Conservative Party* (London: Michael A. Ashcroft, 2005), pp. 94–97.

6   For an overview, see Tim Bale and Paul Webb, 'The Conservative party', in Nicholas Allen and John Bartle (eds), *Britain at the Polls 2010* (London: Sage, 2011), pp. 37–62.

7   See Philip Norton, 'The politics of coalition', in Nicholas Allen and John Bartle (eds), *Britain at the Polls 2010* (London: Sage, 2011), pp. 242–265. A lively journalistic account of the coalition's early years is provided by Matthew d'Ancona, *In It Together: The Inside Story of the Coalition Government* (London: Viking, 2013). For a more systematic scholarly take, see Robert Hazell and Ben Yong, *The Politics of Coalition: How the Conservative-Liberal Democrat Government Works* (Oxford: Hart Publishing, 2012). For an insider account, see David Laws, *Coalition: The Inside Story of the Conservative–Liberal Democrat Coalition Government* (London: Biteback, 2016).

8   See Ben Kisby, 'The Big Society: Power to the people?', *Political Quarterly*, 81 (2010), 484–491.

9   Roland Watson, 'Cameron reels from huge revolt on gay vote', *The Times*, 6 February 2013.

10 See Rebecca Partos and Tim Bale, 'Immigration and asylum policy under Cameron's Conservatives', *British Politics*, 10 (2015), 169–184.

11 See Tim Bale, 'The black widow effect: Why Britain's Conservative–Liberal Democrat coalition might have an unhappy ending', *Parliamentary Affairs*, 65 (2012), 323–337.

12 For a thorough evaluation of the pre-election polls, see Philip Cowley and Dennis Kavanagh, *The British General Election of 2015* (Basingstoke: Palgrave Macmillan, 2015), pp. 232–254.

13 See Peter Naanstead and Martin Paldam, 'The costs of ruling', in Han Dorussen and Michael Taylor (eds), *Economic Voting* (London: Routledge, 2002), pp. 17–44.

14 Matthew Holehouse, 'Boris: Clegg is the PM's prophylactic', *Daily Telegraph*, 8 January 2014.

15 Francis Elliott, 'Cameron fires start gun on Tory leadership race', *The Times*, 24 March 2015.

16 See Anthony King, *Britain Says Yes: The 1975 Referendum on the Common Market* (Washington, DC: American Enterprise Institute, 1977).

17 For accounts of both the negotiations and the subsequent referendum campaign, see Tim Shipman, *All Out War: The Full Story of How Brexit Sank Britain's Political Class* (London: HarperCollins, 2016) and Craig Oliver, *Unleashing Demons: The Inside Story of Brexit* (London: Hodder & Stoughton, 2016).

18 *The Economist*, 'David Cameron strikes a European Union deal', 20 February 2016.

19 House of Commons Debates, volume 606, 20 February 2016, col. 25.

20 BBC News, 'EU vote: Where the cabinet and other MPs stand', 22 June 2016, available at: www.bbc.co.uk/news/uk-politics-eu-referendum-35616946, last accessed 20 October 2017.

21 For an influential aggregate-level analysis, see Matthew Goodwin and Oliver Heath, 'The 2016 referendum, Brexit and the left behind: An aggregate-level analysis of the result', *Political Quarterly*, 87 (2016), 323–332.

22 See Robert Ford and Matthew Goodwin, *Revolt on the Right: Explaining Support for the Radical Right in Britain* (London: Routledge, 2014).

23 Ipsos MORI, 'How Britain voted in the 2016 EU referendum', available at: www.ipsos.com/ipsos-mori/en-uk/how-britain-voted-2016-eu-referendum, last accessed 20 October 2017.

24 By October 2012, one traditional Tory-leaning newspaper had tallied no fewer than 37 U-turns, from backtracking on the decision to levy tax on hot food, the so-called 'pasty tax', to a climb-down on the proposal to sell of England's publicly owned forests. See *Telegraph*, '37 coalition climbdowns, u-turns and row backs', 23 October 2012, available at: www.telegraph.co.uk/news/politics/9617519/37-coalition-climbdowns-u-turns-and-row-backs.html, last accessed 20 October 2017.

25 Quoted in *The Economist*, 'A very big headache', 7 April 2011.

26 Nerys Roberts, *FAQs: Academies and Free Schools*, Briefing Paper 07059 (London: House of Commons Library, 2017), p. 6.

27 HM Government, *The Coalition: Our Programme for Government* (London: Cabinet Office, 2010), p. 15.

28 Sally Gainsbury and Sarah Neville, 'Cash-strapped councils struggle to cope as Osborne's austerity cuts bite', *Financial Times*, 20 July 2015.

29 YouGov's tracker data on 'Government Cuts' can be found on its archive, available at: https://yougov.co.uk/publicopinion/archive, last accessed 20 October 2017.

30 Angela Monaghan, 'Record 910,000 UK workers on zero-hours contracts', *Guardian*, 3 March 2015.

31 Katie Allen and Larry Elliott, 'UK joins Greece at bottom of wage growth league', *Guardian*, 27 July 2016.

32 See, for example, William Keegan, *Mr Osborne's Economic Experiment: Austerity 1945–51 and 2010* (London: Searching Finance Ltd, 2014).

33 On the power of Osborne's narrative, see Andrew Gamble, 'Austerity as statecraft', *Parliamentary Affairs*, 68 (2015), 42–57.

34 See, for example, Michael Wilkinson, 'Public pick Boris but Tories want Osborne', *Daily Telegraph*, 2 October 2015.

35 See, for instance, Macer Hall, 'Tricksy Belle angles for the keys to Number 10', *Daily Express*, 30 April 2016.

36 Neil Johnston and Lucinda Maer, *Leadership Elections: Conservative Party*, Briefing Paper Number 01366 (London: House of Commons Library, 2016), p. 7.

37 According to one study, about one-third of MPs who supported Leave backed Theresa May. See David Jeffery, Tim Heppell, Richard Hayton and Andrew Crines, 'The Conservative party leadership election of 2016: An analysis of the voting motivations of Conservative parliamentarians', *Parliamentary Affairs*, 71 (2018), 263–82.

38 See Thomas Quinn, *Electing and Ejecting Party Leaders in Britain* (Basingstoke: Palgrave Macmillan, 2012).

39 Andy Coulson, 'Theresa, the safe pair of hands, versus Michael, the wit of Westminster', *Daily Telegraph*, 2 July 2016.

40 See Nicholas Allen, 'Labour's third term: A tale of two prime ministers', in Nicholas Allen and John Bartle (eds), *Britain at the Polls 2010* (London: Sage, 2011), pp. 1–36.

41 Laws, *Coalition*, pp. 273, 276.

42   Michael Savage, 'Candid on camera: Clarke derides leadership hopefuls', *The Times*, 6 July 2016.

43   Quoted in Elizabeth Day, 'Theresa May – what lies beyond the public image', *Observer*, 27 July 2014.

44   'Statement from the new Prime Minister Theresa May', 13 July 2016, available at: www.gov.uk/government/speeches/statement-from-the-new-prime-minister-theresa-may, last accessed 20 October 2017.

45   For more information on her initial raft of appointments, see Nicholas Allen, 'Brexit, butchery and Boris: Theresa May and her first cabinet', *Parliamentary Affairs*, 70 (2017), 633–644.

46   Francis Elliott, 'May to EU: give us fair deal or you'll be crushed', *The Times*, 18 January 2017.

47   Oliver Wright, 'Judges make history in Brexit blow to ministers', *The Times*, 25 January 2017.

48   See Philip Norton, 'The Fixed-term Parliaments Act and votes of confidence', *Parliamentary Affairs*, 69 (2016), 3–18.

49   For example of the conventional wisdom, see Martin Kettle, 'There will not be an early general election – and here's why', *Guardian*, 12 August 2016.

50   James Lyons, 'May vows: I won't call snap election', *Sunday Times*, 4 September 2016.

51   Francis Elliott, Sam Coates and Michael Savage, 'Call snap election to crush Labour, cabinet ministers tell May', *The Times*, 8 March 2017.

52   See Allen, 'Labour's third term', pp. 8–11.

53   Sam Coates, 'Cabinet kept in dark by PM over dramatic U-turn', *The Times*, 19 April 2017.

54   Francis Elliott, 'Less a debate, more a dress rehearsal for the campaign', *The Times*, 20 April 2017.

55   YouGov, 'Best Party on Issues (GB)', available at: https://d25d2506sfb94s.cloudfront.net/cumulus_uploads/document/dggt8iprh5/YG%20Trackers%20-%20Best%20Party%20On%20Issues_W.pdf, last accessed 20 October.

56   YouGov, 'Best Prime Minister (GB)', available at: https://d25d2506sfb94s.cloudfront.net/cumulus_uploads/document/qupp7yzyeg/YG%20Trackers%20-%20Best%20Prime%20Minister.pdf, last accessed 20 October 2017.

57   See Harold D. Clarke, David Sanders, Marianne Stewart and Paul Whiteley, *Performance Politics and the British Voter* (Cambridge: Cambridge University Press, 2009).

58   William Hague, 'The case for an early general election: Theresa May should be free to put her Brexit plans to the people', *Daily Telegraph*, 7 March 2017.

59   Oliver Wright, 'Labour put on election footing as Tories press for early poll', *The Times*, 20 March 2017.

60   Harold Wilson, *The Labour Government 1964–1970: A Personal Record* (London: Weidenfeld & Nicolson, 1971), p. 201.

61   Michael Deacon, 'Don't mention the Tories … but Team Theresa needs your support', *Daily Telegraph*, 9 May 2017.

62   'Statement from Downing Street', 18 April 2017, available at: http://press.conservatives.com/post/159746418610/theresa-may-statement-from-downing-street-18th, last accessed 20 October 2017.

63 Kate McCann, 'Labour MPs ditch Corbyn manifesto', *Daily Telegraph*, 12 May 2017.

64 Pamela Duncan and Glenn Swann, 'Analysis shows Theresa May spent half of campaign targeting Labour seats', *Guardian*, 8 June 2017.

65 Ipsos MORI 'Issues Index: 2007 onwards', available at: www.ipsos.com/ipsos-mori/en-uk/issues-index-2007-onwards, last accessed 20 October 2017.

66 See Harold D. Clarke, Peter Kellner, Marianne C. Stewart, Joe Twyman and Paul Whitely, *Austerity and Political Choice* (Basingstoke: Palgrave Macmillan, 2016).

2

Revolt on the left

Labour in opposition

Thomas Quinn

Between 2015 and 2017, Britain's opposition Labour Party underwent a strategic and organisational transformation paralleled only by the Blairite takeover of 1994 in its scope and significance. Under the leadership of Jeremy Corbyn, the party abandoned the last vestiges of centrism associated with 'New Labour' in favour of a radical-left platform and image.

Labour's socialist left wing had enjoyed periods of ascendancy in the past but never as fully as it did after 2015. The Bevanites – followers of Aneurin Bevan, the founder of the NHS – enjoyed support among activists in the 1950s, as did the Bennites – followers of Tony Benn, the technocrat-turned-radical leader of the Labour left – in the 1980s. But neither group captured the party leadership, and both faced strong opposition from Labour's affiliated trade unions. The rise of the left after 2015, in contrast, saw it take over the leadership, the shadow cabinet and virtually every other site of institutional power in the party bar the Parliamentary Labour Party (PLP). Corbyn and his small minority of supporters in the PLP joined in alliance with an impressive array of extra-parliamentary forces. These included the left-wing leader of Labour's largest union affiliate, Len McCluskey of Unite; a slim leftist majority on the party's ruling National Executive Committee (NEC); and, most importantly, a party membership that both expanded and changed out of all recognition. Between 2015 and 2017, Labour's membership surged from under 200,000 to over 500,000. Most of these new recruits were reckoned to be Corbyn loyalists and provided the bedrock of his support. The fact that most Labour MPs opposed Corbyn would have been terminal for the leader's authority in most other contexts, but amid the left-wing takeover, it would be recalcitrant MPs who feared for their positions. This transformation in Labour's factional and institutional balance of power was a consequence of its unexpected response to electoral defeat.

The race to succeed Miliband

Labour had gone into the 2015 general election hopeful of emerging as the largest party in a hung parliament. Instead, the Conservatives pulled off a surprise victory with a slim majority. Labour's leader, Ed Miliband, immediately announced his resignation and his deputy, Harriet Harman, took over as interim leader until a permanent leader was chosen. Miliband had been leader for five years since narrowly defeating his brother, David, in the 2010 Labour leadership contest. Ed was seen as the more left-leaning of the brothers and his victory was heralded as a triumph for Labour's soft-left faction. He had announced that the era of New Labour, associated with Tony Blair, was over, and the expectation was that he would return the party to a more recognisably social-democratic stance.[1]

Labour's policies certainly became more statist under Miliband, and the party was critical of the coalition government's austerity measures.[2] It was a stance that won favour with the Labour left, which became protective of Miliband in the face of Blairite criticism. However, as the 2015 general election approached, the New Labour counsels prevailed. Miliband was persuaded that Labour needed to improve its economic credibility, since it lagged behind the Conservatives in polls of which party would best manage the economy. Miliband and Ed Balls, his shadow chancellor, emphasised more strongly the need to reduce the budget deficit, which had been a major policy issue for five years, as discussed by Nicholas Allen in Chapter 1.[3] This pivot would be crucial in allowing the left to detach itself from Miliband and escape blame for the election defeat.

The outcome of the 2015 election was a shattering blow to Labour. Despite being in opposition and facing a Conservative Party associated with hard-nosed austerity, it suffered a net loss of seats, including an almost complete wipe-out in its Scottish heartlands, where the party lost 40 of its 41 seats to the Scottish National Party (SNP). Many on the left noted that the victorious SNP was more left-wing than Labour on austerity. They reasoned that, had Labour distinguished itself equally clearly from the Conservatives, it could have performed better by mobilising non-voters and bringing back those voters who had defected to the Greens.[4] Instead, they argued, Labour gave voters no positive reason to support it. This analysis stood in contrast to a more centrist argument that Labour lost in 2015 because its leader was weak and the party was not trusted on the economy or immigration, as well as a fear that a minority Labour government would rely on the SNP. Indeed, it was essentially this analysis that formed the basis of a subsequent report into the party's defeat by the former deputy leader, Margaret Beckett.[5]

This centrist narrative propelled early speculation about Miliband's successor.[6] Chuka Umunna, a leading centrist figure, quickly announced he would run, only to backtrack after press intrusion into his family life. Nevertheless, other frontline figures, such as Andy Burnham, the former health secretary, and Yvette Cooper, the former secretary of state for work and pensions, were regarded as strong alternatives, and both declared their candidacies. They were joined by Liz Kendall, a less experienced frontbencher, who emphasised the importance of electability and the need for fiscal discipline.[7]

Labour's radical left also decided to field a candidate. After seeking a standard-bearer, it opted for the 66-year-old veteran backbencher, Jeremy Corbyn. He had entered Parliament in 1983 and was strongly associated with that era's Bennite left. Corbyn had never served on the frontbench in government or opposition and was something of a gadfly to the PLP. He was a long-time campaigner on numerous causes and a supporter of unilateral nuclear disarmament. He was also the chair of the Stop the War Coalition, a left-wing organisation highly critical of British foreign policy and the 'war on terror'. Corbyn was not noted for any particular interest in economics but, insofar as one could tell, was statist. He flatly opposed austerity, whether it was advocated by Conservative or Labour politicians.[8] A natural rebel and outsider, he had voted against the Labour whip more than any other MP in his party between 1997 and 2010. By all conventional measures his was the least plausible candidacy of the four.

Corbyn's bid was not taken seriously by ideological centrists because the left was assumed to represent a small minority in the party. Indeed, he struggled to secure sufficient nominations from Labour MPs to enter the contest. The rules required that all candidates obtain nominations from 15 per cent of the PLP, which meant, in the wake of the election, 35 MPs. He managed to scrape to 36 nominations just minutes before the deadline after 14 MPs 'loaned' him their nominations in a bid to broaden the debate and, more cynically, to oblige the left to fall behind one of the more centrist candidates once Corbyn was eliminated. The other three candidates easily passed the threshold, Burnham securing 68 nominations, Cooper 59 and Kendall 41. Corbyn was regarded as an also-ran.[9]

One of Ed Miliband's key decisions as leader had been to change the system for choosing Labour leaders. Previously, they had been elected through a form of preferential voting by an electoral college comprising MPs/MEPs, party members and trade unionists, with each section carrying the same overall voting weight. This system was replaced in 2014 by one-member-one-vote: the practice of preferential voting was retained, but an MP's vote was now worth the same as that of a grassroots member. Trade unionists were still permitted to vote provided they signed up in time as 'affiliated supporters'. A new category of 'registered supporter' was also created. Members of the public could sign up to Labour's values and, on payment of a small fee (£3 in 2015), vote in leadership contests. Their votes carried the same weight as full party members and, indeed, Labour MPs.[10]

Corbyn's ascent

It quickly became apparent that something unusual was afoot during the campaign.[11] In contrast to his weak support among MPs, Corbyn secured the endorsements of the two largest unions, Unite and Unison. Both leaned to the left and were strongly anti-austerity. Both had been expected to support Burnham, the soft-left candidate. The party also experienced a post-election surge in individual membership, as people signed up in time to vote in the leadership contest. Corbyn's simple message, that Labour needed to abandon austerity and adopt a different foreign policy, was well-received by members attending the hustings. It was not until a YouGov poll of the selectorate in July, however, that the full enormity of what was happening became clear. Corbyn enjoyed a 17-point lead over his nearest rival in first preferences, under the alternative-vote system.[12]

Senior figures in the party began to fear that Corbyn could win. Tony Blair, the former party leader, suggested that anyone whose heart was with Corbyn should 'get a transplant'. There was criticism of those MPs who had nominated Corbyn despite not supporting him, with one Labour press columnist describing them as 'morons'.[13] There were also concerns that the membership surge was indicative of 'entryism', whereby members of other left-wing groups and parties were infiltrating Labour to vote for Corbyn.[14] Some even feared that Conservative supporters were joining Labour to foist on it an unelectable leader. The party scoured the social-media accounts of new members and registered supporters to root out those it suspected of being entryists. But while some applicants were denied votes, most new sign-ups simply appeared to be people enthused by Corbyn.

That enthusiasm – dubbed 'Corbynmania' – was evident among those who attended Corbyn's rallies. These events were packed, with people queuing on the streets to gain entry. Many of the participants were idealistic young people or had little previous interest in party politics. In a nod to Barack Obama's 2008 campaign slogan, they chanted: 'Jez we can!' They also spread his message through social media, where both the fervour and the momentum were maintained.[15]

It is worth pausing here to note the importance of the internet to the organisation of the new left. Online campaigning is now vital in all-member party ballots. In addition to websites established by the candidates, campaigns also have a heavy social-media presence, with Facebook pages and Twitter accounts. Supporters can easily find stories and campaign materials, and engage directly in debates. Online comment sections for newspapers such as the *Guardian* further enable supporters to develop arguments, exchange talking points, criticise opponents and, in some cases, engage in online attacks (as was alleged of some Corbyn supporters or 'Corbynistas').[16] Before the internet these individuals might have felt isolated and unable to organise. The new technology reduced the costs of organisation and mobilisation.

The Corbyn campaign's online presence was much greater than those of the other candidates and it gave him vital momentum. Given Corbyn's initial underdog status, many supporters might have assumed he had little chance of winning. Once it became apparent from online forums that he had lots of vocal support and success was within grasp, it motivated supporters to get

Table 2.1 The 2015 Labour leadership election

	Full members		Affiliated supporters		Registered supporters		Total	
	Votes	%	Votes	%	Votes	%	Votes	%
Corbyn	121,751	49.6	41,217	57.6	88,449	83.8	251,417	59.5
Burnham	55,698	22.7	18,604	26.0	6,160	5.8	80,462	19.0
Cooper	54,470	22.2	9,043	12.6	8,415	8.0	71,928	17.0
Kendall	13,601	5.5	2,682	3.7	2,574	2.4	18,857	4.5
Total	245,520	100.0	71,546	100.0	105,598	100.0	422,664	100.0

Source: Labour Party.

involved, including by joining up as full members or registered supporters. Information on how to do so was spread through social media by Corbyn's supporters, and his official campaign site included a link to the sign-up page on Labour's website. These activities no doubt helped to explain why Labour's membership surged from under 200,000 at the start of the contest to 300,000 by its close, with over 100,000 individuals signing up as registered supporters.

By the time the result was announced in September, there was a sense of inevitability about Corbyn's victory. He won the contest on the first count, taking almost 60 per cent of the vote, 40 points ahead of his nearest rival, Burnham (see Table 2.1). His victory was greatest among the registered supporters but he also came first among full members. According to YouGov's post-contest poll, Corbyn's support was stronger among new members than among longer-standing ones, although he enjoyed a comfortable plurality of the votes even among those who had joined the party before the 2010 election.[17] A Brownite former minister, Tom Watson, was elected deputy leader, replacing Harman, who had stepped down, but it was a small footnote to Corbyn's astonishing triumph.

Corbyn's victory and the rise of the left

The reasons for Corbyn's victory were down to a desire by leftists, both inside and outside the Labour Party, to reorient the party's strategy after the centrism of the Blair years. A poll of selectors during the contest suggested that those who intended to support the three 'moderate' candidates were motivated by such factors as opposing the Conservatives, winning the next election and uniting the party (see Table 2.2).[18] However, Corbyn's supporters did not see his campaign in terms of electability and party unity, but instead as an opportunity to pursue a radical policy agenda and break from New Labour. They wanted to turn Labour into a different type of party from the one it had been for 20 years. Some of

Table 2.2 Selectors' motives for supporting each candidate, 2015

S/he...	Supporters of...				
	All (%)	Burnham (%)	Cooper (%)	Kendall (%)	Corbyn (%)
Will be best opposition to Conservatives	53	52	70	59	43
Has best policies for country	49	29	35	36	70
Has best policies for people like me	36	30	23	21	49
Has best chance of winning in 2020	34	49	58	73	5
Is a break from New Labour and Blair years	33	12	7	8	65
Will unite party	22	48	34	10	5
Is a break from Ed Miliband's Labour Party	9	5	4	31	8

Source: YouGov. Respondents were asked: 'Which two or three, if any, of the following are the main reasons you will vote for [chosen candidate]? (Select up to three)'

Corbyn's supporters spoke of the need to 'purge' New Labour or to 'cleanse' the party. Such language was not representative of the debate but it caused unease among those who did not find themselves in agreement with the left's agenda.

The left's abandonment of Miliband and its insistence that he had ended up adopting Blairite policies was a crucial factor in Corbyn's victory. It enabled the left to avoid responsibility for the 2015 election defeat and to claim that only a radical anti-austerity policy could win. Its own populist narrative pinned the blame for austerity on the bankers and their Conservative political allies. This account had been expounded during the Miliband years by the major trade unions, as well as ginger groups such as the People's Assembly Against Austerity, which included Labour and trade-union figures, and some high-profile personalities such as the journalist Owen Jones. Their argument, which appealed to many on the left, was that poorer people should not be punished with cuts to their benefits and public services because of a recession caused by bankers, who were widely seen to have escaped responsibility for the financial crisis in 2007–08.[19]

Since returning to opposition in 2010, Labour had shifted to the left internally. Most of its largest union affiliates had elected left-leaning executives and leaders over the previous decade.[20] Unite was led by Len McCluskey, a strong voice against austerity and a key supporter of Corbyn. The left also had a thin majority on Labour's NEC, whose members are elected by the party's various stakeholders.[21]

The left's most important powerbase, however, was in Labour's resurgent individual membership, much of which shared the left's critique of austerity

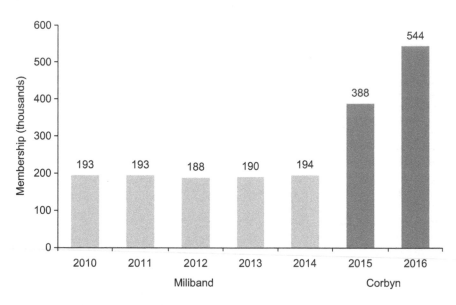

Figure 2.1 Labour Party membership under Miliband and Corbyn, 2010–16
Source: Labour Party Accounts 2011–16. Figures are for year ending 31 December.

and became receptive to its message after the 2015 election. Corbyn's victory in the ensuing leadership election resulted in another influx of members, many of whom could see a great opportunity for the left. By the end of 2015, Labour's membership had doubled over the previous 12 months. Before the general election in 2017 it stood at over 500,000 (see Figure 2.1). That was the highest it had been since the 1970s and it made Labour the largest centre-left party in Europe. Although members tended to be left-wing, the post-2015 members were not much more left-wing than the longer-standing members, although they were somewhat more liberal.[22] Corbyn's supporters, who were disproportionately new members, reported that they were less willing than others to trade off ideological principles for electability.[23]

For some on the left, this huge membership influx promised Labour's transformation into a social movement and the chance to mobilise people in communities.[24] It would involve an alliance with the trade unions and left-wing groups outside of the Labour Party to oppose the government. This vision of extra-parliamentary politics was made more appealing by the reality that Corbyn faced a hostile PLP.

One of the most important new grassroots actors in the Corbyn era was Momentum, an organisation that grew out of his leadership campaign. Founded by Jon Lansman, a veteran Bennite activist, Momentum would regularly be described as Corbyn's 'shock troops'. It sought to mobilise supporters in the membership and pressurise Labour MPs who criticised the leader. It focused on demands for intra-party democratisation to make Labour MPs more answerable to left-wing activists. Centrists feared it wanted to deselect those MPs who opposed Corbyn.[25]

One final factor in Corbyn's victory was his own personal qualities, which appealed to many selectors. Corbyn's strongest personal suit was his authenticity in an era of highly polished politicians. His campaign slogan was 'straight talking, honest politics' and it struck a chord. In television interviews, which were not his strongest format, he generally gave straightforward answers to questions and did not shy away from expressing his opinions on issues, even when they went against public opinion, such as on immigration. Unlike some political leaders on the radical left, Corbyn came across as neither suspiciously charismatic nor opportunistic. Instead, a survey of Labour members in 2016 found that 'principled' was the most commonly chosen term to describe Corbyn (by 76 per cent of respondents), followed by 'honest' (64 per cent) and 'shares my political outlook' (58 per cent).[26] He was also mild-mannered and did not engage in personal abuse, although his critics claimed that he turned a deaf ear to such abuse being meted out by his supporters. They routinely attacked Labour centrists as Blairites or 'Red Tories', and some were accused of levelling personal and sexist abuse at the BBC's political editor, Laura Kuenssberg, after taking exception to her reporting of Corbyn.[27] Overall, Corbyn's principles, his demeanour and possibly his age, together with defensiveness over his treatment by the media, combined to produce a groundswell of enthusiasm among the grassroots for their accidental leader. At times, it could appear close to a personality cult, albeit one that was not promoted by Corbyn himself, who occasionally looked bemused by it.

Corbyn versus the PLP

On becoming leader, Corbyn was immediately faced with a large-scale boycott of the shadow cabinet by senior MPs. Those refusing to serve included Cooper and Kendall, as well as figures from Miliband's shadow cabinet, such as Umunna and Rachel Reeves. Only Burnham among Corbyn's leadership rivals agreed to serve. Angela Eagle was hurriedly appointed shadow first secretary of state after media criticism of Corbyn's chaotic first reshuffle when it was pointed out that there were few women in the most senior positions. Corbyn also appointed a number of left-wingers, including long-serving MPs, John McDonnell, who became shadow chancellor, and Diane Abbott, who took the international-development portfolio. Both were controversial figures among centrists who saw them as divisive and prone to unhelpful comments. Each had sought the leadership in the past: McDonnell failed to secure sufficient nominations to run against Gordon Brown in 2007, while Abbott finished fifth out of five candidates in 2010.[28] To fill vacant positions, Corbyn invited several newly elected left-wing MPs into the shadow cabinet, including Rebecca Long-Bailey, Richard Burgon, Clive Lewis and Angela Rayner.[29]

Corbyn's first year in charge was beset by conflict with his own MPs. There were repeated rumours of centrists forming a breakaway party like the Social Democratic Party (SDP) in the 1980s, though the failure of that party weighed heavily on the minds of would-be defectors.[30] Corbyn's first major confrontation with recalcitrant MPs came three months into his leadership over the government's decision to authorise air strikes on the Islamic State (IS) terrorist group in Syria. Corbyn, a long-time critic of Western foreign policy and chair of the Stop the War Coalition until he became party leader, was strongly opposed to UK involvement in Syria's civil war. Labour's foreign-affairs spokesman, Hilary Benn, supported the proposed attacks. The disagreement was given a dramatic edge because Hilary was the son of Tony Benn, the figurehead of the Labour left in the 1980s and Corbyn's political hero. In a remarkable debate in the House of Commons, Labour's leader spoke against military action while the shadow foreign secretary argued in favour. Benn delivered an impassioned speech, imploring MPs to 'confront this evil' in the form of IS. His speech received a rare standing ovation in the Commons, and in the parliamentary vote, a total of 66 Labour MPs, including Benn, supported the government, which won the vote comfortably.[31]

The Syria vote shone a light on internal Labour dynamics. Corbyn and his advisers had been concerned about the blow to his authority if he imposed a three-line whip on opposing airstrikes only for large numbers of Labour MPs to ignore him. Frontbenchers who rebelled would be obliged to resign their posts. Accordingly, he offered his MPs a free vote, treating the issue as a question of morality and conscience rather than defence policy.[32] Critics pointed out that Labour was now refusing to take a collective position on one of the most important decisions a country can take: whether or not to engage in military action overseas.[33] Nevertheless, it served the internal purpose of avoiding a mass resignation of frontbenchers, including the high-profile Benn.

Such a large-scale revolt would have raised questions about the authority of other leaders but given Corbyn's lack of support among Labour MPs from the start of his leadership, the calculation was different. Significantly, a large majority of Labour MPs – 153 in total, including Corbyn – voted against airstrikes. Some did so because they genuinely opposed military action. Others felt under pressure from activists in their own constituencies: Momentum ran an energetic campaign to mobilise members to write to pro-intervention MPs. The party leadership also undertook a survey of members' views on Syria: 75 per cent opposed British participation in airstrikes.[34] This episode provided another example of how Corbyn used his authority among members in his battles with the PLP. Some activists raised the prospect of deselecting Labour MPs who defied Corbyn, an early warning shot across the bows of his critics.[35] Despite the rebellion, Corbyn could feel satisfied. He had shown his opponents to be on the wrong side of party opinion and a minority within the PLP.

Corbyn repeated the tactic of offering his MPs a free vote in July 2016 on the issue of renewing Britain's nuclear deterrent, Trident. As a lifelong unilateralist, there was never much doubt that Corbyn would oppose Trident, but party policy, as decided by the annual conference and strongly supported by key trade unions, had long been committed to retaining Britain's nuclear arsenal. Fully 140 Labour MPs voted with the government to renew Trident while only 47 opposed it.[36] But one of those was the leader of the opposition, voting against his own party's official policy. In any normal situation, this state of affairs would have led to the leader's resignation. In the extraordinary circumstances that prevailed, Corbyn simply carried on. Labour was now in the uncomfortable position of having a nuclear defence policy but a leader who had already said he would never push the nuclear button. He briefly suggested the nuclear warheads could be scrapped while the submarines that carried them would be retained, to safeguard jobs in the defence sector.[37] Critics accused him of rendering party policy redundant – and with it, a multi-billion-pound weapons system – should Labour win the next election.[38]

Policy differences between the leader and his PLP colleagues were only part of the problem. Many Labour MPs believed that Corbyn was simply not up to the job. That was evident in Corbyn's unsteady early performances at Prime Minister's Questions (PMQs), the weekly question-and-answer session under-taken by the prime minister in the House of Commons, and which became a regular source of lament for Labour MPs. Corbyn seemed ill-suited to forensic questioning or party point-scoring. He initially chose to read out questions he had invited the public to send in to him. With no follow-up questions, David Cameron was easily able to bat them away. Similarly, Corbyn struggled in the media, sometimes appearing to ramble in interviews. He was also criticised for his slightly unkempt appearance. Cameron once mocked Corbyn that his mother would expect the Labour leader to wear a 'proper suit' and do up his tie.[39]

To assist in dealing with the challenges of leadership, Corbyn appointed a team of advisers sympathetic to his aims. His leadership campaign had relied on former staffers of ex-London mayor, Ken Livingstone, a fellow left-winger.[40] As leader, Corbyn made further appointments that drew criticism. Most con-troversially, he chose the *Guardian* journalist, Seumas Milne, as his director of strategy and communications. Milne had a track-record of writing articles highly critical of Western foreign policy. His appointment dismayed Labour centrists.[41] Milne's job was to improve Corbyn's image and message, and deal with hostile press and sceptical broadcasting journalists. Few were impressed and the 'mainstream media' became a constant source of bitter complaint for Corbyn's grassroots supporters.

Corbyn's long history of left-wing activism led the Conservative-supporting media to depict him as an extremist. His past comments, in which he once described the terrorist groups, Hamas and Hezbollah, as 'friends', were held up as evidence, as was his willingness in the 1980s to talk to Sinn Féin politicians in the days before the Northern Irish peace process.[42] Pointed questions were raised over Corbyn's patriotism. These questions were magnified when the lifelong republican was filmed failing to sing the national anthem, 'God Save the Queen', at a service commemorating the Battle of Britain.[43] He was also criticised for saying, in the aftermath of a terrorist attack in Paris, that he was 'not happy' at the thought of the security services adopting a 'shoot-to-kill' policy.[44] Some in the party worried that such faux pas could encourage patriotic white working-class voters, Labour's historic support base, to turn to the United Kingdom Independence Party (UKIP; see Paul Whiteley, Matthew Goodwin and Harold Clarke in Chapter 3).

Corbyn also lacked party management skills at a time when such abilities were sorely needed. Reports surfaced in the press of how he tended to read statements to meetings of his shadow cabinet, but rarely engaged in the cut-and-thrust of debate. He would regularly find himself assailed by angry and despairing Labour MPs at weekly meetings of the PLP. He seemed heavily reliant on a tight-knit team of allies in his office, including Milne and his office manager, Karie Murphy, who had close links to McCluskey and Unite.[45]

Corbyn was accused by centrists of failing to control the abusive and sometimes threatening behaviour of some of his supporters. Labour MPs complained that Momentum was targeting their constituencies and raising the prospect of deselection. They felt that Corbyn did little to confront aggressive left-wing activists. Some Jewish Labour MPs reported receiving anti-Semitic abuse online and in person from party activists. When a Labour MP, Naz Shah, and the former London mayor, Ken Livingstone, were suspended following comments they had made, Corbyn asked Shami Chakrabarti, the former director of the civil-rights group, Liberty, to investigate anti-Semitism and racism in the party. Chakrabarti found some areas of concern but no evidence of a systematic problem in the party. Critics dismissed her report as a 'whitewash'. Their dismay was not eased when Corbyn later nominated Chakrabarti to the House of Lords and appointed her to his shadow cabinet.[46]

The depth of mistrust between Corbyn and the PLP was made clear in March 2016 with the leak of a 'loyalty list' of MPs drawn up by the leader's allies. MPs were classified from 'core', meaning the most supportive of Corbyn, through the slightly less supportive 'core positive', then 'neutral', 'core negative' and finally 'hostile'. Only 19 MPs, mainly on the left, were put in the 'core' group, while 36 were categorised as 'hostile', including Rosie Winterton, the chief whip, the individual responsible for maintaining discipline in the PLP.[47] Unsurprisingly, a feature of Corbyn's first year in charge was an endless stream of press speculation about leadership challenges or coups. The contrast between Corbyn's continued popularity and support among members and the PLP's low estimations of the party leader was without precedent.

Labour's electoral performance in Corbyn's first year was unspectacular but never bad enough to undermine his position. Indeed, some routine electoral victories were taken as triumphs, given the low expectations. Labour comfortably saw off a UKIP challenge in the Oldham West and Royton by-election in

December 2015, increasing its vote share by 7.3 points and assuaging fears that it was losing white working-class voters. In May 2016, Labour's candidate, Sadiq Khan, won the London mayoralty, taking the position back from the Conservatives after the former mayor, Boris Johnson, stood down. Khan, however, had taken care to distance himself from Corbyn during the contest. On the same day, Labour held two parliamentary seats, Ogmore and Sheffield Brightside and Hillsborough, in by-elections, with a third in Tooting following a month later. The party also largely maintained its position in the Welsh Assembly election that year but performed poorly in the elections to the Scottish Parliament at Holyrood, losing second place to the Conservatives. Overall, however, it was difficult for centrists in the PLP to depict Corbyn as an obvious electoral liability.

The most important disagreement between Corbyn and his MPs would come over the EU referendum of June 2016. Since the late 1980s, Labour had been strongly in favour of European integration and went into the referendum solidly behind the campaign to remain in the EU. Only about ten Labour MPs supported leaving the EU, while polls of party members found 90 per cent supported remaining.[48] Corbyn, like many on the party's Bennite left, had opposed the EU as an undemocratic capitalist club. He had voted for Britain to leave what was then the Common Market in the 1975 referendum, and spoken out against the 1992 Maastricht Treaty, which formally created the European Union. More recently, he had criticised the EU for treating Greece 'brutally' after the financial crisis.[49] On assuming the leadership he agreed to continue with Labour's pro-EU stance, partly as a means of reassuring centrist MPs. Critics, however, suspected that he retained his hostility to the EU. Some remained convinced that he had privately backed Leave.

During the referendum campaign, Corbyn's interventions were typically low-key and not always helpful to the Remain cause. Although Labour organised its own campaign to stay in the EU, headed by the former cabinet minister, Alan Johnson, there were complaints that it did not receive timely help from the national party.[50] Corbyn appeared only half-enthused by the campaign. When, during an appearance on a television comedy show, he was asked to rate his enthusiasm for remaining in the EU on a one-to-ten scale, he declared, 'seven, seven-and-a-half'.[51] When the referendum ended in victory for the Leave campaign, Corbyn was subjected to furious attacks from pro-EU Labour centrists that would quickly lead to an attempted coup.

The attempted coup

The referendum result was the cue for a full-blown assault on Corbyn's leadership by irate MPs. Newspaper reports claimed that Hilary Benn was seeking to mobilise shadow-cabinet members for a mass resignation if Corbyn himself would not go. Corbyn ultimately sacked Benn in a late-night phone call, prompting a stream of resignations from frontbenchers over the following days.[52] Twenty members of the shadow cabinet departed, leaving Corbyn to rely on veteran backbenchers, such as the 81-year-old Paul Flynn and the 74-year-old Kelvin Hopkins, to fill vacant positions and keep the party functioning as the official parliamentary opposition. Some shadow-cabinet members had to double-up and take on additional roles.

Corbyn's critics wanted to show his support within the wider PLP had also collapsed. They organised a confidence vote in the leader in which Labour MPs would vote in a secret ballot. Labour has no formal provisions for such votes and so the ballot had no constitutional status, but centrists hoped it would demonstrate the scale of opposition to Corbyn and quicken his departure. Five days after the referendum, Labour MPs voted by 172 votes to 40 to pass a motion of no confidence in their leader.[53]

The conventional wisdom is that when leaders lose the confidence of their senior colleagues, their authority evaporates and they are compelled to resign. However, there was nothing conventional about Corbyn's leadership. He had never enjoyed the confidence of most Labour MPs and so the effect of the resignations and the confidence vote was less than it would have been for other leaders. In a defiant snub to conventional wisdom, Corbyn dismissed the ballot as unconstitutional and repeatedly insisted that the party's members had given him a mandate only ten months earlier. He was urged on by Momentum, which organised demonstrations in support of his leadership.[54] Corbyn rejected attempts by his deputy, Tom Watson, to negotiate a settlement that would see him stand down.[55] As resignation was out of the question, the only constitutional means of removing him was through a formal leadership challenge.

Labour's rules stipulated that a challenger would need to be nominated by 20 per cent of the party's MPs and MEPs (the latter were now included in the calculation after a rule change), meaning that 51 signatures were required. The high threshold had been introduced in 1988 after Tony Benn had challenged Neil Kinnock, the incumbent leader. It was intended to prevent the radical left from mounting frivolous challenges each year, and to that end it succeeded.[56] However, circumstances were now different and with the PLP solidly against Corbyn, there was no trouble in surmounting the barrier.

Centrists thought it would be easier to defeat Corbyn by uniting round a single challenger, but two put themselves forward. One was Angela Eagle, who had just resigned her position as shadow first secretary of state. The other was Owen Smith, who had also just left the shadow cabinet as the party's spokesman on welfare and pensions. After a debate among Labour MPs and MEPs, the centrists chose Smith over Eagle, with the press reporting unofficial tallies of 90 nominations for Smith and 72 for Eagle.[57] Having settled on Smith as the challenger, 173 Labour MPs and MEPs formally nominated him.

Labour's constitution was ambiguous on whether incumbent leaders would require re-nominating in the event of a challenge. Corbyn would have struggled to secure the nominations of 51 Labour MPs and MEPs. A meeting of the

NEC split along factional lines to declare that Corbyn would not require re-nominating. However, after some NEC members had left the room, and in a blow to the left, the executive also decided that a 'freeze date' would be imposed on eligibility to vote in the leadership contest. Individuals who had joined the party after January 2016 would not have the right to vote, ruling out thousands of new members who were largely thought to be Corbyn supporters. They would be entitled to participate as registered supporters, but would be given only two days to sign up. The registration fee was also increased from £3 to £25, which centrists hoped would damage Corbyn's prospects.[58] These decisions were controversial and both the freeze date and the interpretation of the nomination rules were unsuccessfully challenged in court.

The leadership campaign took place over the summer. Corbyn was re-energised after his lacklustre referendum campaign and focused on the left-wing agenda he had set out the previous year. He also emphasised the illegitimacy of MPs attempting to overturn the members' choice of leader. Smith chose not to launch an attack on the left's policy agenda and acknowledged the need to oppose austerity. However, he rejected Corbyn's position on Trident. Smith also vowed to fight for a second Brexit referendum, attempting to tap into the Labour membership's pro-EU leanings. But his principal argument was the need for Labour to re-establish its credibility and electability in the eyes of voters.

Despite the attempted coup by MPs, Corbyn retained the loyalty of the membership and the unions. Polls of the selectorate predicted a comfortable Corbyn victory, and the September result was a foregone conclusion. Corbyn took almost 62 per cent of the half-a-million people who voted, including solid majorities among all classes of selectors, while Smith won 38 per cent (see Table 2.3).

The aggregate figures concealed divisions within the membership. YouGov's post-contest poll found that 63 per cent of full members who had joined the party before the 2015 general election had voted for Smith, and 37 per cent of the same had supported Corbyn. However, the longer-standing members constituted less than half of the total membership and barely a quarter of the entire selectorate. Corbyn won the support of 74 per cent of those members who had joined the party during the previous leadership election in 2015, and 83 per cent of those who had joined since he became leader.[59]

Table 2.3 The 2016 Labour leadership election

	Full members		Affiliated supporters		Registered supporters		Total	
	Votes	%	Votes	%	Votes	%	Votes	%
Corbyn	168,216	59.0	60,075	60.2	84,918	69.9	313,209	61.8
Smith	116,960	41.0	39,670	39.8	36,599	30.1	193,229	38.2
Total	285,176	100.0	99,745	100.0	121,517	100.0	506,438	100.0

Source: Labour Party.

Corbyn's re-election prompted a reshuffle of the shadow cabinet and the return to Labour's frontbench of some, though not all, of those who had resigned in June. Smith and Eagle remained on the backbenches and were joined by some of those figures who had stepped in temporarily, such as Flynn and Hopkins. Nia Griffith and John Healey, who had previously resigned, returned to the shadow cabinet. They were joined by Sir Keir Starmer, the former director of public prosecutions, who became shadow Brexit secretary. The most senior positions were filled by Corbyn loyalists: McDonnell remained as shadow chancellor, Emily Thornberry was the new shadow foreign secretary and Abbott became shadow home secretary, replacing Andy Burnham, who stood down to run for the Greater Manchester mayoralty. Meanwhile, amid some bitterness after the contest among Corbyn's supporters, the prospect of deselecting rebellious MPs was again raised by some, including by the Unite leader, McCluskey.[60]

One consequence of Corbyn's battles with the PLP was enormous churn on Labour's frontbench. Corbyn undertook four major reshuffles in his 21 months in charge before the 2017 election. In Ed Miliband's four-and-a-half years as Labour leader, there were only three major reshuffles. A total of 41 MPs had attended Miliband's shadow cabinets at various points from 2010 to 2015, representing less than one-sixth of Labour MPs. In contrast, 59 MPs, representing one-quarter of the PLP, passed through Corbyn's shadow cabinets before the 2017 election. Amid the turmoil, inexperienced left-wingers who were part of the 2015 intake of MPs quickly became senior figures in the shadow cabinet. The upshot was that Corbyn was eventually able to construct a shadow cabinet more in his own image.

From slump to surge

Corbyn's position was safe for the time being and PLP centrists made a conscious decision to avoid attacking him, for fear of being blamed for poor electoral performance. However, Corbyn seemed to be failing to cut through with voters. Cameron had resigned as prime minister in the wake of the referendum, as described by Nicholas Allen in Chapter 1, and his successor, Theresa May, was enjoying a honeymoon period with voters. A steady gap now opened up between Labour and the Conservatives in the polls. In Corbyn's first year as leader, Labour trailed the Conservatives by a few percentage points but after May became prime minister, the gap widened to anywhere between ten and 20 points. It was an extraordinary position for Labour after seven years in opposition. As Figure 2.2 shows, it compared unfavourably with some other recent opposition leaders' records. Only William Hague's Conservatives endured a weaker performance than Corbyn's Labour in the leader's first 18 months.[61] Corbyn's personal ratings were even worse, as Figure 2.3 shows. His net satisfaction ratings reached -41 after 18 months in charge.[62]

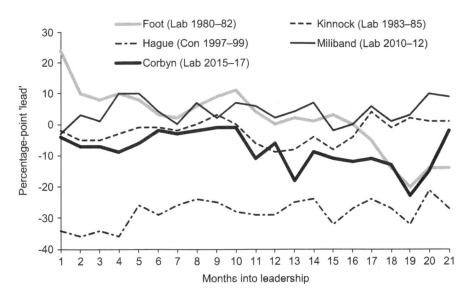

Figure 2.2 The opposition's lead over the governing party, new leaders' first 21 months

Source: Ipsos MORI. Respondents were asked: 'How would you vote if there were a general election tomorrow?' [Opposition % minus government party %] For Miliband, 'government' = Conservatives only. Final data point for Corbyn is the 2017 general election result. IDS is excluded because of mid-series change in polling methodology.

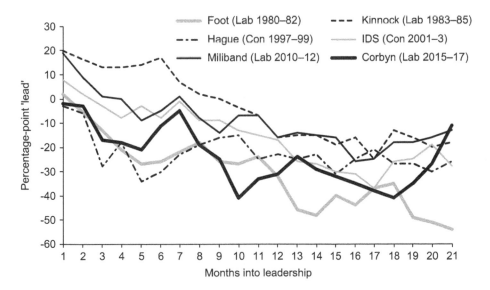

Figure 2.3 Net satisfaction ratings of selected leaders of the opposition in their first 21 months

Source: Ipsos MORI. Respondents were asked: 'Are you satisfied or dissatisfied with the way Mr ... is doing his job as Leader of the Opposition?' [Satisfied % minus Dissatisfied %]

Labour's electoral performances also deteriorated after the referendum. The party's nadir came during the Copeland by-election of February 2017, when it lost a seat it had held since the 1930s.[63] It was the first time the major opposition party had lost a seat in a by-election to a governing party since 1982. Labour did, however, hang on in Stoke Central, partly because of a split in the anti-Labour vote between the Conservatives and UKIP.[64] For concerned Labour MPs, here now was evidence that the party was losing the support of working-class voters put off by Corbyn's perceived softness on immigration and distaste for anything that smacked of patriotism. They began fearing a wipe-out in an early general election. Indeed, both by-elections had been caused by the resignation of centrist MPs, who had disagreed with Corbyn and found more appealing jobs outside of politics.

During the same month, Corbyn endured another parliamentary revolt, this time over the triggering of Article 50 of the Lisbon Treaty to start the UK's withdrawal from the EU. Corbyn imposed a three-line whip on his MPs to support the government's motion, stressing that Labour was respecting the referendum result. However, 52 Labour MPs defied Corbyn to vote against the motion, including Clive Lewis and two other shadow-cabinet members, who all resigned their posts.[65] The resignation of Lewis, previously an ardent supporter of Corbyn, was a sign of divisions on the left thrown up by the referendum.

Many on the left claimed that Labour's poor poll ratings were a consequence of the PLP's coup against Corbyn. Nevertheless, even some of the leader's key supporters started to worry about the party's predicament. In March 2017, McCluskey offered only lukewarm support and suggested that Corbyn's position would be looked at again in 15 months, assuming there was no early election.[66] The *Guardian* journalist, Owen Jones, a vocal proponent of Corbyn's left-wing agenda, called on the leader to resign for the good of the party.[67]

When Theresa May sought an early election, she needed Labour's support to secure the two-thirds parliamentary majority required by the 2011 Fixed-term Parliaments Act. To the dismay of some Labour MPs, Corbyn readily agreed and instructed the PLP to vote for an early poll in June. The MPs' concern was understandable as Labour's prospects looked bleak. They worsened in the first week of the campaign as a collapse in UKIP's support boosted the Conservatives and gave them poll leads of 20 points over Labour. The local elections of May 2017 were disastrous for Labour, with the loss of seven councils and over 380 seats. The party appeared to be heading for a catastrophic defeat in the general election.

What happened instead is the subject of analysis elsewhere in this volume. Suffice to say the most remarkable and consequential election campaign in recent British history saw Labour come back from the dead to register its biggest percentage vote increase since Attlee's party in 1945 and to deprive the Conservatives not only of a predicted landslide but of any majority at all. A big part of the explanation lies with the complacent and uninspiring campaign run by the governing party. But Labour's revival was also down to its own campaign, which was rich on policy detail and played to its leader's strengths as a campaigner.

Labour's manifesto

The turnaround in the party's fortunes began with the leak of Labour's draft manifesto a few days in advance of its official launch. Since Corbyn's elevation to the leadership, the party had engaged in little policy development, partly because of its preoccupation with internal divisions and partly because, with the next election expected in 2020, there was no need to rush through policies. The snap election changed all that and necessitated the rapid production of a manifesto.

The story emerging from leaked drafts of the manifesto proved to be accurate. The official 128-page document, entitled 'For the Many, Not the Few', attempted to be both radical and reassuring. Indeed, its title was taken from Clause IV of Labour's constitution as it had been rewritten by Tony Blair.[68] The manifesto was packed with populist policies that would appeal to both Labour activists and ordinary voters. These included: £30 billion in extra funding for the NHS; the abolition of university tuition fees; a higher minimum wage; the extension of free childcare; the reversal of some welfare cuts introduced by previous governments; building one million homes; and further infrastructure spending. The manifesto revived public ownership of industry as a Labour objective by promising to renationalise the railways, the energy and water companies, and Royal Mail. These pledges represented a major expansion in the size of the state and a firm rejection of austerity as had been advocated by the Conservatives and tolerated by Labour.

Labour's spending commitments were based on the proposition that the 'few' could pay for the 'many'. To this end, it advocated increasing taxes on the wealthy – those earning over £80,000 per year – and raising levels of corporation tax. The party claimed 95 per cent of people would not see their taxes increased. The highly respected Institute for Fiscal Studies suggested that the manifesto's £50 billion in extra taxes would increase the UK's annual tax burden to its highest level for 70 years, although it doubted that the corporation-tax rises would bring in as much as Labour hoped, as firms cut investment.[69]

In other respects, the manifesto eschewed populism for prudence. It promised to renew Trident and to maintain the UK's NATO commitment to spend 2 per cent of GDP on defence – although there was also a promised post-election strategic defence and security review. On Brexit, Labour affirmed its acceptance of the referendum result and of leaving the EU. A Labour government's negotiating aims would prioritise 'retaining the benefits of the single market and the customs union', but there was no commitment to maintain membership of either, as some centrists demanded. A 'meaningful vote' in Parliament was promised on the Brexit deal, but there was no offer of a second referendum. Labour also guaranteed the rights of EU citizens living in the UK to remain, whilst acknowledging that freedom of movement with the EU would end after Brexit. This strategic ambiguity, coupled with the decline in the Liberal Democrats and UKIP, enabled former Remainers and Leavers alike to return to Labour.

The leaked draft manifesto electrified Labour's campaign. The formal launch of the final version a few days later enabled the party to maximise media coverage of its proposals. Grassroots activists were ecstatic. Momentum emailed supporters, describing the document as 'brilliant'. The manifesto had been drawn up quickly because of the snap election and so there was little consultation with the wider party. Despite the demand of many activists for more intra-party democracy, the lack of consultation did not seem to matter: in this instance, the oligarchic process was less important than the outcome of a manifesto aligned with members' views.

The manifesto put clear red water between Labour and the Conservatives, and, especially with its commitment to renationalisation, represented a sea-change in the party's thinking compared with Blair's centrist manifestos. It arguably helped to energise thousands of party members, enabling Labour to exploit its biggest resource advantage over the Conservatives – its much larger and more active party membership. They were also evident at rallies and walkabouts by Corbyn, creating strong images of a positive and popular campaign. Many centrist MPs felt able to endorse the manifesto, although lots effectively chose to run their own local campaigns. Others who were sceptical of the manifesto's proposals kept their own counsel: with a left-wing leader and a left-wing manifesto, they were determined that the left should take the blame for Labour's expected defeat.

Yet Labour began to close the gap in the polls. Corbyn's satisfaction ratings started to improve too. At the beginning of the campaign, the ratings of both the party and the leader had resembled those of the Michael Foot years. In the event, Labour finished only two points behind the Conservatives on polling day, while Corbyn's personal standing was transformed (see Figures 2.2 and 2.3). It was an extraordinary turnaround and challenged the conventional wisdoms that campaigns do not matter and that public perceptions of leaders are fixed in their first six months.

Thanks to its own efforts, as well as a poor Tory campaign, Labour succeeded in scooping up most of the anti-Conservative vote. It won 262 seats, a net increase of 30, and prevented the Conservatives from securing a parliamentary majority. Even more remarkably, Labour's vote share increased by ten percentage points, the biggest increase by either of the two major parties since 1945. Although Labour would not form the next government, the result felt like a victory to many in the party. Set against the pre-campaign expectations, that was understandable.

Conclusion

The period between the 2015 and 2017 general elections was a remarkable one in Labour's history. It began with a left-wing insurgency that many commentators thought could not last and ended with the left completely in the ascendant. Jeremy Corbyn, whose position was under constant threat before polling day, became the first major-party leader since Neil Kinnock in 1987 not to come under pressure to resign after an election defeat.

The dominance of the left held open the possibility of a more functional relationship between Labour's parliamentary and extra-parliamentary wings. The election appeared to show that Corbyn was not the enormous liability that many Labour MPs assumed he was, perhaps reconciling them more to his leadership. The greater strength and assertiveness of the unions and the membership, especially Momentum, pointed towards a party in which the PLP's power had been checked. Threats of deselection and other rule changes had played their part. After the election, several centrist MPs signalled they were now prepared to serve in the shadow cabinet, and while Corbyn called only on Owen Smith to do so, there was at least the prospect of others being invited later.

Possible flashpoints remained, however. One was defence policy and Labour's position on Trident. Another was Brexit, where Labour adopted an ambiguous position during the election, accepting the referendum mandate but hinting at a softer policy than the Conservatives'. This strategy enabled Labour to keep together its electoral coalition of working-class voters in the Midlands and the North, who were more likely to have voted Leave, and Remain-supporting professionals, students and ethnic minorities in metropolitan areas, especially London. Labour thus held off UKIP in the North and the Liberal Democrats in more prosperous areas. But the advance of Brexit negotiations will require Labour to adopt a less ambiguous position and risk alienating some of its supporters and causing internal ructions.

Despite these potential threats to unity, Labour is a party transformed. It offers an object lesson in how political power can be transferred between intra-party factions in a short space of time. It demonstrated that there is nothing inevitable about the decline of party membership, even if it remains to be seen how well membership levels hold up.[70] It also showed that the PLP is not always ascendant. Labour aborted in the most comprehensive way Tony Blair's mission to remake the party in a centrist image. The question that will be answered in the coming years is whether this radical reinvention can make the credibility leap from a project of opposition to a genuine prospect for government.

Notes

1   Thomas Quinn, *Electing and Ejecting Party Leaders in Britain* (Basingstoke: Palgrave Macmillan, 2012), pp. 64–82.
2   Tim Bale, *Five Year Mission: The Labour Party under Ed Miliband* (Oxford: Oxford University Press, 2015).
3   Patrick Wintour and Rowena Mason, 'Election debate: Ed Miliband pressured to toughen stance against austerity', *Guardian*, 16 April 2017.

4   Diane Abbott, 'If you think Ed Miliband was too leftwing you weren't paying attention', *Guardian*, 13 May 2015.

5   Rowena Mason, 'Beckett report: Labour lost election over economy, immigration and benefits', *Guardian*, 14 January 2016.

6   For a more detailed account of Labour's leadership election in 2015, see Thomas Quinn, 'The British Labour party's leadership election of 2015', *British Journal of Politics and International Relations*, 18 (2016), 759–778.

7   Patrick Wintour and Nicholas Watt, 'The Corbyn earthquake – how Labour was shaken to its foundations', *Guardian*, 25 September 2015.

8   Peter Dorey and Andrew Denham, '"The longest suicide vote in history": The Labour Party leadership election of 2015', *British Politics*, 11 (2016), 259–282, p. 272.

9   Quinn, 'The British Labour party's leadership election of 2015', pp. 762–763.

10 The system was proposed in a report on Labour's links with its affiliated trade unions. See Ray Collins, *Building a One-Nation Labour Party: The Collins Review into Labour Party Reform* (London: Labour Party, 2014).

11 A detailed account of behind-the-scenes events in the Corbyn campaign can be found in Wintour and Watt, 'The Corbyn earthquake'.

12 YouGov, 'YouGov/The Times Labour leadership (day one)', 22 July 2015, available at: https://d25d2506sfb94s.cloudfront.net/cumulus_uploads/document/ul79cmahd5/LabourLeadership_150721_day_one_W.pdf, last accessed 20 October 2017.

13 Wintour and Watt, 'The Corbyn earthquake'.

14 Tim Ross, 'Jeremy Corbyn backers plunge Labour into new "entryism" row', *Daily Telegraph*, 23 August 2015.

15 Toby Helm and Daniel Boffey, 'Jez we did: How Labour rank outsider Jeremy Corbyn swept to victory', *Observer*, 13 September 2015.

16 Quinn, 'The British Labour party's leadership election of 2015', p. 764.

17 YouGov, 'YouGov Labour leadership', 15 September 2015, available at: https://d25d2506sfb94s.cloudfront.net/cumulus_uploads/document/h4c7aqabu7/LabourSelectorate_TopLine_W.pdf, last accessed 20 October 2017.

18 YouGov, 'YouGov/The Times Labour leadership (day two)', 23 July 2015, available at: https://d25d2506sfb94s.cloudfront.net/cumulus_uploads/document/94enqtd1fz/LabourLeadership_150721_day_two_W.pdf, last accessed 20 October 2017.

19 Owen Jones, 'How the People's Assembly can challenge our suffocating political consensus – and why it's vital that we do', *Independent*, 24 March 2013. On the financial crash, see Michael Moran, Sukhdev Johal and Karel Williams, 'The financial crisis and its consequences', in Nicholas Allen and John Bartle (eds), *Britain at the Polls 2010* (London: Sage, 2011), pp. 89–119.

20 Thomas Quinn, 'New Labour and the trade unions in Britain', *Journal of Elections, Public Opinion and Parties*, 20 (2010), 357–380.

21 Stephen Bush, 'Jeremy Corbyn secures his first big victory of Labour party conference', *The Staggers* (*New Statesman* blog), 29 September 2015, available at: www.newstatesman.com/politics/elections/2015/09/jeremy-corbyn-secures-his-first-big-victory-labour-party-conference, last accessed 20 October 2017.

22 This finding was from an ESRC-funded survey, organised by Tim Bale, Paul Webb and Monica Poletti. Their data is available at: https://esrcpartymembersproject.org/.

23 Peter Kellner, 'Corbynistas stay loyal, but few others share his views', *YouGov*, 24 November 2015, available at: https://yougov.co.uk/news/2015/11/24/analysis-corbynistas-stay-loyal-few-others-share-h/, last accessed 20 October 2017.

24 For a critique, see Paul Thompson, 'Corbynism isn't a social movement and Labour shouldn't be one', *The Staggers* (*New Statesman* blog), 24 August 2016, available at: www.newstatesman.com/politics/uk/2016/08/corbynism-isn-t-social-movement-and-labour-shouldn-t-be-one, last accessed 20 October 2017.

25 Ewen MacAskill, 'At home with Momentum: The rise of "Corbyn's shock troops"', *Guardian*, 8 March 2016.

26 YouGov, 'YouGov/The Times Labour selectorate', 30 August 2016, available at: https://d25d2506sfb94s.cloudfront.net/cumulus_uploads/document/0cpa7iw5l7/TimesResults_160830_LabourSelectorate.pdf, last accessed 20 October 2017.

27 Andrew Grice and Oliver Wright, 'Jeremy Corbyn supporters accused of launching SNP-style cyber attacks on Labour leader rivals', *Independent*, 12 August 2015.

28 See Quinn, *Electing and Ejecting Party Leaders in Britain*, pp. 64–72.

29 Patrick Wintour, 'Corbyn gathers his shadow cabinet and makes first moves to rally MPs', *Guardian*, 14 September 2015.

30 Ivor Crewe and Anthony King, *SDP: The Birth, Life and Death of the Social Democratic Party* (Oxford: Oxford University Press, 1995).

31 Patrick Wintour, 'Britain carries out first Syria airstrikes after MPs approve action against Isis', *Guardian*, 3 December 2015.

32 Patrick Wintour and Rowena Mason, 'Syria airstrikes: Jeremy Corbyn gives Labour MPs free vote', *Guardian*, 30 November 2015.

33 Dan Hodges, 'Syria will be the spark for an open Labour rebellion', *Daily Telegraph*, 26 November 2015.

34 Patrick Wintour, 'Majority of Labour members oppose Syria airstrikes, poll finds', *Guardian*, 30 November 2015.

35 Rowena Mason and Damien Gayle, 'Jeremy Corbyn denounces activists accused of threatening Labour MPs', *Guardian*, 3 December 2015.

36 Ben Riley-Smith and Laura Hughes, 'MPs vote to renew Trident', *Daily Telegraph*, 19 July 2016.

37 Christopher Hope and Laura Hughes, 'Jeremy Corbyn says he would keep submarines patrolling the world without any nuclear weapons', *Daily Telegraph*, 17 January 2016.

38 Dan Hodges, 'Labour can either care about defending Britain or support Jeremy Corbyn', *Daily Telegraph*, 9 February 2016.

39 Nicholas Watt, 'David Cameron launches personal attack on Jeremy Corbyn's appearance', *Guardian*, 24 February 2016.

40 Wintour and Watt, 'The Corbyn earthquake'.

41 Kate McCann, 'Jeremy Corbyn appoints top advisor who once defended terrorism', *Daily Telegraph*, 20 October 2015.

42 Leo McKinstry, 'Jeremy Corbyn is anti-British and a friend to terrorists', *Daily Express*, 15 May 2017.

43 Caroline Davies, 'Corbyn stands silent for national anthem at Battle of Britain service', *Guardian*, 15 September 2015.

44 Ben Riley-Smith, 'Jeremy Corbyn: I'm "not happy" with shoot-to-kill policy if terrorists are attacking Britain', *Daily Telegraph*, 16 November 2015.

45 Dan Hodges, 'Guess who's set to be Labour's REAL leader? Clue: It definitely won't be Jeremy Corbyn', *Mail on Sunday*, 19 February 2017.

46 Christopher Hope and Laura Hughes, 'Shami Chakrabarti handed peerage weeks after suppressing Jeremy Corbyn interview from "whitewash" anti-Semitism report', *Daily Telegraph*, 5 August 2016.

47 Anushka Asthana and Heather Stewart, 'Labour MPs hostile to Corbyn named in leaked party document', *Guardian*, 23 March 2016.

48 Chris Curtis, 'Corbyn loses support among Labour party membership', *YouGov*, 30 June 2016, available at: https://yougov.co.uk/news/2016/06/30/labour-members-corbyn-post-brexit/, last accessed 20 October 2017.

49 Jeremy Wilson, 'Jeremy Corbyn wants Britain to remain in the EU – but here are all the times he said it was bad', *Business Insider UK*, 14 April 2016, available at: http://uk.businessinsider.com/jeremy-corbyn-is-making-a-big-speech-saying-we-should-remain-in-the-eu-heres-all-the-times-he-said-the-eu-was-bad-2016–4, last accessed 20 October 2017.

50 John McTernan, 'Jeremy Corbyn sabotaged the pro-EU campaign, and is doing much worse to Labour', *Daily Telegraph*, 8 August 2016.

51 Caroline Mortimer, 'Jeremy Corbyn on *The Last Leg*: Enthusiastic about staying in the EU but won't share a platform with Cameron', *Independent*, 10 June 2016.

52 Daniel Boffey, Claire Phipps and Anushka Asthana, 'Labour in crisis: Shadow ministers resign in protests against Corbyn', *Observer*, 26 June 2016.

53 Anushka Asthana, Rajeev Syal and Jessica Elgot, 'Labour MPs prepare for leadership contest after Corbyn loses confidence vote', *Guardian*, 28 June 2016.

54 Ewen MacAskill, Caelainn Barr and Matthew Holmes, 'Momentum and unions prepare for new Corbyn campaign after revolt', *Guardian*, 28 June 2016.

55 Peter Walker and Anushka Asthana, 'Labour leadership: Tom Watson calls on MPs to step back from the brink', *Guardian*, 2 July 2016.

56 Quinn, *Electing and Ejecting Party Leaders in Britain*, p. 60.

57 Anushka Asthana and Jessica Elgot, 'Owen Smith to face Corbyn in Labour leadership challenge', *Guardian*, 19 July 2016.

58 Heather Stewart, Rajeev Syal and Ben Quinn, 'Labour executive rules Jeremy Corbyn must be on leadership ballot', *Guardian*, 13 July 2016.

59 YouGov's polling data is available at: https://d25d2506sfb94s.cloudfront.net/cumulus_uploads/document/a8ttjt0lgq/ElectionDataResults_160923_FinalCall.pdf, last accessed 20 October 2017.

60 Heather Stewart and Jessica Elgot, 'Len McCluskey: Disloyal MPs "asking for it" and will be held to account', *Guardian*, 18 September 2016.

61 Ipsos MORI, 'Voting intention trends', available at: www.ipsos.com/ipsos-mori/en-uk/voting-intention-trends, last accessed 20 October 2017.

62 Ipsos MORI, 'Party leaders', available at: www.ipsos.com/ipsos-mori/en-uk/party-leader, last accessed 20 October 2017.

63 The seat was called Whitehaven until 1983.

64 Jessica Elgot, Josh Halliday and Heather Stewart, 'Labour ousted by Tories in Copeland byelection but sees off Ukip in Stoke', *Guardian*, 24 February 2017.

65 Heather Stewart and Anushka Asthana, 'Clive Lewis quits shadow cabinet as Brexit bill passes with huge majority', *Guardian*, 9 February 2017.

66 Andrew Sparrow, 'Corbyn has 15 months for a Labour recovery, says McCluskey', *Guardian*, 26 March 2017.

67 Owen Jones, 'Jeremy Corbyn says he's staying. That's not good enough', *Guardian*, 1 March 2017.

68 Labour Party, *For the Many, Not the Few: The Labour Party Manifesto 2017* (London: Labour Party, 2017).

69 Phillip Inman, 'IFS makes damning assessment of Tory and Labour manifestos', *Guardian*, 26 May 2017.

70 Ingrid van Biezen, Peter Mair and Thomas Poguntke, 'Going, going, … gone? The decline of party membership in contemporary Europe', *European Journal of Political Research*, 51 (2012), 24–56.

3

The Liberal Democrats

Remaining in the doldrums

John Curtice

On 8 May 2015, the hopes and aspirations of the Liberal Democrats were in tatters. After five years in coalition with the Conservatives, the first time it had enjoyed UK governmental office since the end of the Second World War, the party's share of the vote fell from 23 per cent at the previous election in 2010 to a little under 8 per cent. Its number of MPs dropped from 57 to just eight. Even its traditional position as the third largest party in British politics was usurped, with the Scottish National Party (SNP) outperforming it in terms of seats and the United Kingdom Independence Party (UKIP) outpolling it in terms of votes. The party was weaker electorally than it had been at any time since the early 1970s.

The decision to enter into coalition with the Conservatives had been far from uncontroversial. Although often described as a 'centre party', in between its two far bigger rivals, left-leaning Labour and the right-inclined Conservatives, the party often thought of itself as being part of the 'progressive' wing of British politics, happier dealing with Labour than the Conservatives.[1] Indeed, under the leadership of Paddy Ashdown, it explicitly stated in the run-up to the 1997 general election that it would only be willing to sustain a Labour-led government in the event that no party secured an overall majority, thereby ruling out the possibility of sharing power with the Conservatives.[2] Labour and the Liberal Democrats even agreed a joint programme of constitutional reform shortly before the 1997 ballot.[3] Moreover, the party's success in expanding its parliamentary representation from just 20 seats in 1992 to as many as 62 in 2005 had rested primarily on winning constituencies from the Conservatives rather than Labour, often with the help of erstwhile Labour supporters who were persuaded to vote tactically for the Liberal Democrats in seats where they, rather than their own party, appeared better able to defeat the Conservatives locally.[4]

However, by the time the 2010 election came around, the Liberal Democrats, now under the leadership of Nick Clegg, had reverted to their traditional stance of 'equidistance' between Labour and the Conservatives. Relations between Labour and the Liberal Democrats had been cool ever since the Labour government decided shortly after the 2001 election to join in the US-led invasion of Iraq, a decision that the Liberal Democrats opposed.[5] In any event, there seemed little point in hitching the party's wagon to a party and a Labour government that had long since lost its electoral sheen. At the same time, the party had also moved somewhat to the right economically. Whereas in 1997 and 2001 the Liberal Democrats were campaigning in favour of increasing the basic rate of income tax in order to spend more on education, by 2010 they were championing the idea of reducing taxation for the less well-off by raising the threshold (known as the personal allowance) at which people began to pay income tax.

Meanwhile, although the outcome of the 2010 election, in which no one party had secured an overall majority, gave the party the kind of post-election bargaining power that it had long craved, it did not quite leave it as the 'hinge' that could simply choose to strike a deal with whichever party made it the better offer.[6] The Conservatives had 306 seats, 20 short of the 326 needed for an overall majority. Labour, in contrast, had just 258. If the 57 Liberal Democrat MPs joined forces with the Conservatives the resultant coalition would have a substantial overall majority of 76.[7] Any coalition with Labour, however, would have only 315 seats, leaving it dependent on the support of a rainbow collection of SNP, Plaid Cymru, Green and Northern Irish MPs. In the event the Conservatives proved to be the more ardent suitors too, and five days after the election a coalition was formed.[8]

The Liberal Democrats anticipated that the coalition would prove the gateway for further electoral progress.[9] The party would show that it could govern effectively, and thereby overcome claims that – as the country's perpetual third party – it was an irrelevance. The electoral reverses often suffered by junior coalition partners elsewhere might, perhaps, have given the party some pause for thought, and especially so given that hitherto it often seemed to profit from 'protest' voting, winning (albeit usually temporarily) the support of voters discontented with the performance of the party in government.[10] Meanwhile, it was hardly the best of times to come to power. It was just two years after the financial crash of 2008 that had created a large hole in Britain's public accounts and was concurrently resulting in a sovereign debt crisis in more than one European country.[11] As Nicholas Allen describes in Chapter 1, the new government committed itself to reducing the fiscal deficit and to do so primarily by cutting public expenditure – and thus to potentially unpopular cuts in public services.[12]

One early decision of the coalition designed to help cut the deficit was to cause the Liberal Democrats particular grief. The party had fought the 2010 election (as it had done the two previous elections) committed to scrapping the tuition fees that were paid by students at English universities.[13] These had been introduced in 1998 and now stood at £3,000. The party's stance reflected the fact that it tended to be relatively popular among university graduates – according to the British Social Attitudes survey as many as 36 per cent of them voted for the party in 2010, twice the equivalent proportion among non-graduates. Meanwhile, the party's policy had seemingly helped it win a number of constituencies with relatively large numbers of students, such as Cardiff Central, Cambridge and Leeds North West. But in the autumn of 2010 it was announced that far from eliminating tuition fees, the coalition was to increase them to up to £9,000. The decision to enter the coalition had already cost the party support in the polls – by September 2010 on average just 16 per cent said that they would vote for the party, eight points down on the party's tally in the general election – but after the tuition fees decision support fell to just 11 per cent, as the party was accused of being willing to break a key election pledge in order to obtain the keys to power. It never recovered from this blow. Indeed support fell yet further in the middle of 2014 in the wake of UKIP's success in coming first in that year's European election (see Paul Whiteley, Matthew Goodwin and Harold Clarke in Chapter 4). The party lost both a third of its membership, leaving it with just over 40,000 members, and nearly 2,000 seats in local council elections as the substantial base the party had developed in local government came crashing down. There seemed to be nothing the party could do to avoid the disaster that was the 2015 general election.[14] In contrast their Conservative coalition partners went on in the election to win a narrow overall majority of 12 seats, thanks not least to their success in gaining 27 seats from the Liberal Democrats.

A new leader

Unsurprisingly on hearing the outcome of the 2015 election, the party's leader, Nick Clegg, immediately announced his resignation. The position of being his successor, in which all members of the party had a vote, was contested by Tim Farron, a former president of the party who had not been a minister in the coalition government, and Norman Lamb, who had been a parliamentary private secretary to Nick Clegg in the early years of the coalition and subsequently a junior employment and then health minister. The contest inevitably came to some degree to be a referendum on the coalition, which the coalition outsider, Tim Farron, won by 56.5 to 43.5 per cent. However, it was a contest in which Farron, an evangelical Christian, came under fire due to his apparent reluctance to back same-sex marriage and his support for reducing the period during which an abortion could be undertaken.[15] His stance on such issues potentially put the new leader at odds with many of the party's supporters, who, though they may be in the centre on economic issues, are inclined to adopt a socially liberal stance on moral issues. For example, according to the 2014 British Social Attitudes survey 77 per cent of those who identified with the Liberal Democrats supported same-sex marriage, compared with 49 per cent of Conservatives and 65 per cent of Labour identifiers.

The immediate challenge facing the new leader was how to pick up the pieces. To some extent the apparent answer was provided for him by two key developments. The first was the election in September 2015 of Jeremy Corbyn as Labour leader, a development that was widely regarded as an indication that the Labour Party was moving to the left. Labour subsequently struggled to rise in the polls much above the 31 per cent that it had secured in 2015. As noted earlier, Liberal Democrats were often inclined to reach an accommodation with Labour, and indeed after the 2015 election some, such as Sir Vince Cable, business secretary in the coalition, and the former leader, Paddy Ashdown, seemed keen to revive the idea of creating some kind of 'progressive alliance' with Labour (and, indeed, the Greens).[16] But at the same time the party has also often contemplated the prospect of displacing Labour as the main party of the centre left (much as Labour had displaced the then Liberal Party, the forerunner of the Liberal Democrats, from that position in the 1920s).[17] Jeremy Corbyn's apparent unpopularity (including among his own parliamentary colleagues) and Labour's seeming 'lurch' to the left made it a tempting target for the Liberal Democrats. It was, perhaps, not surprising that the Liberal Democrat leader talked openly at his party's conference in September 2015 of his hopes that Labour MPs would defect to the party and announced plans to give grants to young entrepreneurs, a policy that was reported to be a 'land grab for those Labour voters who understand and care about Britain's economic stability and who look at Corbyn's offering and despair'.[18]

But by this stage the second key development was also looming. This was that the new majority Conservative government was committed to holding a referendum on the UK's membership of the EU. The Liberal Democrats – and before them the Liberals - had long been the keenest supporters of continued membership. True, during the coalition the party had acquiesced in legislation that required that a referendum be held if there was any future proposal to transfer significant powers from the UK to the EU. Nevertheless, the party had vetoed the idea of a referendum on whether or not the UK should remain a member. Thus, it was not surprising that Jeremy Corbyn's apparent lack of enthusiasm for remaining in the EU (the Labour leader had voted to leave in the 1975 referendum) was also part of the charge that Tim Farron laid at Corbyn's door.[19]

Just nine months later, in June 2016, the referendum had been held and a majority had voted to leave the EU. The issue of how to respond to that vote now became the central issue of British politics. Tim Farron's initial instinct was to say that the Liberal Democrats would fight the next election on a promise to overturn the referendum result and stay in the EU.[20] By September, however, the position had morphed into a promise that a second referendum should be held in which voters would be able to choose between accepting the terms of withdrawal that were eventually agreed with the EU, or staying in the Union, a proposal that was clearly aimed at framing the choice put before voters in such a way that staying in the EU was more likely to win.[21] In contrast, Jeremy

Corbyn, after throwing off a challenge to his leadership from Owen Smith, who also supported the idea of a second referendum, indicated that the Labour Party accepted the result of the referendum, though it subsequently distanced itself from the stance on Brexit taken by the Conservative government, which prioritised securing control over immigration from the EU over remaining part of the EU single market.

Here then seemed to be the beginnings of a golden opportunity for the Liberal Democrats to restore their fortunes. True, not everyone who voted for the party in 2015 voted to stay in the EU, but as many as three in four had done so.[22] (Indeed, three of Tim Farron's own parliamentary colleagues abstained on key votes on whether the government should instigate steps to leave the EU.) Meanwhile, around two in three Labour supporters had voted Remain. Labour's acceptance of Brexit, the unpopularity of Jeremy Corbyn, and the divisions within the Labour Party suggested there was plenty of scope for the Liberal Democrats to win votes from Labour. There also seemed to be a good chance of winning over the two in five or so of Conservative supporters who had voted Remain. At the same time, this was an issue where the party's stance seemed likely to help it reconnect with much of its core demographic of university graduates, the vast majority of whom had voted Remain and tended to take a socially liberal stance including, not least, on immigration.[23]

The initial signs were promising. During the autumn of 2016 the party's poll ratings began to climb back into double figures. The party made some notable, and indeed sometimes spectacular, gains in local government by-elections, and increased its share of the vote by 24 points in a parliamentary by-election in Witney occasioned by the resignation of the former prime minister, David Cameron, following the referendum vote to leave the EU.[24] Above all, the party captured the seat of Richmond Park from the Conservatives in a December 2016 by-election. The Liberal Democrat candidate, Sarah Olney, won a constituency in which no less than 72 per cent had voted Remain, although it was also a seat with a long history of Liberal and Liberal Democrat strength and had, indeed, been held by the party between 1997 and 2005.[25] Meanwhile, by the end of 2016 party membership had climbed to nearly 80,000, almost twice the level to which it had fallen during the darkest days of the coalition.[26]

Moreover, the increase in the party's support in the polls occurred entirely among Remain voters. According to YouGov, support for the party among Remain voters increased from 13 per cent in the summer of 2016 to 19 per cent by January 2017, and held at more or less that level throughout the winter.[27] In contrast, support among those who voted Leave stayed constant at just 3 per cent. Moreover, much of the Liberal Democrats' new-found support seemed to be coming from former Labour voters, leaving Labour support in the polls below even the 31 per cent that the party had won in 2015. The Liberal Democrats' distinctive stance on Brexit seemed to be slowly helping the party out of the doldrums.

Indeed, by the time of the party's spring conference in March 2017 its strategic course appeared to be clear. Tim Farron joined the long line of party leaders who sought to displace Labour as the principal alternative to the Conservatives, saying that, 'I want us to replace the Labour Party as the main opposition to the Conservatives ... so that we can replace the Conservatives as the Government of our country'.[28] The Conservatives were attacked for their 'isolationist', 'introverted' stance on Brexit, Labour written off as too extreme and divided to be able to win under Jeremy Corbyn's leadership. At the same time, in line with its anti-Conservative stance, the party seemed to signal something of a swing back to the left as it embraced once more a proposal to increase the basic rate of income tax, this time in order to increase funding for the NHS.

In practice, however, the party was aiming for a niche market of those who were most opposed to leaving the EU. At the turn of the year, polls conducted by ComRes, Opinium and YouGov all suggested that only around a third of all voters – and no more than two-thirds of those who had voted Remain – actually supported the idea of a second referendum. But, if the party could attract the support of just half of this group, this would enable it to double the share of the vote it won in 2015 and put it discernibly back on the road to recovery. Given many of these pro-second referendum voters were young, socially liberal graduates, a demographic group among whom, as we have already noted, the party has always performed relatively well, such an ambition seemed wholly reasonable.

The campaign

The centrepiece of the Liberal Democrats' manifesto was therefore a proposal for a second referendum – and a call in the meantime for the UK government to seek a much softer Brexit than it currently had in mind, with the UK staying in the single market and the customs union.[29] To this was added not only a proposal for a one penny increase in income tax, but also the legalisation of cannabis, the protection of spending per school pupil in real terms, the restoration of maintenance grants for less well-off university students (these had been cut by the Conservatives after the coalition ended) and an end to the 1 per cent pay cap that the government was imposing on pay increases in the public sector, a 'rent to own' scheme for young people struggling to get on the housing ladder, a ban on the sale of diesel cars by 2025, and a reduction of the voting age to 16.[30] Although there was no promise to scrap tuition fees – this was a stance that Labour adopted instead – only a promise to commission a review of university finances, all in all these measures read like proposals that were aimed at reinforcing the party's appeal among the kind of young professional voter who had voted Remain.

But in practice their reach and popularity proved to be somewhat less than the party had hoped and imagined. Table 3.1 shows the responses that

Table 3.1 Attitudes towards Liberal Democrat manifesto policies (%), Remain and all voters

	Remain voters		All voters	
	Good idea (%)	Wrong priority (%)	Good idea (%)	Wrong priority (%)
Increase the basic rate of income tax from 20 per cent to 21 per cent and spend the money raised on the NHS and social care	66	22	56	28
Ban the sale of diesel cars and vans by 2025	45	36	35	42
Allow cannabis to be sold legally through licensed outlets	40	47	35	52
Hold a second referendum on the EU after negotiations are complete, to decide if Britain accepts the deal or wants to remain in the EU after all	58	31	34	54
Reduce the voting age to 16	42	47	29	60

Source: YouGov.

YouGov received when, shortly after the Liberal Democrat manifesto was unveiled, they presented their respondents with some of the proposals that it contained and asked them whether they were a 'good idea' or a 'wrong priority'.[31] The table shows the responses both of voters as a whole and of those who had voted Remain in particular. First of all, we can see that, in line with the findings of other polls, only one in three of all voters and no more than around three in five of those who had voted Remain backed the idea of a second referendum. Meanwhile, even Remain voters were far from enthusiastic about the legalisation of cannabis, banning the sale of diesel cars or reducing the voting age. Rather more popular was the party's proposal to increase the basic rate of income tax in order to spend more on health. Over a half of all voters and two-thirds of Remain voters supported this idea. What, however, is less clear is whether voters appreciated that this was where the party now stood on taxation and spending – as we have seen, it represented yet another volte-face on the issue. According to the British Election Study Internet Panel that took place during the 2017 election campaign, just 10 per cent of those who felt that cuts to NHS spending had gone too far intended to vote Liberal Democrat. This figure was no higher than it had been in 2015.

Perhaps just as importantly this package generally proved less popular – including not least among Remain voters – than that put forward by Labour.

For example, YouGov found that 60 per cent of Remain voters supported the abolition of university tuition fees, 66 per cent Labour's policy of increasing income tax on those earning more than £80,000 a year, while 71 per cent supported imposing a cap on increases in housing rents. In short, far from presenting the electorate with a manifesto that was regarded as unacceptably left-wing, Labour presented a manifesto that seemed more than capable of competing with the Liberal Democrats for the support of Remain voters.[32]

That meant that it was even more important that the party's leader should be making best use of the campaign to put himself and his party forward. The party has long relied on the ability of its leader to make an impression on voters, and thereby make best use of the fact that the rules on broadcast coverage of elections ensured that the party secured more air time than its current tally of eight MPs could normally obtain. All five of Tim Farron's predecessors, Jeremy Thorpe, David Steel, Paddy Ashdown, Charles Kennedy and Nick Clegg, had – in their different ways – been charismatic characters who had enabled their party to punch above its weight at election time.

Tim Farron proved not to be their equal. His apparent reluctance to endorse same-sex marriage came back to haunt him and he was persistently pursued throughout the campaign as to whether he regarded homosexuality as a sin or abortion as wrong.[33] Such question marks over his views were not designed to enhance his appeal among those of a socially liberal disposition. But more generally Tim Farron sometimes came across as rather diffident and lacking in confidence when, in truth, he needed to create an exaggerated presence on the stage and in the television studio. In any event, he was certainly no more successful at persuading voters that he was an effective party leader than he had been during the previous two years. In five polls conducted by Opinium between the beginning of 2017 and the calling of the election, on average just 15 per cent had said that they approved of his performance as Liberal Democrat leader, while 34 per cent stated that they disapproved. Half simply said that they neither approved nor disapproved. In eight polls that the company conducted during the election campaign, the proportion who told Opinium that they approved of Tim Farron's leadership simply oscillated between 14 per cent and 18 per cent and in the company's final poll stood at 16 per cent, little different from what it had been before the election was called. At the same time, the proportion who said they disapproved, which varied between 35 per cent and 40 per cent and ended up at 37 per cent, was, if anything, slightly higher than it had been immediately before the election. It was Jeremy Corbyn, not Tim Farron, who managed during the campaign to improve his image in the eyes of voters.

Meanwhile, if what was intended to be the party's calling card at this election, its proposal for a second referendum on leaving the EU, was going to persuade voters to switch to – or in some cases, come back to – the party, it needed to be communicated to those who had voted Remain. The party seems to have struggled

Table 3.2 Perceptions of the parties' Brexit stances among Remain voters (%)

	Conservatives	Labour	Liberal Democrats	UKIP
They are opposed to Brexit and would like Britain to remain in the European Union	4	12	26	1
They opposed Brexit and would like to have a second referendum once negotiations are complete	2	9	28	0
They accept Brexit, but would like Britain to have a 'soft Brexit' and retain the benefits of the single market	21	37	6	1
They support Brexit and would like Britain to leave the European Union completely and negotiate a new trade deal	41	4	1	70
They do not have any clear policy	20	23	11	14
Not sure	11	15	28	14

Source: YouGov.

to do so. True, as Table 3.2 shows, many a voter struggled to identify where any of the parties stood on Brexit.[34] However, while as many as 41 per cent thought that the Conservatives supported Brexit and wanted the UK to confine its future relationship with the EU to a new trade deal, and 37 per cent thought that Labour would like a 'soft' Brexit, only 28 per cent reckoned that the Liberal Democrats would like a second referendum once the negotiations are complete. Almost as many, 26 per cent, thought that the party simply wanted Britain to remain in the European Union.

Perhaps, just as importantly, Remain voters did not necessarily recognise where the party stood on one of the central issues in the Brexit debate, immigration. In the same YouGov poll, just 34 per cent of Remain voters said that the Liberal Democrats wished to maintain the current level of immigration, considerably less than the 45 per cent who reckoned that was where Labour stood, let alone the 62 per cent who associated the Conservatives with a reduction in immigration. No less than 48 per cent said that they either were not sure what the party's stance on immigration was or that it was not clear. It seems as though one of the central reasons why the party wanted the UK to stay in the EU – to retain freedom of movement – was not appreciated by many voters. In those circumstances, there was evidently a risk that the party's stance on Brexit would not have the resonance that the party anticipated.

The dynamics of the campaign

And so it proved. The party's support actually fell back during the campaign. An initial average poll rating of 11 per cent had by the end of the campaign fallen to just 7 per cent, only a little below the party's actual tally when the ballot boxes were opened of 7.4 per cent across the United Kingdom. This was the first time since 1987 that the party had seen its support end up lower at the end of an election campaign than it had been at the beginning.[35] The drop was not the result of Leave voters taking fright at its support for a second independence referendum. According to a large poll conducted by YouGov immediately after the election, at 3 per cent the party's level of support among such voters was exactly the same on polling day as it had been when the election was called. Rather, the party lost ground among the very group to which it was trying to appeal, that is, those who voted to remain in the EU. Just 12 per cent of this group voted for the party, well down on the 20 per cent who, according to YouGov, were minded to do so when the election was first called.[36] ICM identified much the same pattern, with support for the party among Remain voters falling from 16 per cent in March and early April to 12 per cent during the last fortnight or so of the campaign.[37]

It was Labour, not the Liberal Democrats, who gained ground among Remain voters during the campaign. When the election was called, just 36 per cent of Remain voters (according to YouGov) said they intended to vote Labour. By polling day that figure had increased to no less than 55 per cent.[38] Although Labour also made gains among those who voted to Leave, the increase in support among this group, at 11 points, was little more than half the 19-point increase among Remain supporters. Moreover, Labour's successful pitch to Remain voters appears to have had a direct impact on Liberal Democrat support. At the outset of the campaign, just 11 per cent of those who said they voted for the Liberal Democrats in 2015 indicated that they would now vote Labour; by polling day, no less than 34 per cent had decided to make that switch. Equally, whereas when the election was called 13 per cent were minded to switch from having voted Labour in 2015 to voting Liberal Democrat this time around, in the event just 5 per cent did so.

In short, it was not just Theresa May's hopes for the election that were scuppered by the dramatic increase in Labour support during the 2017 election campaign – so were those of the Liberal Democrats. Labour, which we have seen was quite widely regarded as being in favour of a relatively soft Brexit, made a successful pitch for the very kind of voter that the Liberal Democrats had been targeting. Indeed, it looks as though during the campaign Labour reclaimed from the Liberal Democrats much of the support among Remain voters that Jeremy Corbyn's party had seemed to lose to the Liberal Democrats during the previous autumn. The hopes generated by the Richmond Park by-election were well and truly dashed.

The outcome in perspective

At 7.4 per cent, the Liberal Democrats' share of the national vote was actually half a point below what the party secured in 2015. It thus represented the lowest share of the vote for the Liberal Democrats (and the Liberals before them) at any election since 1970 – and in 1970 the party fought only just over half of all the constituencies, rather than, as in 2017, all bar three. Indeed, once we take into account the number of seats fought, the performance in 2017 was probably second only to the 1951 election in the party's league table of worst performances. True, the party did secure a modest increase in its tally of seats, from eight to 12, but, 2015 apart, this still left the party with fewer seats than at any election since 1970. No less than half of the seats the party was defending were lost, including former leader Nick Clegg's Sheffield Hallam constituency and the recent by-election gain in Richmond Park. Meanwhile, although a collapse in UKIP support meant that the party was restored once more to its position as the third largest party in England, it still found itself conceding to the SNP the position of third largest party in the House of Commons.

The party's attempt to woo Remain voters brought it relatively little reward. A number of surveys and polls found that support for the party among this group grew only a little. True, the British Election Study Internet Panel found that, at 14 per cent, support for the party among those who voted to remain in the EU was three points higher than it was among this group in 2015, whereas support fell back a point, to 4 per cent, among those who voted Leave. However, according to YouGov the 12 per cent support that the party secured among Remain voters was just one point above what it had secured among the same group of voters two years previously, while the 3 per cent support registered among Leave voters represented a two-point drop.[39] Similar polling conducted on and around polling day by Lord Ashcroft suggests the party made even less relative progress among Remain voters. His data suggest the party had the same level of support, 14 per cent, among Remain voters as it had had in 2015, while its popularity slipped just a little, from 5 per cent to 4 per cent, among Leave supporters.[40]

Much the same pattern emerges if we look at the party's relative performance in different kinds of constituency. On average its share of the vote fell back by 1.1 points in seats where it is estimated that 55 per cent or more of the EU referendum vote went to Leave, its vote dropped a little less, by half a point, in seats where the Leave vote was between 45 per cent and 55 per cent, while it only just about increased – by 0.3 of a point – in the most pro-Remain constituencies where Leave won less than 45 per cent. Although, as we shall see below, there were some kinds of pro-Remain constituencies where the party did make a notable advance, across Britain as a whole the party made only slightly more progress in Remain voting areas.

In other respects too, the party's vote looks much as it did two years earlier. There is, for example, little consistent evidence that it made particular progress among those demographic groups, such as younger voters and university graduates, where support for Remain was highest. True, Ipsos MORI's collation of all the polls it conducted during the election campaign suggests the party's vote increased by a point or two among the under-35s, while falling back slightly among those aged 45 and over.[41] There is also a similar pattern in the data collected by British Election Study Internet Panel. However, none of the polling exercises conducted by Lord Ashcroft, Opinium or YouGov on or shortly after polling day replicate this finding. The party did perform relatively well among university graduates, but there is no consistent evidence that it did so to any greater extent than it had done two years previously. For example, the 11 per cent support among this group registered by YouGov is exactly the same as the company obtained in an equivalent exercise immediately after the 2015 election – as was the 14 per cent registered by the British Election Study Internet Panel.[42] Equally all the polling evidence suggests that the party performed better among middle-class voters than their working-class counterparts, but again not to any significantly greater extent than it had done two years previously.

That said, the party did perform relatively well in seats with relatively large numbers of graduates. On average its vote increased by 1.6 points in constituencies where more than a third of the adult population have a degree (according to the 2011 census), whereas elsewhere it fell on average by just over a point. In part (though only in part) this reflects the fact that such constituencies were also more likely to have registered a relatively large Remain vote in 2016. In addition, as Table 3.3 shows, the party also performed relatively well in London and the South East – and to a lesser extent in the South West and the Eastern region too – regions with relatively large numbers of graduates and of Remain voters (especially so in the case of London). However, none of these regional differences

Table 3.3 Liberal Democrat performance by government region

	% vote 2017	Change in % vote since 2015
Scotland	6.8	−0.7
North East	4.6	−1.9
Yorkshire and Humberside	5.0	−2.1
North West	5.4	−1.1
East Midlands	5.3	−0.3
West Midlands	4.4	−1.1
Eastern	7.9	−0.2
London	8.8	+1.1
South East	10.5	+1.0
South West	15.0	−0.1
Wales	4.5	−2.0
United Kingdom	7.4	−0.5

Note. The party did not contest two seats in the South East (one in 2015) and one in Yorkshire and Humberside. It also did not contest any seats in Northern Ireland.
Source. Author's calculations.

can simply be accounted for by the distinctive demographic composition or referendum histories of the regions in question. These regional patterns help illustrate why the party lost four seats across the North West, Yorkshire and Wales,
while five of the eight gains that it made were in London, the South East and the
South West. The remaining three gains in Scotland were the product of a sharp
decline in SNP fortunes rather than any marked improvement in the party's
own support.

Gains and losses

The key to understanding why the party won some seats but lost others is,
however, to be found above all by looking at the political character of the seats
in question. The first clue lies in the fact that all five of the gains that the party
made in England were at the expense of the Conservatives, while two of the
three losses were to Labour. This suggests that perhaps the party prospered
relatively well in constituencies where the Conservatives were strong. This is
confirmed by Table 3.4 which breaks down the change in the Liberal Democrat
vote between 2015 and 2017 by (a) the outcome of the EU referendum and
who won the seat in 2015, and (b) the proportion of graduates and who won the
seat in 2015. In both cases, the party performed relatively well in seats that were
being defended by the Conservatives as compared with those with a similar
demographic mix or referendum vote being defended by Labour. However,
this is above all the case in seats with a relatively large number of graduates
and those with a large Remain vote in 2016. The party may not have advanced
much in general in seats with large numbers of Remain voters, but it did do so
in Conservative-held seats that contained many a Remain voter.

Table 3.4 Change in Liberal Democrat share of constituency vote, 2015–17, by proportion
of graduates and EU referendum vote

Mean change in % Liberal Democrat vote 2015–17	Conservative-won seats in 2015	Labour-won seats in 2015	All seats in 2015
Leave vote 2016			
Less than 45%	+5.0	–1.6	+0.3
45–55%	–0.1	–1.3	–0.5
More than 55%	–0.5	–2.0	–1.1
Graduates			
Less than 25%	–0.5	–1.9	–1.1
25–33%	–0.4	–1.6	–1.1
More than 33%	+3.4	–1.3	+1.6
All seats	+0.3	–1.8	–0.5

Source: Author's calculations.

This distinction between Conservative- and Labour-held seats also proves to be important when we look at the impact of another phenomenon that we might expect to be important in accounting for where the party was and was not able to win. Votes won on the basis of the personal popularity of the local candidate (and often very intense local campaigning) have long been important to the party's ability to win and defend seats. However, in the event the personal popularity of its incumbent MPs only helped the party to retain a handful of seats in 2015.[43] Nevertheless, the drop in the Liberal Democrat share of the vote in seats that the incumbent MP was defending at that election was still markedly lower than it was in seats where the party had put in a strong performance in 2010 but where the local party candidate was not the incumbent MP – in these seats the party's vote often plummeted.[44] We thus might anticipate that in seats where the former incumbent Liberal Democrat MP was trying to regain a seat they lost in 2015 – as 19 of them were trying to do – the party might perform relatively well, thanks to the ability of the ex-MP to register once again their local, personal support (especially as they had only stopped being the local MP quite recently). Equally, the party might also be expected to perform relatively well in the seven constituencies where the current incumbent Liberal Democrat MP was seeking re-election. Conversely, the party might struggle to maintain its vote in seats where a former incumbent Liberal Democrat MP was no longer trying to retain their seat after having lost it in 2015, or indeed in the one seat (Southport) that was no longer being defended by the existing Liberal Democrat MP.

However, these expectations were only partially realised (see Table 3.5). In seats where the party was battling things out locally with Labour, both incumbent and ex-incumbent Liberal Democrat MPs struggled to maintain their share of the vote. Indeed, in seats that the party lost to Labour in 2015, the Liberal Democrat vote fell heavily irrespective of whether or not the former Liberal Democrat MP was trying to regain the seat. In contrast, in seats where either a current or former Liberal Democrat MP was doing battle with a Conservative challenger, the party's vote on average increased by between three (in the case of incumbent MPs) and six (ex-incumbent MPs) points. In both cases this performance was much better than it was where a new candidate was attempting to recapture a seat from the Conservatives; in these instances, the party's vote on average fell back slightly (and, indeed, especially so – by 3.2 points – where the incumbent Liberal Democrat MP had defended the seat in 2015), while in the one seat (Southport) in which a new candidate was attempting to defend a seat the party already held, the party's vote fell back by 4.6 points.

So, the presence of a substantial Remain vote, the existence of a large number of university graduates, and the presence of a current or former Liberal Democrat MP all only proved conducive to a relatively strong Liberal Democrat performance in seats where the party was in competition locally with the Conservatives. Perhaps this means that the party was able to win over some disaffected, pro-Remain Conservatives, in places where it was locally credible? However, Table 3.6 casts doubt on this explanation. On average the Conservative vote increased just

Table 3.5 Mean change in Liberal Democrat share of the constituency vote, 2015–17, by candidate status and principal challenger

Seat being fought for Lib Dems by:	Principal challenger		
	Conservatives	Labour	All seats
Incumbent MP	+3.3	–3.6	+0.4
Ex-incumbent MP	+5.7	–11.2	–1.4
New candidate in seat lost in 2015	–0.6	–10.6	–4.7
New or old candidate in seat not won in 2010	+0.1	–1.2	–0.3

Note: Principal challenger refers to the party that won the seat in 2015 or which was second to a Liberal Democrat victor at that election.
Source: Author's calculations.

Table 3.6 Mean change in all parties' share of the vote, 2015–17, by status of Liberal Democrat candidate and principal challenger

Seat being fought for Lib Dems by:	Change in % vote since 2015 in Lib Dem/Con battlegrounds			Change in % vote since 2015 in Lib Dem/Lab battlegrounds		
	Con	Lab	Lib Dem	Con	Lab	Lib Dem
Incumbent or ex-incumbent MP	+4.6	+4.1	+5.2	+4.9	+14.9	–9.5
New candidate in seat won in 2010	+7.8	+8.5	–0.8	+6.8	+16.2	–10.6
New or old candidate in seat not won in 2010	+4.5	+10.1	+0.1	+5.8	+10.6	–1.2

Source: Author's calculations.

as much in Liberal Democrat/Conservative battleground seats where an existing or former Liberal Democrat MP was standing as it did in Conservative-held seats that the Liberal Democrats did not win in 2010. Rather it is Labour that made relatively little progress in seats where the Liberal Democrats were primarily in competition with the Conservatives. At just over four points the average increase in the Labour vote in these seats was some six points below what it was in seats that the Liberal Democrats did not hold before the 2015 election.

Indeed, this tendency for the Liberal Democrats to perform relatively well at Labour's expense was also evident in some Conservative-held seats where Remain won more than 55 per cent of the vote in 2016 but the Liberal Democrats did not win the seat in 2010. In four such seats where the Liberal

Democrats started off this election in second place, their vote increased on average by as much as 8.0 points, while Labour's vote increased by no more than 5.4 points. (These figures exclude Richmond Park, but there again it is evident that the Labour vote was squeezed.) There are even signs of this behaviour in a few pro-Remain seats where the Liberal Democrats had been third to Labour in 2015, but no more than five points behind; in six seats that fall into this group the party's vote increased on average by 6.2 points, while Labour's advance was only 7.0 points. Not surprisingly, given the high Remain vote in these seats the Conservatives also performed poorly (their vote fell on average by one point), but given that such seats were usually places where Labour advanced most, the Labour performance has to be regarded as surprisingly modest. And it is this ability to stem the Labour vote that helps to explain why, as we saw in Table 3.4, the Liberal Democrats performed relatively well in Conservative-held seats where there was a large Remain vote in 2016.

There were then some circumstances in which the Liberal Democrats were able to stem the advancing Labour tide: that is, in seats where the party might have been thought better able to mount a challenge to the local Conservative candidate, and especially where, as a result, potential Labour supporters often faced a choice between voting for a Labour candidate who seemingly had little chance of winning and a relatively well-known Liberal Democrat candidate. Here the Liberal Democrats were able to take advantage of their strategic position locally (and to do so even in seats where there was a large Leave vote in 2016). At the same time the party also managed to compete with Labour in some Conservative-held seats where there was a large proportion of Remain voters. But the fact that the party's relative successes were often the product of a weaker Labour performance underlines the earlier argument that the party found itself at this election primarily in a battle for votes with Labour, a battle that in all but limited circumstances the party lost.

Conclusion

The outcome of the 2017 election represented a considerable disappointment for the Liberal Democrats. Despite the apparent progress that the party had made in the months after the referendum, the party actually went backwards in many respects, and certainly enjoyed little in the way of an electoral recovery. Its attempt to win over Remain voters who were upset at the prospect of Brexit by promising a second referendum largely fell flat. Too few voters were aware of a policy stance that, perhaps, focused too much on process rather than substance. Meanwhile, the party had relatively little else to offer that the electorate regarded as attractive, and it was hampered by a leader who, despite his best endeavours, proved unable to make much impact on the electorate and whose stance on some moral issues appeared to be something of a handicap. As a result, many of the voters whose support the party hoped to gain switched to a Labour Party that was thought to favour a soft Brexit, had a range of popular policies, and a leader who did succeed in showing during the election campaign that perhaps he was not so bad after all. Only in very limited circumstances – seats where Labour locally was weak and where there was a large pro-Remain constituency and/or a current or former Liberal Democrat MP was standing – did the party enjoy some apparent measure of success in stemming the Labour tide. Still, that limited success did help provide a silver lining in the form of a slightly enlarged parliamentary party, including the swift return to the House of Commons of three MPs with extensive experience of government, Sir Vince Cable, Sir Ed Davey and Jo Swinson. Indeed, following Tim Farron's resignation as party leader, it was to Sir Vince Cable that the party turned as its leader in the hope that he could be more successful in steering a course out from the doldrums.

Notes

1   Paul Webb, *The Modern British Party System* (London: Sage, 2000).
2   David Denver, 'The Liberal Democrats in "constructive opposition"', in Anthony King (ed.), *Britain at the Polls 2001* (New Jersey: Chatham House Seven Bridges Press, 2002), pp. 143–163.
3   The agreement is set out in Robert Blackburn and Raymond Plant (eds), *Constitutional Reform: The Labour Government's Constitutional Reform Agenda* (London: Longman, 1999), pp. 468–490.
4   John Curtice and Michael Steed, 'Appendix 2: The results analysed', in David Butler and Dennis Kavanagh, *The British General Election of 1997* (Basingstoke: Palgrave Macmillan, 1997), pp. 295–325; John Curtice and Michael Steed, 'Appendix 2: An analysis of the results', in David Butler and Dennis Kavanagh, *The British General Election of 2001* (Basingstoke: Palgrave Macmillan, 2001), pp. 304–338; Thomas Quinn, 'Third-party strategy under plurality rule: The British Liberal Democrats and the New Zealand Social Credit Party', *Political Studies*, 65 (2017), 740–763.
5   Thomas Quinn and Ben Clements, 'The Liberal Democrats: Realignment in the centre', in Nicholas Allen and John Bartle (eds), *Britain at the Polls 2010* (London: Sage, 2011), pp. 63–88.
6   Quinn and Clements, 'The Liberal Democrats'.
7   Philip Norton, 'The politics of coalition', in Nicholas Allen and John Bartle (eds), *Britain at the Polls 2010* (London: Sage, 2011), pp. 243–265.
8   See David Laws, *22 Days in May: The Birth of the Lib Dem-Conservative Coalition* (London: Biteback, 2010); Andrew Adonis, *5 Days in May: The Coalition and Beyond* (London: Biteback, 2013).
9   Nick Clegg, *Politics: Between the Extremes* (London: Vintage, 2017).
10 Andrew Russell and Ed Fieldhouse, *Neither Left nor Right: The Liberal Democrats and the Electorate* (Manchester: Manchester University Press, 2005); Tim Bale, 'The Black Widow effect: Why Britain's Conservative–Liberal Democrat coalition might

have an unhappy ending', *Parliamentary Affairs*, 65 (2012), 323–337; Craig Johnston and Alia Middleton, 'Junior coalition parties in the British context: Explaining the Liberal Democrat collapse at the 2015 general election', *Electoral Studies*, 43 (2016), 63–71.

11 See Michael Moran, Sukhdev Jodal and Karel Williams, 'The financial crisis and its consequences', in Nicholas Allen and John Bartle (eds), *Britain at the Polls 2010* (London: Sage, 2011), pp. 89–119.

12 HM Government, *The Coalition: Our Programme for Government* (London: Cabinet Office, 2010), p. 15.

13 The Liberal Democrats, *Manifesto 2010* (London: The Liberal Democrats, 2010). The manifesto (p. 33) said: 'We will scrap unfair university tuition fees so everyone has the chance to get a degree, regardless of their parents' income.'

14 Philip Cowley and Dennis Kavanagh, *The British General Election of 2015* (Basingstoke: Palgrave Macmillan, 2015).

15 Frances Perraudin, 'Tim Farron: My religion would not be an issue if I were Jewish or Muslim', *Guardian*, 3 July 2015.

16 Pippa Simm, 'Lib Dems must build "progressive alliance" – Lord Ashdown', *BBC News*, 19 September 2016, available at: www.bbc.co.uk/news/uk-politics-37410523, last accessed 30 October 2017.

17 Paul Adelman, *The Decline of the Liberal Party, 1910–1931* (London: Longman, 1995); Ross McKibbin, *The Evolution of the Labour Party, 1910–1924* (Oxford: Oxford University Press, 1974); Martin Pugh, *The Making of British Politics, 1867–1939* (Oxford: Blackwell, 1982); Alan R. Ball, *British Political Parties: The Making of a Modern Party System* (London: Macmillan, 1981).

18 Mark Leftly, 'Tim Farron makes "unashamed land grab" for centre Labour voters who "look at Jeremy Corbyn's business policy and despair"', *Independent on Sunday*, 20 September 2016.

19 See 'Tim Farron's Lib Dem Conference speech in full', Politics.co.uk, 23 September 2015, available at: www.politics.co.uk/comment-analysis/2015/09/23/tim-farron-s-lib-dem-conference-speech-in-full, last accessed 30 October 2017. Farron said: 'There's been a lot of nonsense written about Jeremy Corbyn's patriotism following a service at St Paul's a week ago. Is it a threat to Britain if the leader of the Labour party doesn't sing the national anthem? Not really. Is it a threat to Britain if the leader of the Labour party is ambivalent about Britain's future in Europe? Absolutely!'

20 Jennifer Rankin, 'Liberal Democrats will fight election on halting Brexit, says Farron', *Guardian*, 28 June 2016.

21 BBC News, 'Tim Farron on second EU referendum over Brexit deal', 19 September 2016, available at: www.bbc.co.uk/news/av/uk-politics-37408662/tim-farron-on-second-eu-referendum-over-brexit-deal, last accessed 30 October 2017.

22 John Curtice, 'Why Leave won the UK's EU referendum', *Journal of Common Market Studies*, 55 (2017), 19–37.

23 For example, asked to place their views on a scale where 0 meant immigration generally undermines Britain's cultural life and 10 that immigration enriches that life, respondents to the 2013 British Social Attitudes survey who were graduates gave themselves a score on average of 6.2, whereas non-graduates on average gave themselves a score of just 3.9.

24 BBC News, 'Witney by-election: Tory majority slashed in David Cameron's former seat', 22 October 2016, available at: www.bbc.co.uk/news/uk-politics-37719170, last accessed 30 October 2017.

25 Francesca Gillet, 'Richmond Park by-election result: Zac Goldsmith stunned as Lib Dem Sarah Olney wins seat', *Evening Standard*, 2 December 2016.

26 See Mark Pack, 'Liberal Democrat membership figures', 9 October 2017, available at: www.markpack.org.uk/143767/liberal-democrat-membership-figures/, last accessed 3 November 2017.

27 John Curtice, 'Is Brexit causing voters to switch parties?', *What UK Thinks: EU*, 21 February 2017, available at: https://whatukthinks.org/eu/is-brexit-causing-voters-to-switch-parties/, last accessed 3 November 2017.

28 Tim Farron, 'Speech to the Liberal Democrat Spring Conference', 19 March 2017, available at: www.libdems.org.uk/tim-farron-conference-speech, last accessed 3 November 2017.

29 See Liberal Democrats, *Change Britain's Future: Liberal Democrat Manifesto 2017* (London: The Liberal Democrats, 2017), pp. 9–10: 'when the terms of our future relationship with the EU have been negotiated (over the next two years on the Government's timetable), we will put that deal to a vote of the British people in a referendum, with the alternative option of staying in the EU on the ballot paper. We continue to believe that there is no deal as good for the UK outside the EU as the one it already has as a member.'

30 Liberal Democrats, *Change Britain's Future*.

31 YouGov, 'YouGov/Sunday Times survey results, 18–19 May 2016', available at: https://d25d2506sfb94s.cloudfront.net/cumulus_uploads/document/wvyc3lofp5/SundayTimesResults_170519_VI_W.pdf, last accessed 3 November 2017.

32 Matthew Smith, 'How popular are the parties' policies?', *YouGov*, 22 May 2017, available at: https://yougov.co.uk/news/2017/05/22/how-popular-are-parties-manifesto-policies/, last accessed 24 October 2017.

33 Perraudin, 'Tim Farron: My religion would not be an issue'.

34 YouGov, 'YouGov/Sunday Times survey results, 9–10 May 1017', available at: https://d25d2506sfb94s.cloudfront.net/cumulus_uploads/document/1b8yww4g1l/SundayTimesResults_170512_VI_W.pdf, last accessed 3 November 2017.

35 See Ivor Crewe and Anthony King, *SDP: The Birth, Life and Death of the Social Democratic Party* (Oxford: Oxford University Press, 1995).

36 See John Curtice, 'A Brexit election after all?', *What UK Thinks: EU*, 7 June 2017, available at: https://whatukthinks.org/eu/a-brexit-election-after-all, last accessed 3 November 2017. See also Chris Curtis and Matthew Smith, 'How did 2015 voters cast their ballot at the 2017 general election?', *YouGov*, 22 June 2017, available at: https://yougov.co.uk/news/2017/06/22/how-did-2015-voters-cast-their-ballot-2017-general, last accessed 3 November 2017.

37 Curtice, 'A Brexit election after all?'. The analysis there has been updated to include the results of the final ICM poll conducted 6–7 June 2016: https://www.icmunlimited.com/wp-content/uploads/2017/06/2017_guardian_prediction_PRELIM_1500.pdf, last accessed 3 November 2017.

38 Curtice, 'A Brexit election after all?'; Curtis and Smith, 'How did 2015 voters cast their ballot'.

39 Curtis and Smith, 'How did 2015 voters cast their ballot'.

40   Michael Ashcroft, 'How did this result happen? My post-vote survey', 9 June 2017, available at: http://lordashcroftpolls.com/2017/06/result-happen-post-vote-survey/, last accessed 3 November 2017. Equally, a mixed mode panel conducted by NatCen Social Research found that support for the Liberal Democrats increased by just one point among Remain voters (to 15 per cent), while it fell back a point (to 5 per cent) among Leave supporters.

41   Ipsos MORI, 'How Britain voted in the 2017 election', available at: www.ipsos.com/ipsos-mori/en-uk/how-britain-voted-2017-election, last accessed 30 October 2017.

42   Peter Kellner, 'General Election 2015: How Britain really voted', *YouGov*, 8 June 2015, available at: https://yougov.co.uk/news/2015/06/08/general-election-2015-how-britain-really-voted/, last accessed 3 November 2015.

43   John Curtice, Stephen Fisher and Robert Ford, 'Appendix 1: The results analysed', in Philip Cowley and Dennis Kavanagh, *The British General Election of 2015* (Basingstoke: Palgrave Macmillan, 2016), pp. 387–431.

44   John Curtice, 'The Liberal Democrats and the 2015 election', *Journal of Liberal History*, 88 (2015), 64–69.

4

The rise and fall of UKIP, 2010–17

Paul Whiteley, Matthew Goodwin and Harold D. Clarke

It is impossible to understand the outcome of the 2017 general election without reference to the remarkable rise in support for the United Kingdom Independence Party (UKIP) that occurred during the period of coalition government after the 2010 general election. The high point of UKIP's success was the referendum on British membership of the European Union (EU) in June 2016. The party's downfall came only one year later when it was virtually wiped out at the 2017 general election. In 2015 UKIP had fielded 624 candidates and received nearly 13 per cent of the national vote. In 2017, by contrast, it fielded just 377 candidates and its share of the UK vote crashed to 1.8 per cent. In 2015 the party polled at least 10 per cent of the vote in 450 constituencies. In 2017 it achieved this milestone in only two. While UKIP's growth was rooted in long-term social changes, it has turned out to be a 'flash' party, a term political scientists use to describe new parties that are here today and gone tomorrow.[1]

In its rise and fall, UKIP resembles the Social Democratic Party (SDP) of the 1980s. The SDP had been formed in 1981 after a widely publicised ideological schism split the Labour Party. Although the SDP quickly became a prominent player, it failed to 'break the mould' of British party politics, as its founders intended, and was eventually taken over by the Liberals in the newly formed Liberal Democrats. Its long-term impact was negligible.[2] In contrast, UKIP's impact on British politics has been profound. Its rapid success prompted David Cameron to call a referendum on EU membership, and there is a strong case for arguing that the United Kingdom would not have voted to leave the EU in 2016 without UKIP.

This chapter has two objectives. The first is to identify the factors that explain the remarkable rise in support for UKIP after the 2010 general election, in particular the party's electoral success in the 2014 European Parliament elections and 2015 general election, as well as its contribution to the victory for the Leave campaign in the 2016 referendum.[3] The second task is to explain why the party crashed so spectacularly in the 2017 general election. Explanations of both its rise and fall can be divided into long- and short-term factors, the former associated with deeper social changes 'baked in' over a relatively long period, and the latter associated with various events and conditions that occurred over the past decade.

The structure of the chapter is as follows: it first examines changes in support for UKIP over time to identify the trends that need to be explained. Next, it identifies the forces that underpinned the rise in support for the party and that are relevant for understanding right-wing populism more generally. It then presents empirical evidence on trends that have helped to drive support for UKIP over time. Finally, it considers the party's performance in 2017, when the gains made after 2010 were reversed. The conclusion speculates about UKIP's future and the possible re-emergence of a populist right-wing party in British politics.

Trends in UKIP support, 2010 to 2017

In the 2010 general election, UKIP fielded 558 candidates, 459 of whom lost their deposits, and won only 3.1 per cent of the national vote. The party came nowhere near winning a seat in the House of Commons: its best result was recorded in the Speaker's constituency of Buckingham, a seat which is traditionally not contested by the main parties, where UKIP's former and soon-to-be-again leader Nigel Farage won 17.5 per cent of the vote. As the Conservatives and Liberal Democrats formed their coalition government, UKIP was very much on the fringes of British politics. The partial exception to this picture was the party's success in the 'second-order' 2009 European Parliament elections, which had taken place under a more proportional regional party-list electoral system.[4] In these elections, and against the backdrop of a parliamentary expenses scandal, UKIP came second, receiving almost 2.5 million votes and winning 13 seats.[5] This was a sign of things to come, even though this performance was not repeated in the 2010 general election.

Nigel Farage, who had reassumed the party's leadership in November 2010, was determined to change this state of affairs. In a speech at the party's 2011 spring conference, he announced that:

> The Liberal Democrats are no longer the voice of opposition in British politics – we are. Between now and the next general election our aim is to replace them as the third party in British politics.[6]

In purely electoral terms, UKIP easily achieved this objective, winning 3.9 million votes and one seat in the 2015 general election. In contrast, the Liberal Democrats won only 2.4 million votes, although they still won eight seats. Figure 4.1 uses data from the Essex Continuous Monitoring Survey (ECMS), to show trends in general-election voting intentions for UKIP from April 2004 to April 2015. Before 2010 UKIP support fluctuated at around 4 per cent and showed no sign of increasing over time, apart from two bursts of increased

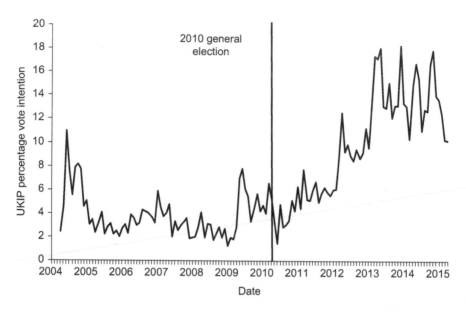

Figure 4.1 Percentage intending to vote UKIP in next general election, April
2004–April 2015

Source: Essex Continuous Monitoring Survey.

popularity during the 2004 and 2009 European Parliament elections. It is also
worth noting that during this earlier period UKIP was competing for votes with
the far-right British National Party (BNP), which often out-performed UKIP
at the local level.[7] In sharp contrast, after 2010, and following the collapse of the
BNP, UKIP's support began to trend upwards.

The real breakthrough election for UKIP was not the 2015 general election,
but the European Parliament elections in May 2014, a contest that saw the
party campaign heavily against membership of the European Union, migrant
workers from other EU member states and the other main Westminster parties.
The party topped the poll with more than 4.3 million votes, or 26.6 per cent
of the UK vote, and won 24 seats. This was the first time a party other than
Labour or the Conservatives had won the most seats in a nation-wide election
since 1910, the year of two narrow general-election victories for the old Liberal
Party. The European Parliament elections of 2014 were a watershed for UKIP
and provided the springboard for the party's improved performance in the 2015
general election. UKIP's strong showings in these elections paved the way for
the unexpected Leave victory in the 2016 referendum.

The next section examines why the remarkable change in UKIP's electoral
fortunes took place between 2010 and 2016, only to quickly unravel in 2017.
Explanations can be divided into two broad types: those that emphasise forces
arising from long-term trends in the British economy and society; and those
that focus on short-term forces associated with particular election campaigns.

The former go well beyond British politics and involve global economic and social changes that are affecting the politics of many advanced democracies. In contrast, the latter are associated with specific events and conditions in British electoral politics. We begin by examining the long-term factors that apply to Britain and other democracies in Europe and elsewhere.

Explaining support for right-wing populist parties

There are two broad types of explanations for the growth in support for insurgent right-wing populist parties, such as UKIP.[8] The first focuses on a syndrome of grievances based on the economic marginalisation of individuals, perceived threats from immigrants, refugees and ethnic-minority groups, and identity politics. It has its roots in social and economic change brought about by globalisation and has been reinforced, at least in Europe, by the growing competences of the EU. The second type of explanation emphasises voters' growing disillusionment with the performance and effectiveness of mainstream political parties, and declining trust in politicians and democratic institutions. It is largely driven by perceptions that political parties and state institutions, such as parliaments, no longer deliver what people want. Together these developments interact in important ways to bring about growing discontent with the status quo. They also create opportunities for populist parties of both the left and right to attract public support.

Populist parties tend to offer simple solutions to complex problems. They are often led by charismatic individuals who tend to focus on communicating clear goals but who are usually less clear about the details of policy implementation. Since its founding in 1991 by the academic Alan Sked, initially as the Anti-Federalist League, UKIP has portrayed itself as a 'common-sense' party that vigorously champions the interests of ordinary people – interests that it claims are being progressively undermined by unresponsive economic and political elites. According to this populist narrative, self-serving elites dominate Britain's mainstream political parties. The elites are said to have given sovereignty away to the EU, so that Britain is increasingly subservient to an unelected, unresponsive and unaccountable Brussels bureaucracy that threatens to drown British democracy in a sea of vexatious regulations. These developments are also said to put traditional political and social institutions and cultural values at grave risk. UKIP has always argued that as long as Britain remained a member of the EU it faced an insurmountable 'democratic deficit' and loss of control over its own destiny.

This narrative is not without substance. The 2007 Lisbon Treaty, which came into force two years later, gave the EU exclusive competence over a wide range of policy areas, including the EU customs union, competition rules, monetary policy for members of the Eurozone, the conservation of marine species under the common fisheries policy, commercial policy and the negotiation of some international agreements.[9] Further shared competences were introduced in which member states were unable to make changes once the rules had been agreed with the EU. These applied to a very broad range of policies, including the internal market, agriculture, the environment, transport, energy, security and justice. The policy area that had the most immediate resonance in the context of British electoral politics was the free movement of labour. This is one of the four founding freedoms of the EU, along with the free movement of capital, goods and services. It gives all EU citizens from across the other 27 member states the right to work in Britain – and vice versa – and it has made immigration a very potent political issue.

Free movement of labour represents both an economic and a cultural challenge to British society. Economic theory and a considerable body of evidence suggest that labour mobility brings about economic growth and boosts employment.[10] In Britain, however, there is some evidence that it has had a differential effect on domestic wage levels, reducing those at the level of semi-skilled and unskilled labour. For example, one study suggested that a 1 per cent increase in the ratio of immigrant to UK-born workers in the working-age population produced a 0.7 per cent decline in the wages of the 5 per cent of lowest paid workers.[11] The same study found that immigration produced an increase in the wages of higher paid workers, so it has distributional effects that widen inequalities in the labour market. In part, this explains why different occupational groups had different views about membership of the EU in the 2016 referendum (see Nicholas Allen in Chapter 1). Highly educated individuals in skilled jobs tended to support remaining in the EU, whereas poorly educated people in low-skilled jobs and the unemployed largely opted for Brexit.[12]

There is also evidence that free movement of labour affects the employment prospects of UK-born people. Research by the Migration Advisory Committee, an independent body that advises government on migration policy, investigated the impact of immigration on employment using data from the Labour Force Survey. The study produced evidence that immigration was undermining UK-born employment opportunities but this applied to immigration in general rather than just migration from the EU.[13] In addition, the negative impact of immigration on the employment of UK-born workers was greatest during economic downturns. So the employment effects of free movement were made worse by the 'great recession' that followed the financial crisis of 2007–08.[14]

There is also a cultural challenge arising from free movement. The arrival of large numbers of immigrants brings different cultural, linguistic, values and religious practices that can be radically at odds with those of established communities. Rapid immigration can transform neighbourhoods in relatively short periods of time in ways that can be quite challenging for long-standing residents. This can produce what sociologists call a 'culture shock' that impacts the indigent population, particularly if there is little attempt by newcomers to integrate into the wider society.[15] As one would expect, the cultural impact of immigration depends on its speed and the numbers involved, since communities have greater difficulty adjusting to change when larger numbers arrive over a shorter period of time. These issues all helped to stimulate support for UKIP. They would also stimulate support for Brexit in the run-up to the 2016 referendum. Indeed, research suggests that support for Brexit was significantly higher in communities that experienced above-average rates of demographic turnover in the ten-year period before the referendum.[16]

One important theoretical idea that has been used to explain protest behaviour in the past and is relevant for understanding growing support for UKIP is 'relative deprivation'.[17] This is the notion that people make comparisons between what they expect out of life and what they actually experience, and that a sense of deprivation occurs when the latter falls short of the former. Expectations are formed, in part, when people compare themselves with others who are rather similar to themselves. Thus blue-collar workers tend to compare themselves with other workers in occupations like their own. They will not, as a rule, compare themselves with middle-class professionals or rich entrepreneurs who are seen as being remote from their own circumstances. If such comparisons produce large gaps between expectations and actual experiences, this sense of deprivation will lead to frustration and aggression. This may in turn trigger political action in the form of protests and voting for anti-establishment populist parties like UKIP.

Relative deprivation can operate in people's personal lives arising from their social status and standards of living, but it can also focus on the political system in general. If the system is seen as being unresponsive to the concerns of ordinary people and failing to deliver equity and fairness, this will trigger a sense of relative deprivation. The larger the gap between people's expectations of government performance and their perceptions of its actual performance, the greater will be their sense of deprivation and, again, the more likely it is that they will vote for a populist party like UKIP.

Relative deprivation can influence specific perceptions, such as the feeling that the economy does not work for ordinary people, or that immigrants receive special treatment when they come to Britain. Alternatively, it can influence general feelings, such as the belief that politicians and the government do not listen to ordinary people but do listen to the 'rich and powerful' and to lobbyists. It is important to note that objective measures of deprivation such as low income or unemployment do not necessarily translate into political action. Poverty and deprivation can produce apathy and a desire to withdraw from politics or cynicism about the value of participating in politics. So there is no simple relationship between low income, low status and poverty, and support for parties like UKIP. It is only when the indicators of objective deprivation trigger a sense of injustice and psychological deprivation, and a party succeeds in giving voice to these concerns, that they translate into political action. The role of political parties and leaders in articulating this sense of deprivation is crucial for providing an appealing narrative that makes sense to people and mobilises them to enter the political arena. In Britain, UKIP succeeded in giving voice to many of these concerns.

Another aspect of UKIP's appeal was a perception that successive British governments had presided over a loss of control of policy making in an increasingly globalised world. UKIP has focused its grievances on the EU but the argument applies well beyond Europe. Research in the 1980s acknowledged the growing importance of globalisation but argued that it had not fundamentally eroded the ability of states to pursue independent policies. As one scholar observed, 'the impact of electoral politics has not been dwarfed by market dynamics'.[18] However, more recent research has tended to contradict this conclusion, suggesting that the autonomy of the state is now quite limited in many aspects of policy-making, particularly in relation to the economy.[19]

The general erosion of nation-state autonomy through globalisation has been reinforced in EU member states by the growing importance of policy-making at the EU level, and with it perceptions of a democratic deficit. National parliaments have ceded major powers to the European Union whose one elected institution, the European Parliament, is viewed by many as being remote and subservient to the powerful bureaucracy in Brussels. These perceptions help to explain the decline in turnout across the EU in European Parliament elections over time. Turnout in EU elections averaged 62 per cent in the first round of direct elections in 1979, but only 43 per cent in the eighth round in 2014.[20] Since elected bodies are seen as lacking power and influence fewer people are willing to vote for them.

A sense of public alienation from democratic institutions was given a significant boost by the 2008 financial crash and the subsequent lengthy recession. The massive economic setback had a serious effect on many EU member states. In the case of southern European countries such as Italy, Greece, Spain and Portugal, the impact was very damaging. Although the recession's effects were far from uniform, it significantly reduced living standards and increased unemployment throughout much of the EU, including Britain.

The performance of the British government in managing the economy and immigration and a generalised feeling among the public that Britain has lost control of its ability to make independent policy choices are all aspects of the mix of attitudes that has led to the rise of UKIP. A poor performance by an incumbent party, either as a consequence of mistaken policies or because it has limited ability to influence outcomes, creates opportunities for an insurgent party like UKIP to pick up votes. The drivers of UKIP support are, therefore, 'Euroscepticism, hostility to immigration, dissatisfaction with the performance of existing parties and a pessimistic outlook on life'.[21] These factors are related to the long-term developments in the economy and society discussed earlier, with origins in economic deprivation, growing inequality and the cultural challenges posed by mass immigration, as well as an accompanying sense of political alienation among marginalised groups.

While these long-term factors created favourable conditions for an insurgent party like UKIP, its rapid rise after the 2010 general election was also a product of a number of short-term factors. In the 2014 European Parliament elections and 2015 general election, negative judgements about the coalition government's performance, especially with regard to the economy, the National Health Service (NHS) and immigration, worked very much to UKIP's advantage. Labour had not recovered from being in office during the financial crisis and was still seen as unfit to run the economy. The Conservatives were penalised for their economic record as well, since real wages were flat-lining and many people felt their own financial situation was not improving as a result of chancellor George Osborne's programme of 'austerity'. Equally, many people were unhappy with the Conservatives' handling of the NHS, and an upsurge in net immigration from the EU. This development further played into UKIP's narrative that Britain has lost control of its borders.

The UKIP leader Nigel Farage also played a key role in the rise in support for his party in 2014 and 2015. Farage had long been a polarising politician with people tending either to like him or loathe him, but his anti-establishment message and 'common bloke' demeanour reached out to many and boosted support for UKIP. Positive feelings about Farage helped to mobilise discontented voters who were concerned about immigration and felt left behind because they had not kept pace with economic conditions in the country as a whole. Later, the 2016 referendum provided the same individuals with a long-awaited opportunity to strike a blow at what they regarded as unresponsive, self-serving elites at Westminster.

Another short-term factor spurring the rise of UKIP was the tens of thousands of people who joined what Farage liked to call his 'people's army'. Survey research on UKIP party members shows that the vast majority were middle-aged or older white men who became active out of a strong desire to leave the EU and reduce immigration. They provided foot soldiers in the party's election campaigns, articulating its full-throated message on the doorstep and through social media. Although demographically distinctive, their populist views about rapacious banks and corporate greed struck a chord among the wider public. Equally, their hostility to immigration and dislike of minority ethnic and religious groups closely resembled attitudes in the public in general.[22]

A final factor that helped UKIP after 2010 was the decision by Liberal Democrat leader Nick Clegg to join David Cameron's Conservatives in a coalition government. By doing so, the Liberal Democrats vacated their traditional position in the party system as a political receptacle for protest voters. Few felt a sense of attachment to the Liberal Democrats, but many more disliked both the Conservatives and Labour, and voting Liberal Democrat had been a convenient way to register a 'none of the above' sentiment. With the Liberal Democrats now in government, UKIP was the obvious alternative for the many people wishing to cast a protest vote.

In summary, a number of factors explain the increase in UKIP support after the 2010 election. They include public attitudes to membership of the EU, the performance of the economy and public services, feelings about the party leaders, and concerns about immigration. There was also the feeling among some people that Britain was losing control of its destiny and that the political establishment was responsible for this state of affairs. Equally significant were short-term factors arising from the formation of the coalition government and the policies it pursued.

UKIP support before the EU referendum

In this section we examine in greater detail the drivers of support for the party over time. UKIP's touchstone issue has always been Britain's membership of the EU, and, not surprisingly, there is clear evidence of a growth in Euroscepticism and increasing support for UKIP after 2010. Drawing on ECMS data, Figure 4.2 charts the monthly percentages of respondents who approved or disapproved of EU membership from April 2004 to April 2016, two months before the referendum. After the 2010 general election Euroscepticism grew rapidly. Those who disapproved of EU membership continued to outnumber those who approved of it until the 2014 European Parliament elections. Thus, in the run-up to UKIP's breakthrough election, Britain was a relatively Eurosceptic country. Many people turned to UKIP during this period, and a sizable portion stayed with the party through to the general 2015 general election, even though levels of Euroscepticism had started to wane by that time.

The background to mounting levels of Euroscepticism was the Eurozone debt crisis. In the wake of the 2007–08 financial crisis, a number of EU member states, notably Greece, Portugal and Ireland, were unable to repay or refinance their government debt or to bail out their over-indebted banks. As a result, they sought support from other Eurozone countries, the International Monetary Fund (IMF) and the European Central Bank (ECB). The ECB in particular was slow in responding to the crisis, and did so initially by pursuing pre-Keynesian austerity measures that only made things worse.[23]

Back in Britain, the 2010 Conservative–Liberal Democrat coalition government also decided to pursue a policy of austerity, which involved large-scale cuts in public expenditure and a freeze on public sector pay and other measures, as Nicholas Allen outlines in Chapter 1.[24] Research has shown that many voters do not distinguish between the British government and the EU when it comes to attributing responsibility for economic performance. Instead, they tend to bundle these together with both being rewarded for a good performance and punished for a bad one.[25] This meant that many voters did not distinguish between the Eurozone crisis and the consequences of domestic austerity policies. The crisis and the austerity policies worked together to produce an anti-EU backlash that is evident in Figure 4.2. Indeed, had a referendum on EU membership been held in early 2012 it probably would have produced a landside majority for Leave. In contrast by 2015 the British economy had emerged from recession, and the resulting change in economic perceptions helped to stimulate a revision of attitudes to EU membership. Had the referendum taken place at the same

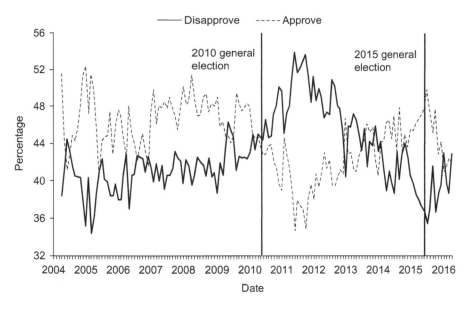

Figure 4.2 Attitudes towards EU membership, April 2004–April 2016
Source: Essex Continuous Monitoring Survey.

time as the 2015 general election, there probably would have been a Remain majority. But in the earlier period leading up to the 2014 European Parliament elections, many voters concluded that the EU was a failing enterprise and so were open to the idea supporting UKIP.

Figure 4.3 shows the relationship between intending to vote UKIP and perceptions that no party is best at managing the economy in Britain. It is clear that UKIP voting intentions tracked the perception that none of the major parties could do a good job on the economy.[26] One can readily appreciate why the perception that no party could manage the economy was growing at the time. The great recession had damaged Labour's reputation for economic management when the party was in office before 2010, so voters continued to be sceptical about the party after that election. The Conservatives suffered from the same perception after the election as a result of their austerity policies. Voters were increasingly likely to think that none of the major parties were up to the job of managing the economy and some of them turned to UKIP.

The effects of economic conditions on Conservative support involved the phenomenon of relative deprivation discussed earlier. Here, the gap between perceptions of national and personal economic circumstances is key. The ECMS measured personal economic optimism with a question asking people about the financial prospects for themselves and their families over the coming year. It measured national economic optimism with a question asking people about their views of the state of the economy as a whole, again over the coming year. As Britain came out of recession in 2013, optimism about the national economy

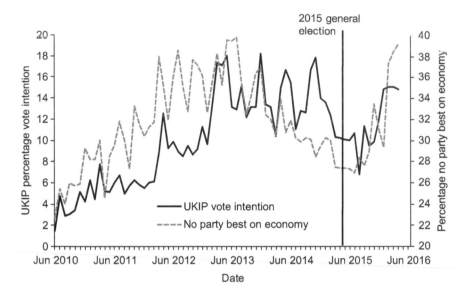

Figure 4.3 UKIP vote intentions and perceptions that no party is best at managing the UK economy, June 2010–May 2016

Source: Essex Continuous Monitoring Survey.

soared. Personal economic optimism also increased, but much more slowly. As Figure 4.4 shows, these differences – calculated by subtracting the proportion of those saying the national economy was getting better from the proportion saying their personal finances were getting better – produced a growing gap between people's judgements about how they were doing compared with the country as a whole. This gap is important for generating feelings of relative deprivation. Although judgements about national and personal economic conditions became more sanguine, unfavourable comparisons between personal circumstances and those for the country at a whole became more common. As this gap grew, so did support for UKIP.[27]

A third important issue that helped to increase support for UKIP was the sensitive topic of immigration. Concerns about rising immigration had been growing across the EU during this period, and were given a significant boost by German chancellor Angela Merkel's decision to throw open Germany's borders to over one million immigrants from the Middle East and Africa in 2015.[28] This decision led to the partial suspension of the Schengen Agreement, the policy of open borders across Europe, and it triggered growing support for right-wing populist parties like UKIP. As Figure 4.5 shows, ECMS data showed an upward trend in perceptions that immigration was getting worse during this time – a perception that was reinforced by a large growth in net immigration into Britain from the EU.[29] In the 1990s flows of migrants between Britain and the rest of the EU had been below 100,000 a year and were largely self-cancelling. By 2015, immigration from the EU was running at nearly 300,000 a year, nearly two-and-a-half

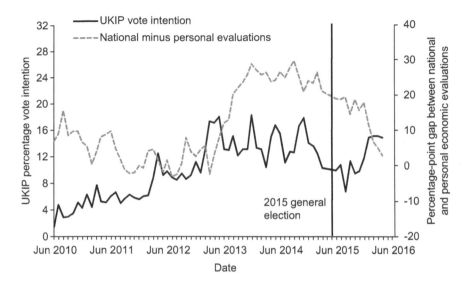

Figure 4.4 UKIP vote intentions and gap between national and personal economic conditions, June 2010–May 2016

Source: Essex Continuous Monitoring Survey.

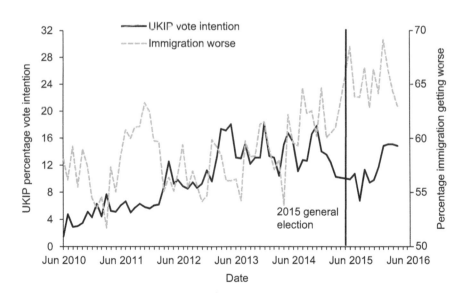

Figure 4.5 UKIP vote intentions and perceptions that immigration is getting worse, June 2010–May 2016

Source: Essex Continuous Monitoring Survey.

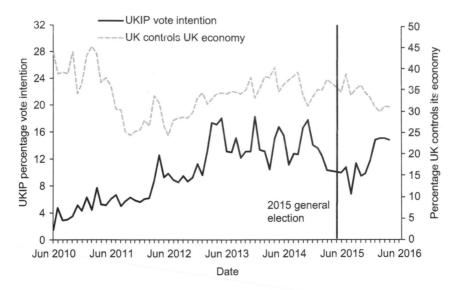

Figure 4.6 UKIP vote intentions and perceptions that the UK government controls the country's economy, June 2010–May 2016

Source: Essex Continuous Monitoring Survey.

times greater than emigration to the EU, which was about 125,000 a year.[30] In addition, the upsurge in arrivals from the EU was largely economic, reflecting the country's emergence from recession earlier than the Eurozone.[31] The suggestion that migrant workers were undercutting domestic wage levels was a particularly controversial aspect of debates over immigration and reinforced the salience of this issue.

One of the drivers of support for UKIP and Euroscepticism more generally was the perception that the UK was losing control of its destiny. The UK had lost control of its borders and economy, so the argument runs, while the democratic accountability of Parliament had been weakened by the effects of globalisation and European integration. This perception can be investigated by a question in the ECMS surveys which asked respondents about the UK government's control of the British economy.[32] The relationship between it and UKIP voting intentions is shown in Figure 4.6. Perceptions that the government controlled the economy rapidly declined during the early years of austerity following the general election, and this coincided with increased support for UKIP.[33] By the start of 2013 the perceived ability of the government to control the country's economy revived, although it did not return to earlier levels. During this later period the percentage of people saying they intended to vote UKIP levelled off but did not decline.

One of the themes in Nigel Farage's speeches and UKIP campaigning more gen-erally was that the three big parties in Westminster politics were not to be trusted

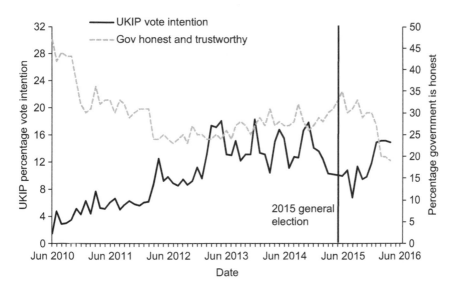

Figure 4.7 UKIP vote intentions and perceptions that the government is honest and trustworthy, June 2010–May 2016

Source: Essex Continuous Monitoring Survey.

since they failed to deliver on their promises and ran a cosy cartel that served Britain badly. Figure 4.7 displays the relationship between UKIP voting intentions and perceptions that the British government was honest and trustworthy. This variable provides a general indicator of dissatisfaction with government institutions. The change of government in 2010 produced a huge increase in perceptions that the government was honest, something that had happened following previous changes of government.[34] But once the new coalition government was in place, perceptions that it was honest and trustworthy declined quickly as the austerity policies started to bite. Some voters were perhaps also mindful of the Liberal Democrats' broken commitment to abolish university tuition fees. Once again, this period coincided with a rise in support for UKIP, and when perceptions of honesty stabilised after the start of 2013, support for the party levelled off.[35]

A final factor noteworthy for understanding the rise in UKIP support relates to identity politics, especially national identity. Despite its name, the *United Kingdom* Independence Party has always done better in some parts of Britain than others. For instance, in the 2014 European Parliament elections, the party won on average 29.2 cent of the vote in England, 27.6 per cent of the vote in Wales and only 10.5 per cent of the vote in Scotland. Similarly, in the 2015 general election, the party won 14 per cent of the vote in England and a similar proportion of the vote in Wales. In Scotland, however, UKIP won only 1.6 per cent of the vote. Compared to the rest of mainland Britain, Scotland has tended to be a no-go area for UKIP. The party's messages never resonated with Scottish identity.

The link between national identity and support for UKIP's cause can also be seen in patterns of voting in the 2016 EU referendum. A majority of voters in England and Wales (53.4 per cent and 52.5 per cent respectively) gave their backing to Leave, whereas a majority of voters in Scotland and Northern Ireland (62.0 per cent and 55.8 per cent) backed Remain. Identity also mattered in England: survey research has consistently shown that individuals who said they thought of themselves as 'British' were quite likely to vote Remain, whereas those who said they thought of themselves as 'English' were more likely to vote Leave.[36] That said, national identity cannot easily explain the *rapid* rise in support for UKIP after 2010 because identities change slowly over time. National identity has worked in the background to influence attitudes towards the EU, and it has also structured support for the party, but it did not by itself cause a short-term boost in support for UKIP.

A multivariate statistical analysis of UKIP voting shows that several explanatory variables affected support for the party in the 2015 general election and voting in the EU referendum a year later.[37] After the 2010 election UKIP entered a virtuous circle of electoral success followed by increasing media coverage in a context in which Euroscepticism was increasing over time. These factors had the effect of generating further electoral success as previously inattentive voters started paying attention to what UKIP was saying.[38] Some of them found the party's messages appealing.

After the EU referendum UKIP entered a turbulent period and the support that it had built up in the earlier period largely disappeared. We tell this story in the next section.

UKIP and the 2017 general election

The 2017 general election produced an apparent return to two-party politics in Britain. As discussed at greater length by John Bartle in Chapter 8 the Conservatives secured 42.4 per cent of the vote, an increase of 5.5 percentage points on 2015, but the party lost a net total of 13 seats. At the same time, Labour won 40.0 per cent of the vote, a 9.6-point increase, and gained a net total of 30 seats. The two main parties increased their share of the vote at the expense of the other parties – none more so than UKIP. Its vote share collapsed from 12.6 per cent to 1.8 per cent, with the party losing nearly 3.5 million votes across the UK. The party's sole MP, Douglas Carswell, had previously quit the party after Theresa May had triggered Article 50. UKIP slumped to a distant third place in Carswell's old seat of Clacton. Indeed, while the party had come second in 120 seats in 2015, it finished no higher than third in any seat in 2017.

Given that UKIP had also won a larger vote share in both 2005 (2.2 per cent) and 2010 (3.1 per cent), the 2017 result signalled a sharp reversal in public support. Part of the reason for UKIP's abrupt decline was that it contested only 317 seats, well down from the 624 it had fought in the 2015 election. The party clearly had trouble recruiting candidates, suggesting that the decline in its support was well under way before the general election took place.

One interesting question to ask is where did the 2015 UKIP vote go to in 2017? We can get an idea of which parties gained most from UKIP's electoral demise by looking at constituency voting in the two elections. If a fall in the UKIP vote was strongly associated with a rise in the Conservative vote, but only weakly associated with an increase in the Labour vote, that would imply that the Conservatives gained more from the collapse of UKIP than did Labour.

The correlation between changes in the Conservative and UKIP vote shares in the 317 constituencies that UKIP contested was -0.38. In other words the collapse in the UKIP vote helped the Conservatives, but it was not a one-to-one relationship. As far as the other parties were concerned, changes in the Green Party's vote share had a modest negative relationship with changes in the UKIP vote (-0.29). In the case of Labour the relationship was negative but relatively weak (-0.13) and for the Liberal Democrats it was negligible (0.06). The Conservatives were clearly the winners from the sea-change in UKIP's fortunes. These numbers are consistent with the finding that many former Conservative voters who had switched to UKIP in 2015 returned to the fold in 2017.

There are essentially three reasons why the party did so badly in the 2017 election: leadership, internal conflicts and Brexit. In terms of leadership, Nigel Farage had stepped down immediately after the 2016 referendum. This was always likely to hurt UKIP since he had been such a dominant figure in the 2015 election and had effectively mobilised support. He had also kept the party more or less united. Farage backed Diane James as his successor in the subsequent leadership contest and she duly won. She was a former UKIP councillor in Waveney and was subsequently elected to the European Parliament in 2014. However, James stepped down after only 18 days in the job claiming that she lacked the authority to see through the changes she had planned. Soon afterwards, she left the party altogether, though she remained an independent MEP. This development was a clear sign that infighting had engulfed UKIP after the referendum.

These internal conflicts went public after James stepped down, and they started to influence UKIP's standing among the public. Steve Woolfe, an MEP, got into a fight with Mike Hookem, a fellow UKIP member of the European Parliament, in October 2016 over allegations that Woolfe was planning to defect to the Conservatives.[39] Rumours about this surfaced after Woolfe was prevented from running for the leadership contest on a technicality by the party's National Executive Committee. In addition, Douglas Carswell, UKIP's only MP, had been in conflict with Farage over party strategy for some time but this dispute went public after the referendum vote had been won. In early 2017 Farage claimed that Carswell had undermined UKIP's policy agenda from the beginning and called for him to be expelled from the party. Carswell left the party in March 2017 and sat briefly as an independent MP before leaving the House of Commons at the 2017 general election. Shortly afterwards, another former UKIP MP, Mark Reckless, who had defected from the Tories, also resigned his party membership. Reckless had won the Rochester and Strood by-election for UKIP in late 2014 but had lost his seat to the Tories in the 2015 general election.

Paul Nuttall won the leadership contest held after Diane James resigned. Nuttall was an activist from northern England who sought to take the party in a more right-wing direction. He also talked more about the issue of radical Islam, always a sensitive issue, and courted accusations of Islamophobia. Nuttall lacked Farage's political acumen and campaigning skills. He was also less popular among voters. This mattered because voters' reactions to party leaders are an important factor in influencing vote choice. Leader images constitute a 'fast and frugal' heuristic or cue which voters use to evaluate a party without knowing a great deal about its policies or performance. During the 2015 and 2017 election campaigns, the ECMS asked respondents to score the party leaders on an 11-point likeability scale where 0 meant that they strongly disliked a leader and 10 meant that they strongly liked them. Neither Farage nor Nuttall were particularly popular across the electorate as a whole. Farage's average score in 2015, however, was significantly higher (3.5) than Nuttall's in 2017 (2.5). This is a significant difference for this type of measure and suggests that Nuttall's unpopularity contributed to the collapse of his party's vote.

A sign of things to come was provided by the local government elections in May 2017. UKIP won a single seat from Labour in Lancashire but lost all 145 of the council seats it was defending. This devastating loss prompted the party's millionaire donor Arron Banks to call for the party to be wound up, blaming Paul Nuttall for the heavy losses. In a statement he said: 'If we use the analogy of UKIP as a racing car, Nigel was a skilled driver who drove the car around the track faster and faster, knowing when to take risks, delighting the audience. The current leadership has crashed the car, at the first bend of the race, into the crowd, killing the driver and spectators.'[40]

A month later in the general election, Nuttall ran a distant third in the Boston and Skegness constituency, winning only 7.7 per cent of the vote and 24,000 fewer votes than the winning Tory candidate. This result compared very badly with UKIP's performance in 2015 when the party came second in the seat on 33.8 per cent of the vote, just 4,300 votes behind the Conservatives. Nuttall had chosen this seat precisely because it looked like it could be won by UKIP, but the result in 2017 turned out very differently from his expectations. As the dust cleared from the general election, Nuttall announced his resignation as leader.

The unpopularity of UKIP's leader was not the whole story, however. UKIP also lost ground in the eyes of the public between 2015 and 2017. Using a similar 'likeability' scale to measure public attitudes towards the parties shows that by the time of the 2017 general election, UKIP was becoming a 'nasty' party in the eyes of many of its previous sympathisers. The upshot was that both the leader and the party suffered significant losses in public esteem between the two elections. The post-referendum infighting in the party undoubtedly produced a large amount of unfavourable publicity and damaged the public's perception of the party.

Although the change in leadership and infighting were important, the most significant factor in UKIP's sudden decline was the result of the EU referendum. In effect, the party suffered from a 'winner's curse': it had achieved its main objective, and so many of its former supporters, especially those who had voted Leave in the EU referendum, decided that UKIP was no longer needed. This perception was reinforced by Theresa May's Lancaster House speech in January 2017 where she set out her government's priorities for the Brexit negotiations. This speech called for an end to membership of the single market and the jurisdiction of the European Court of Justice. Britain would also leave the EU's customs union and reclaim the right to negotiate trade agreements with countries outside the EU. Perhaps even more importantly for some former UKIP supporters, the UK would reassert control over its borders and immigration. May's promise of, in effect, a 'hard' Brexit greatly weakened UKIP's argument that the Conservatives could not be trusted to respect the referendum result.

During the EU referendum campaign, the Leave campaign, like UKIP, had made great use of the slogan 'take back control'. It had proven very effective, and May had clearly accepted the need to respect the sentiment. Under May, the Tories had also moved to accommodate other UKIP ideas, such as supporting the promotion of new grammar schools and the rejection of social liberalism. At the autumn 2016 Conservative party conference, May had enraged many social liberals by declaring: 'if you believe you're a citizen of the world, you're a citizen of nowhere'.[41] In the 2017 election campaign UKIP was reduced to the rather lame claim that it would 'keep an eye on the Conservatives' as the Brexit process unfolded. With May's government seemingly committed to a hard Brexit, UKIP's promise was unlikely to inspire many, particularly since the party had always had a tiny – and, after Carswell's resignation, non-existent – presence in the House of Commons.

Conclusion: rise and fall

UKIP's story has been remarkable. For years after its creation it remained stuck on the fringes of British politics, making occasional inroads at successive European Parliament elections. Then, the 2007–08 financial crisis, the great recession and the arrival of the coalition government in 2010 opened up the political space for the party to prosper. Under Nigel Farage, it took full advantage of this opportunity and became, briefly, a major force to be reckoned with.

In the wake of the 2016 Brexit referendum and especially the devastating blow of the 2017 general election, its significance has all but evaporated. Although UKIP still has some elected representatives in the Welsh Assembly, local government and, ironically, in the European Parliament, it may not survive in its present form.

Despite its recent setbacks, the party continues to represent a distinct if small group of mostly elderly white men who feel they have been left behind by economic and cultural changes in British society over the last quarter of a century. This group is not going anywhere in the near future and so there is a continuing support base for the party, even if it is unlikely to permit a repeat of its success in the 2015 election. In the social characteristics of its supporters, UKIP has much in common with other populist parties in Europe, such as France's National Front and Germany's Alternative für Deutschland, the latter doing particularly well in the 2017 German elections. UKIP has previously tapped into public concerns about rising immigration, a loss of control by national governments, a distrust of elites and above all the flat-lining wages and failure of government to manage the economy successfully after the great recession. If these conditions persist into the future then the party has a narrative which could appeal to many voters and enable it to rebuild.

For the time being, the Conservative stance on Brexit has left little space for UKIP to articulate an alternative position and appeal to Eurosceptic voters. However, Theresa May's loss of her party's parliamentary majority in the 2017 general election has greatly weakened her hand in the negotiations. It is going to be very hard for the government to get a 'hard' Brexit through Parliament. Paul Nuttall's successor as UKIP leader, Henry Bolton, rejected any shift towards an anti-Islamic agenda and signalled his commitment to focusing on Brexit. In doing so, he aligned himself more closely with Nigel Farage's general stance. Bolton's leadership was to prove short-lived, however. In February 2018, following a scandal over racist text messages sent by his girlfriend, he was forced to resign, raising further questions about the party's future strategy. If negotiations with the EU fail and there is no deal, there could be an anti-EU backlash that could create an opportunity for UKIP to articulate successfully an alternative, more confrontational approach to Brussels. In short, circumstances could yet favour the re-emergence of a right-wing populist party in British politics in the near future. Whether this will be a reinvigorated UKIP – perhaps led, once again, by Farage – or an offshoot party under another name, or even an entirely new party, remains to be seen.

Notes

1   For an overview of these social changes, see Robert Ford and Matthew Goodwin, *Revolt on the Right: Explaining Support for the Radical Right in Britain* (London: Routledge, 2014).

2   For the definitive account of the party's short history, see Ivor Crewe and Anthony King, *SDP: The Birth, Life and Death of the Social Democratic Party* (Oxford: Oxford University Press, 1995).

3   See Harold D. Clarke, Matthew Goodwin and Paul Whiteley, *Brexit: Why Britain Voted to Leave the European Union* (Cambridge: Cambridge University Press, 2017).

4   Second-order elections generally refer to those other than general elections in the United Kingdom. But see Robert Johns in Chapter 5 of this volume on the changing character of elections for the Scottish Parliament.

5   Dennis Kavanagh and Philip Cowley, *The British General Election of 2010* (Basingstoke: Palgrave Macmillan, 2010), p. 352.

6   BBC News, 'UKIP leader says they "will replace Liberal Democrats"', 5 March 2011, available at: www.bbc.co.uk/news/uk-politics-12658045, last accessed 20 October 2017.

7   Matthew Goodwin, *New British Fascism: Rise of the British National Party* (Abingdon: Routledge, 2011).

8   A sizable literature on support for European right-wing populist parties has appeared over the past two decades. See, for example, Cas Mudde, *Populist Radical Right Parties in Europe* (Cambridge: Cambridge University Press, 2007); Daniel Oesch, 'Explaining workers' support for right-wing populist parties in Western Europe: Evidence from Austria, Belgium, France, Norway, and Switzerland', *International Political Science Review*, 29 (2008), 349–373; and Kai Arzheimer, 'Contextual factors and the extreme right vote in Western Europe, 1980–2002', *American Journal of Political Science*, 53 (2009), 259–275. More general studies relevant to understanding possible openings for minor parties in the British party system include Cees Van der Eijk and Mark N. Franklin, 'Potential for contestation on European matters at national elections in Europe', in Gary Marks and Marco R. Steenbergen (eds), *European Integration and Political Conflict* (Cambridge: Cambridge University Press, 2004), pp. 32–50; Jack H. Nagel and Christopher Wlezien, 'Centre-party strength and major-party divergence in Britain, 1945–2005', *British Journal of Political Science*, 40 (2010), 279–304; and Daniel Stevens, 'Issue evolution in Britain: The debate on European Union integration, 1964–2010', *European Journal of Political Research*, 52 (2013), 536–557.

9   See Jean-Claude Piris, *The Lisbon Treaty: A Legal and Political Analysis* (Cambridge: Cambridge University Press, 2010).

10 See Daron Acemoglu, *Introduction to Modern Economic Growth* (Princeton: Princeton University Press, 2009).

11 Christian Dustmann, Tommaso Frattini and Ian P. Preston, 'The effect of immigration along the distribution of wages', *Review of Economic Studies*, 80 (2013), 145–173.

12 See Clarke *et al.*, *Brexit*.

13 See Migration Advisory Committee, *Analysis of the Impacts of Migration* (London: Home Office, 2012).

14 See Michael Moran, Sukhdev Johal and Karel Williams, 'The financial crisis and its consequences', in Nicholas Allen and John Bartle (eds), *Britain at the Polls 2010* (London: Sage, 2011), pp. 89–119.

15 See Adrian Furnham, Colleen Ward and Stephen Bochner, *The Psychology of Culture Shock* (London: Routledge, 2001).

16 See Matthew Goodwin and Oliver Heath, 'The 2016 referendum, Brexit and the left behind: An aggregate-level analysis of the result', *Political Quarterly*, 87 (2016), 323–332.

17 See W.G. Runciman, *Relative Deprivation and Social Justice* (Berkeley: University of California Press, 1966).

18 Geoffrey Garrett, *Partisan Politics in the Global Economy* (Cambridge: Cambridge University Press, 1998), p. 2.

19 See for example Timothy Hellwig, *Globalization and Mass Politics: Retaining the Room to Maneuver* (Cambridge: Cambridge University Press, 2014).

20 European Parliament, 'Results of the 2014 European elections: Turnout', available at: www.europarl.europa.eu/elections2014-results/en/turnout.html, last accessed 20 October 2017.

21 Ford and Goodwin, *Revolt on the Right*, p. 187.

22 Clarke *et al.*, *Brexit*, pp. 191–193.

23 See Mark Blyth, *Austerity: The History of a Dangerous Idea* (Oxford: Oxford University Press, 2013).

24 See also Harold D. Clarke, Peter Kellner, Marianne C. Stewart, Joe Twyman and Paul Whiteley, *Austerity and Political Choice in Britain* (London: Palgrave Macmillan, 2016).

25 Mark Franklin, Michael Marsh and Lauren McLaren, 'Uncorking the bottle: Popular opposition to European unification in the wake of Maastricht', *Journal of Common Market Studies*, 32 (1994), 455–473.

26 The Pearson's *r* coefficient for the two series is +0.55, indicating a moderate positive correlation.

27 The Pearson's *r* coefficient for these two series is +0.46, again indicating a moderate positive correlation.

28 Kate Conolly, 'Angela Merkel defends Germany's refugee policy after attacks', *Guardian*, 28 July 2016.

29 Because high levels of concern about immigration preceded growing support for UKIP, the Pearson's *r* coefficient (+0.24) shows only a weak positive correlation.

30 Office for National Statistics, *National Population Projections, 2012-Based Reference Volume* (Titchfield: ONS, 2016).

31 Clarke *et al.*, *Brexit*, pp. 191–193.

32 Alternative possible responses included the options that the EU controls the economy or that no one controls it.

33 Across the period as a whole, however, the Pearson's *r* coefficient (-0.09) shows no correlation.

34 Paul Whiteley, Harold D. Clarke, David Sanders and Marianne C. Stewart, 'Why do voters lose trust in governments? Public perceptions of government honesty and trustworthiness in Britain 2000–2013', *British Journal of Politics and International Relations*, 18 (2016), 234–254.

35 The Pearson's *r* coefficient for these two series is -0.68, indicating a strong negative correlation between perceptions of honesty and UKIP support.

36 Clarke *et al.*, *Brexit*, pp. 159–160.

37 Clarke *et al.*, *Brexit*, pp. 111–145.

38 UKIP was accorded 'major party' party status by Ofcom in March 2015. This meant the party was awarded two party election broadcasts in 2015 and opened the door to Nigel Farage's participation in the two televised leaders' debates.

39 Jessica Elgot, Josh Halliday and Jennifer Rankin, 'Steven Woolfe "smiling and well" after alleged fight with Ukip MEP', *Guardian*, 6 October 2016.

40 The statement is repeated in Danny Boyle, 'Arron Banks: Under Nigel Farage, Ukip was a racing car – Paul Nuttall has "crashed the car at first bend of the race"', *Daily Telegraph*, 5 May 2017, available at: www.telegraph.co.uk/news/2017/05/05/arron-banks-nigel-farage-ukip-racing-car-paul-nuttall-has/, last accessed 20 October 2017.

41 Theresa May, 'Theresa May's conference speech in full', *Daily Telegraph*, 5 October 2016, available at: www.telegraph.co.uk/news/2016/10/05/theresa-mays-conference-speech-in-full, last accessed 20 October 2017.

5

Squeezing the SNP

The election in Scotland

Robert Johns

General elections are the United Kingdom's national elections. But the UK is made up of nations and regions, each with its own distinctive political institutions and interests, and their dynamics are part of the story of every general election. Just as many voters in Scotland feel both British and Scottish, so each general election in Scotland is about both UK politics and the specific interests and issues at play in Scottish politics. The importance of the Scottish dimension has strengthened considerably in recent decades. First, there was devolution and the creation in 1999 of a separate Scottish Parliament at Holyrood, which was endowed with primary law-making powers, and an executive. Then there was an intensely fought independence referendum in 2014 that not only left Scotland's constitutional future uppermost in Scottish voters' minds, but also made that future a live issue in broader British politics.

Constitutional upheaval has certainly brought rapid electoral change in Scotland. The backdrop to the 2017 general election there was barely recognisable from just ten years before, and would have been unthinkable 20 years earlier. In 1997, Labour cruised to a victory in Scotland even more comprehensive than its win south of the border, winning 46 per cent of the vote and 56 of the 72 seats then available.[1] The Conservatives, supposedly the UK's other major party, were wiped out entirely. The pro-independence Scottish National Party (SNP), while doubling its seat tally, still sent only six MPs to Westminster, and many in the Labour Party believed that any threat posed by the SNP was shortly to be extinguished by the creation of a Scottish Parliament. George (now Lord) Robertson was not the only senior Labour figure who thought that devolution would 'kill nationalism stone dead'.[2]

Robertson's prediction proved spectacularly wrong. In the 2014 referendum, some 44.7 per cent of the Scottish electorate voted 'Yes' to independence from the rest of the UK. In the 2015 general election, the SNP achieved a near 'yellow-wash' of the Scottish electoral map, taking all but three of the 59 seats

Table 5.1 Results of the 2017 UK general election in Scotland

	Vote share (%)	Change	Seats (N)	Change
SNP	36.9	−13.1	35	−21
Conservative	28.6	13.7	13	12
Labour	27.1	2.8	7	6
Liberal Democrat	6.8	−0.8	4	3
Others	0.7	−2.6	0	0
Turnout	66.4	−4.7		

Source: House of Commons.

now available and winning 50 per cent of the vote. Such electoral dominance is unheard of in modern British politics (and, for that matter, in competitive elections almost anywhere else). In particular, the SNP achieved a complete takeover of the urban 'central belt', an area stretching from Glasgow in the west to Edinburgh in the east, much of which used to be Labour's own one-party fiefdom. The SNP simultaneously prevented any Conservative or Liberal Democrat inroads in rural areas.

Against any other backdrop, the SNP's 2017 result – a majority of Scottish seats and a vote share in the high 30s, as shown in Table 5.1 – would have been hailed as a triumph. It was by far the party's second best showing in a Westminster election after 2015. But success quickly creates expectations, and expectations drive assessments of electoral performance. Hence it was not the SNP but the Conservatives, who almost doubled their vote share and surged from fourth to second place, who came away from the 2017 election with a sense of triumph. Likewise, Labour, whose expectations were in the basement following their 2015 collapse, could find solace in winning seven seats despite finishing behind the Conservatives in a general election in Scotland for the first time since 1955.

This chapter investigates these dramatic shifts in the parties' fortunes. It begins with an overview of the post-1999 devolution settlement and the SNP's emergence as a party of power at Holyrood, suggesting that its new prominence was a useful but not sufficient condition for success in Westminster elections. It then contrasts the 2015 and 2017 elections in terms of the strategic choices facing voters, attributing the SNP's weaker performance in 2017 in large part to its limited potential influence on the anticipated Tory majority. The chapter then considers the relative impact of the 2014 'Indyref' and 2016 'Brexit' referendums, suggesting that the first of these left a much deeper imprint on voters and was the major reason for the Conservative resurgence. In essence, the SNP lost ground and the Tories made gains, not because of any decline or weakening in support for independence but because the Conservatives' 'we said no and we meant no' message appealed to unionists, while many left-leaning 'Yes' supporters set aside their constitutional preferences and joined Jeremy Corbyn's battle against the Conservatives.

Devolution and the SNP surge

With hindsight, devolution was the key to the SNP surge that left the party dominant – and with everything to lose – ahead of the 2017 election. Had the many Scots in the upper echelons of the Labour Party foreseen anything like what would happen, they might have filed away the proposal for a Scottish Parliament in the same drawer as electoral reform for Westminster on the grounds that it, too, would hurt them and help other parties. Instead they intended and expected the opposite, as shown in the words of George Robertson: by associating Labour with this recognition of Scotland's distinctive interests and preferences, they hoped to preserve their dominance north of the border and head off Scottish nationalism at the pass. If, with hindsight, this sounds fanciful, it is worth noting that some senior SNP figures had shared the same analysis, fearing that devolution would prove a cul-de-sac for the party.[3]

There are a number of reasons why devolution provided a road to power for the SNP in Scotland and ended Labour's dominance. Some of these relate to the nature of devolution itself, and were thus at play from the first Scottish Parliament election of 1999. Others relate to the parties' subsequent strategies and policies, and were thus more contingent. The SNP did not immediately surge to dominant status; it got off to a rather slow start.

The first and most basic reason why devolution helped the SNP is what might be termed 'geographical viability'. Put bluntly, before devolution there was rarely much point in voting for the Nationalists in UK-wide elections since they were contesting only around one in ten of the seats.[4] In Scottish Parliament elections, however, this potent 'wasted vote' argument was eliminated. The SNP immediately went from being one of the 'Others' to being one of the important players. It could also now appeal to habitual Labour voters whose principal goal had been to defend the interests of Scotland against the Conservatives. In the constituency contests in the inaugural election in 1999, Labour lost seven percentage points from its 1997 general-election vote share, and the SNP gained seven points. Much of that was a direct transfer between these two parties.[5]

Second, the mixed-member proportional (MMP) system adopted for devolved elections – which enables voters to elect a constituency MSP and cast an additional vote for a party on a regional list – did the SNP two important favours. Previously, the single-member plurality system used for UK general elections – Britain's 'other national lottery', as discussed by John Bartle in Chapter 8 – had rewarded Labour's concentrated support in the central-belt region of Scotland with super-majorities of seats, but had punished the SNP's more evenly spread support. Under MMP, however, the SNP could pick up regional-list seats everywhere, even in Labour heartlands. Four-fifths of the party's seats in the inaugural Holyrood contest – including that of current party leader and first minister, Nicola Sturgeon – were won on regional lists. Another 'wasted vote' argument could thus be dismissed. Moreover, proportionality also meant that single-party government was highly unlikely.[6] Back in the 1990s, Labour was still the dominant party, but MMP denied them an entrenched majority and thereby offered the SNP, like all parties elected to the new parliament, the potential for negotiating and entering a coalition.

If the possibility of office seemed rather remote in 1999, it was partly because the SNP had performed well and looked more like a rival than a junior coalition partner. This brings us to the third key effect of devolution: it created a distinct party system, specific to Scottish elections, in which Labour initially remained dominant but the SNP was demonstrably the second force. While there is no official opposition in the Holyrood system, there are institutional trappings. In 1999, for example, the then SNP convenor Alex Salmond secured the right to ask the first two of the weekly first minister's questions. Having become the de facto opposition to the Labour–Liberal Democrat coalition that formed the Scottish executive in 1999, the SNP was best placed to profit should Labour start to lose its electoral grip.

There was reason to suppose that Labour's grip would loosen. Labour had flourished in Scotland during the 1980s and 1990s partly because it had been in opposition at Westminster. But Labour was the UK government from May 1997 and after 1999 was in office in both London and Edinburgh. It was thus subject to the 'costs of ruling', the price generally paid by governing parties in terms of electoral popularity, twice over.[7] In the Scottish devolved elections of 2003, the UK government was still perceived as holding sway in most key issue areas, and so Labour in Scotland largely escaped this penalty. Four years later, however, Scottish Labour were incurring this cost. Contemporary survey data reveal a striking contrast: in 2003, the likelihood of someone voting Labour was more influenced by evaluations of the UK government than by evaluations of its Scottish counterpart; in 2007, it was evaluations of the Scottish government that mattered more.[8]

It was the creation of this new and distinctively Scottish political arena that was the fourth way in which devolution allowed the SNP to prosper. This arena extended beyond formal institutions. The Scottish media increasingly divided its attention between Westminster and Holyrood, gifting the party greater exposure. This was most obviously true during election campaigns but the SNP and Labour were also on a more equal footing in media reporting of everyday politics. Devolution also enforced professionalisation on the party: it had hitherto been more 'amateur-activist' than 'professional-electoral'.[9] More SNP parliamentarians were elected in the first Holyrood election in 1999 than in every previous Westminster election put together, and their number required an organisation – and especially an election campaigning machine – that was better resourced, better coordinated and more coherent in its message. The drive for professionalisation and centralisation was symbolised in 2004 when the party changed its constitution to refer explicitly to a 'leader' rather than a 'convener'.

These developments took time. Devolution, in a phrase coined by Labour's former Welsh secretary, Ron Davies, is 'a process, not an event'. The Scottish institutions slowly became more influential as they reached for more of the

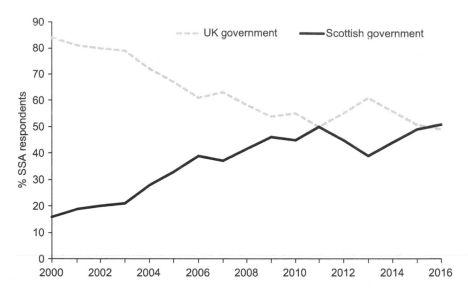

Figure 5.1 Trend in perceived relative importance of UK and Scottish governments, 2000–16

Note: The italicised figures are not survey results; they are halfway points between the real data points either side (to ensure that the trend line continues in the graph).Hence there are no markers for 2008 and 2014 on the graph.

Source: Scottish Social Attitudes Survey (SSA).

powers made open to them by the 1998 Scotland Act. In 2007, for instance, the incoming minority SNP executive rebranded itself as the Scottish government, which was formally renamed as such when the Westminster Parliament passed the 2012 Scotland Act. This highlights a psychological dimension to the process: Holyrood was not only doing more but over time came to be seen to be doing more, as shown in Figure 5.1. The graph is based on a question from the long-running Scottish Social Attitudes series that asks voters to choose which level of government – Westminster, Holyrood, their local council or the EU – 'has the most influence over the way Scotland is run'. The graph excludes the relatively small numbers choosing the latter two options. It shows a clear and generally steady increase in the perceived influence of the Scottish government, which, by 2016, was on a par with the UK government.[10]

The upshot of this change is that voters have come to care more about the outcome of Scottish Parliament elections. In psephological parlance, these have moved along the continuum from second- to first-order elections.[11] Scottish elections are now less like local or European elections, in which relatively little is at stake, and more like Westminster elections, in which who wins really matters. Put another way, Scottish elections are increasingly about assessing the policies and performance of the principal authority and its likely challengers. This is not to say that Westminster casts no shadow over Holyrood contests; indeed, relations between the two are always a prominent theme. Yet the character of that theme has changed, again in a way that suggests a flexing of devolved muscle. In the first couple of Scottish elections, voters were often registering their views on the new constitutional settlement itself.[12] As devolution became a fact of political life, however, voters started to focus more on the question of which parties would best use the new institutions to promote Scottish interests, including in dealings with Westminster. This shift benefited the SNP, whose constitution gives 'the furtherance of all Scottish interests' equal billing alongside independence. At the 2007 devolved elections, when the SNP first overtook Labour in the popular vote, 74 per cent of Scottish Election Study (SES) respondents said that they trusted the SNP to look after Scotland's interests either 'very' or 'fairly closely'. The equivalent figure for Labour was 50 per cent, well above the Conservatives' 23 per cent, but far behind the Nationalists on a criterion that was increasingly important in Scottish elections.[13]

The SNP benefited in this context from being a Scottish-*only* party that was primarily focused on the new Scottish arena. All six of its MPs elected in 1997 stood for the Scottish Parliament in 1999. By contrast, the ambitions of Scottish politicians in the Conservative, Labour and Liberal Democrat parties focused on London. Their Westminster-centrism did not inspire confidence that they would stand up for Scottish interests within the UK. It also led to invidious comparisons between the number and seniority of Scots around Labour's cabinet table at Westminster and the shortage of what this book's dedicatee would have called 'big beasts' at Holyrood.[14] Scottish Labour's subsequent struggles and the high rate of turnover among its leaders – seven came and went between October 2000 and August 2017 – only reinforced the impression of it being a struggling 'branch office' of the London party, unwilling or unable to stand up for Scotland's interests in the way the SNP claims to.[15]

Devolution was therefore the launch-pad from which the SNP replaced Labour as Scotland's dominant party. It automatically turned the Nationalists into major players with a structural advantage in a distinctively Scottish arena. Of course, agency mattered as well as structure. The timing and scale of the SNP surge owed plenty to Alex Salmond's return to the leadership in 2004 and, in turn, the image of competence that his party was able to project.[16] The party downplayed independence in its election platform, both by emphasising other issues and by promising a referendum on independence, one that all polls suggested would be lost. The party also benefited from some pure good luck. The SNP's majority win in 2011 owed much to the 'no alarms and no surprises' nature of its term in minority government, yet the party had edged out Labour by just one seat in 2007. Had just a handful of votes gone the other way in a few key seats – or, more bizarrely, had an error not been spotted at the last minute at the Highlands and Islands regional count, when the returning officer had been poised to assign the final regional list seat incorrectly to Labour – then the SNP might not have had that springboard of office.[17]

At this point, readers may well be asking themselves why the narrative has focused primarily on the SNP surge rather than Labour's decline. After all, the two developments are closely related, in that all parties gain by exploiting their rivals' weaknesses. The answer to this question is twofold. First, there was a clear pattern to the transfer of voters and seats after 1999. The Nationalists' gains up to 2011 were made across the board and at the expense of all parties. By contrast, Labour lost votes and seats overwhelmingly to the SNP.[18] If the main story to be explained was Labour's troubles, we would expect to observe the reverse pattern: general Labour losses, with only a portion of their votes going to the SNP. But this was not what happened.

Second, it is worth emphasising that Labour was structurally vulnerable from the outset in the devolved context. There was no reason to expect them to carry their Westminster dominance into purely Scottish elections. By the late 1990s, thanks to class dealignment and ideological convergence, Labour's dominance in Scotland had ceased to be based on mass party allegiance.[19] Instead, it was based on a party system in which their main rival was the widely disliked Conservative party, and an electoral system that kept other challengers firmly at bay. In Westminster elections, what counted was that Labour was far ahead of the Tories on the question of which party was most likely to stand up for Scotland's interest. It mattered little that the SNP was rated even higher. In the devolved party system, however, the ranking of the parties was the same but the pertinent comparison had changed. With hindsight, the SNP was always likely to take advantage.

Explaining SNP success – and failure – at Westminster

If devolved elections were tailor made for the SNP's agenda, Westminster elections continued to pose a challenge. Figure 5.2 highlights just how challenging they have been. From the first devolved election onwards, a pattern emerged in which the SNP would increase their vote share in a Holyrood contest but then slip back at the ensuing general election. This pattern was interrupted by the extraordinary referendum-fuelled outcome in 2015 – although even this election conformed to some other established patterns – but resumed after 2016. As this section will make clear, the 2017 general election in Scotland marked something of a return to normal service as far as party competition was concerned.

The 2015 election was a perfect storm in Scottish politics in that it resoundingly met the three key conditions necessary for SNP success in a Westminster election.[20] First, some factor or event has to bring the 'Scottish question' – that is, some divergence of interests between Scotland and the rest of the UK – to the top of voters' minds. In the October 1974 election, for example, the only previous occasion when the party had surpassed 30 per cent of the vote, that factor had been North Sea oil.[21] In 2015, it was the independence referendum. The

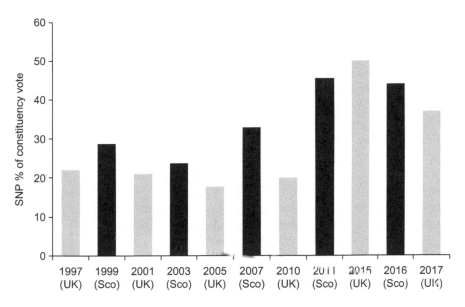

Figure 5.2 SNP constituency vote shares in UK general and Scottish Parliament elections, 1997–2017

Source: House of Commons.

long referendum campaign had focused minds not only on the constitutional question but also on whether Scotland had incompatible values with the rest of the UK (often longhand for England), usually summarised as Scotland being further to the left. The SNP was firmly positioned as the defender of Scottish interests on both counts. British Election Study (BES) data confirm that voters placed the party appreciably to the left of Labour (at 3.3 compared to 4.1 on a 0–10 left-right scale).[22] On the constitution, short-term attention had turned to whether and when the Scottish Parliament would receive the extra powers grandiosely 'vowed' to it by the Westminster party leaders a few days before polling in a bid to keep Scotland in the Union.[23] A month before the 2015 election, Scots were asked the following question in a YouGov poll: 'Thinking about the MPs elected from Scotland at the next general election, which party would be most effective at securing increased powers for the Scottish Parliament?' In response, fully 75 per cent chose the SNP.

One crucial reason for this confidence was the widespread expectation of a hung parliament ahead of the 2015 general election. This brings us to the second condition for SNP success at Westminster: a close contest. If either of the major UK parties, the Tories or Labour, is set for a clear win, there is not much that Nationalist MPs can do to pursue Scottish interests. In 1974, for example, the earlier February general election had resulted in a hung parliament, and it seemed that the October re-run could leave the SNP holding the balance of power. In 2015, the same prospect not only seemed feasible but was a central element of the Conservative campaign. The Tories produced posters and cartoons showing Labour leader Ed Miliband literally in the pockets of SNP leader Nicola Sturgeon and her predecessor Alex Salmond, all of which was intended to draw English votes away from Labour. Needless to say, the Tories' approach only helped the SNP, whose own campaign strategy was exactly to emphasise the sway that it might exert on Scotland's behalf. One in ten SNP votes in 2015 came from Scots who had voted 'No' to independence just eight months before (see Table 5.2), and the explanation is straightforward: they saw the SNP as the most reliable defenders of Scottish interests within the Union.

As it turned out, of course, there was no hung parliament and, according to the inquiry into the pollsters' collective failure, the polls had probably been wrong all along.[24] Had the eventual Conservative majority been more widely expected, the dynamics of the campaign may have been very different, especially in Scotland, and not in the SNP's favour. It is not outrageous to suggest that many of the Nationalist MPs who won by narrower margins in 2015 owed their seats to the pollsters. In any event, the crucial point is that the SNP tends to do better in Westminster elections come when voters expect an inconclusive national outcome, regardless of the accuracy of those expectations.

The third condition for SNP success at Westminster is that it must already be seen as a viable electoral force. If this sounds a rather circular argument it is because there is a virtuous circle at work: success breeds prominence and influence, which in turn boosts success. In February 1974, the SNP had already made a breakthrough, doubling its vote share and winning seven seats. This made it much more difficult come October for the SNP's opponents to play the 'wasted vote' card against it. In 2015, likewise, success was owed partly to the prospect of a hung parliament but also to the widespread belief that the Nationalists would be a significant force within it. The SNP entered the campaign with an unambiguous lead in the opinion polls, a lead that only widened as polling day approached. It did the SNP no harm that each fresh poll was accompanied by a lurid graphic showing just how yellow those results would turn the Scottish electoral map. Even sceptical voters could hardly doubt that the SNP was set for big gains and its largest ever presence at Westminster.

How far did those three conditions apply in 2017? While much was similar to 2015, there were important differences that go a long way to explaining why the SNP lost ground. In the case of the third condition of viability, there was obviously no change. The SNP's poll rating in the run-up to 2017 did not scale the heights of 2015 but it was still easily the largest party, bound for another sizable cohort of MPs, and competitive in every one of Scotland's 59 seats. If voters moved against the SNP in 2017, it was not due to fears of its irrelevance.

On the second condition, the closeness of the race between the two major Westminster parties, there was a major change. As the campaign began, the only question being asked was just how big a landslide Theresa May and the Tories would win, as Nicholas Allen describes in Chapter 1. Even as the race narrowed, few believed that the Conservatives would be denied a majority. In both 2015 and 2017, the polls were drastically misleading – albeit in different ways – about the likelihood of a hung parliament. In 2017, this error worked strongly to the SNP's disadvantage. If the Conservatives were set to win with ease, then the Nationalists' scope for influence was severely limited.

The polls not only changed the strategic calculation of voters but cost the Nationalists prominence. In 2015, expectations of a hung parliament and especially the Conservatives' preoccupation with the SNP gave the Nationalists an unusually high profile in election coverage, especially in the UK-wide broadcasting system that remains a large part of many Scots' media diet. Nicola Sturgeon, for instance, featured prominently in the televised leaders' debates of that year. Being talked about as a pivotal player was obviously ideal for the SNP, but merely being talked about was useful in itself. Two years later, aside from Sturgeon's presence in the televised debates, the party was largely absent from the narrative of the UK election. That narrative increasingly took the form of a two-party horse race, with Labour coming back at the Conservatives in the final furlongs. The SNP was back to being an also-ran.

Expectations of an easy Tory win also had a knock-on effect on the first condition, the salience of the Scottish dimension. One possible misconception about Westminster elections in Scotland, especially after the 2014 referendum, is that voters are simply registering their opinion on the independence issue. They are not. Scottish voters care about jobs, taxes, immigration, pensions, which UK governments are responsible for. Scottish voters also care about hospitals and schools; and even though policy responsibility for these areas has been devolved to Edinburgh, fiscal responsibility still lies mostly with Westminster. Just six months after the referendum, when a TNS-BMRB poll in February 2015 asked voters to choose from a list of issues those that would be 'very important to you when considering how you will vote' in the upcoming general election, only 24 per cent cited independence. Every one of the six issues listed just above was chosen more often. The point about the 2015 election, then, is not that the referendum distracted Scottish voters from other more everyday issues. Rather, a combination of the referendum and the expected hung parliament gave the SNP unprecedented prominence, and they used this to emphasise diverging Scottish and English interests on those bread-and-butter issues, in particular a Scottish rejection of English fiscal austerity.

On this account, the key difference between the 2017 and 2015 general elections is not the time that had elapsed since the referendum but that the electoral context had changed. Some of the giddiness of the post-referendum atmosphere had dissipated, to be sure, but the battle lines were still clearly drawn. The 2017 SES found clear majorities agreeing that the Scottish Parliament should be given control over taxes and welfare benefits, a large minority believing that Scotland receives less than its fair share of UK government spending, and half of respondents (including 27 per cent of those who had voted *against* independence) agreeing that 'In Scotland our values make us different from the rest of the UK'. Plenty of voters were thus receptive to the same message as in

2015. The problem was that the SNP found it much harder to get that message across. Rather than reflecting on the limitations of Westminster government, many Scottish voters in 2017 were too busy choosing one.

It is hard to quantify how much of the SNP's 13-point loss in vote share between 2015 and 2017 was due to the change in electoral context, but some sense can be gleaned from the short campaign in 2015. The SNP's poll-of-polls rating hovered around the 45 per cent mark for most of the six months leading up to the 2015 general election, but in the final weeks, when attention fell closely on the strategic implications of a hung parliament, support reached 50 per cent. It is reasonable to infer that, had there been no prospect of a hung parliament, the SNP would not have gained those five percentage points and may well have lost ground had voters refocused on the Labour–Conservative battle. Seen in this light, we are well on the way to explaining the sharp fall in SNP support in 2017 with barely a mention of independence, and none at all of Brexit.

The 2014 effect

The 2014 independence referendum was a transformative moment in Scottish party politics and its impact is still strongly felt. What is less clear, however, is how far that referendum can explain electoral change between 2015 and 2017. After all, the vote shares for what are now the leading parties on either side of the independence issue, the SNP and the Conservatives, changed by far more between 2015 and 2017 than did support for independence over the same period. Every shiver in opinion-poll measures of the latter was hailed by one side's zealots as *the* moment when opinion had shifted definitively in their direction, but in reality support for independence more or less flat-lined. That is no surprise. The length and fervour of the referendum campaign were such that opinions were bound to have become deeply entrenched. By the same token, it would be wrong to attribute the electoral tremors in Table 5.1 to any shift in the constitutional tectonics beneath. There was no shift.

What *has* changed since 2015, as Table 5.2 indicates, is a loosening of the association between support for independence and party choice. Even then, however, this change was both limited and asymmetric. Overall, the proportion of voters choosing a party that had taken a different line from them in the 2014 referendum increased from 10 per cent to 15 per cent between the two elections, but this increase was largely down to pro-independence or 'Yes' voters switching to a 'No' party. The proportion of 'No' voters crossing to a 'Yes' party – which included the Scottish Greens as well as the SNP – actually declined, as if the referendum effect was strengthening on the unionist side.

Attitudes to independence still exert a powerful anchoring effect on vote choice but the short-term features of an election can shift some voters across

Table 5.2 Voting in UK general elections by 2014 referendum vote

How voted in election	2015 general election		2017 general election	
	Voted No in 2014 (%)	Voted Yes in 2014 (%)	Voted No in 2014 (%)	Voted Yes in 2014 (%)
Voted for a No party	87.8	7.8	92.0	23.4
Voted for a Yes party	12.2	92.2	8.0	76.6
Total voted 'across' 2014 lines	10.2		14.9	
SNP	10.1	89.4	7.7	76.0
Conservative	26.1	1.2	47.8	7.3
Labour	43.9	4.3	32.1	13.9
Liberal Democrat	13.6	1.8	10.9	2.0
Others	6.3	3.3	1.5	0.9
Turnout	76.7	79.1	73.6	70.8
N	2,151	1,872	1,206	966

Sources. British Election Study Internet Panel; Scottish Election Study 2017.

the divide. In May 2015, as already noted, one in ten 'No' voters were willing to vote SNP to maximise Scottish influence in the anticipated hung parliament. In 2017, they and many 'Yes' voters may have switched away from the SNP because there seemed to be no prospect of a hung parliament, and they were looking to promote Scottish influence through one of the major parties instead. On this logic, the difference between the two elections is not so much their psychological distance from the referendum, as the passage of time allowing other considerations to crop up.

The party-specific data in Table 5.2 hint at what some of those other considerations might be. Brexit looks the likeliest explanation for the small group of 'Yes' voters backing the Conservatives in 2017. Less than a quarter of that already small group had previously voted Tory in either 2005 or 2010, which suggests that something new had converted most of them. The Conservatives' hardening position on Brexit under Theresa May was almost certainly it. Among the larger group of 'Yes' switchers to Labour, the change was more often a switch back: 47 per cent had voted for the party in either 2005 or 2010. Some of the remainder may have been returning after even longer away. Voters in both categories may have been attracted by Labour's leftwards shift under its new leader, Jeremy Corbyn, which Thomas Quinn describes in Chapter 2. Many such voters had rejected Tony Blair and New Labour moderation and had used the freedom of Scottish elections – those posing no threat of a Tory victory – to defect to more unambiguously left-wing parties such as Solidarity or the Greens. Many had gone on to vote 'Yes' in 2014 and SNP in 2015. The changed circumstances of 2017 – a clear fight between the Tories and a Corbyn-led Labour Party – tempted many of them back.

At the same time, as Table 5.2 shows, Labour's success in winning back many 'Yes' voters was offset by its haemorrhaging support among 'No' voters. The party's gains came almost entirely from the SNP; the losses went largely to the Conservatives. Since these losses had much to do with the Conservative Party's success in presenting itself as *the* unionist party, as we shall see, they are a sign of the continuing power of the 2014 effect.

There was one area in which the impact of the referendum seemed to diminish, however, and that was turnout. The energy and apparent narrowness of the 2014 campaign translated into a turnout of 85 per cent, an extraordinary figure by recent British standards.[25] This new enthusiasm carried over into the 2015 election: turnout in Scotland rose to 71.1 per cent, up seven points on 2010, compared to 66.4 per cent across the UK as a whole and an average increase of just over a point. In 2017, turnout in Scotland fell five points and ended up a couple of points below the average UK level, which had generally been the case in previous contests. General elections are less able than keenly fought referendums to tempt people to the polls.[26] In 2017, with the participatory fervour of the referendum receding in memory, turnout continued its predictable drift back to normal.

Declining turnout unquestionably cost the SNP. The final row in Table 5.2 shows that, while 'Yes' voters were more likely to turn out in the post-referendum 2015 election, they were more likely to stay at home in 2017. This large fall in turnout among a group that constitutes almost half of the electorate and votes overwhelmingly for the SNP accounts for a sizable proportion of the party's overall losses. While it could also be interpreted as a decline in enthusiasm for independence, it is extremely risky to extrapolate from electoral behaviour to constitutional preferences. The key point about these voters is that they are, socioeconomically speaking, the kinds of people who typically do not vote. In other words, 2017 was 'back to normal' in terms not just of *how many* but also of *which* people voted. Like Heineken, whose brewers promise that it refreshes 'the parts other beers cannot reach', the independence referendum reached those parts of the electorate that elections normally do not reach, with the result that the typically strong correlations between an area's socioeconomic characteristics and its turnout almost vanished. These correlations re-emerged in 2015 and, by 2017, were back up to their pre-referendum strength.[27] This was bad news for the SNP.

The Tory resurgence

On the long view, the most striking feature of the 2017 general election in Scotland was not the large losses sustained by the SNP but the large gains made by the Tories. Between 1997 and 2015, the Conservative polling trend in Scotland was the flattest line in British electoral politics, static in the mid-teens.

Their 28.6 per cent in 2017 was thus a startling performance. The party had last achieved a similar result – 11 seats and 25.6 per cent of the vote – in 1992. Since then, Scotland had become almost a no-go area for the Tories, at least when it came to electing MPs to Westminster. Many explanations have been put forward for the party's sudden resurgence in 2017, some deserving longer shrift than others.

Two pieces of background information are crucial here. The first is that, as per Table 5.2, most of Conservatives' gains came among 'No' voters, many of whom had voted Labour in 2015. Second, the resurgence was already clearly in progress at the time of the Scottish Parliament election in May 2016, an election at which the Tories achieved a surprise second place (on the regional list vote, at least) and a doubling of their overall seat tally. Back then, the party was largely backing 'Remain' in the ongoing European referendum campaign – voting would take place on 23 June – and the Scottish Conservative leader Ruth Davidson was one of the most vocal advocates of staying in the EU. On sequencing alone, if the Conservative revival is a tale of two referendums, then it has much more to do with the 2014 independence vote than the 2016 Brexit vote.

Table 5.2 suggests that about 85 per cent of Scottish voters in 2017 chose parties that had been on the same side as them in the 2014 referendum. An intense and divisive campaign has realigned Scottish electoral politics around the independence question, leaving Labour and the Conservatives fighting primarily for voters on the 'No' side. Moreover, given the polarised state of public opinion on this issue, there was a major strategic advantage to being seen as the party with the most extreme position. Many 'No' voters were looking for a party as strongly and unambiguously opposed to independence as they felt. This was the position that the Conservatives in Scotland had carved out for themselves, over both the long term – as a unionist party, they had even initially opposed devolution after 1997 – and over the short term, with a heavy emphasis on the issue and effective campaign slogans like 'we said no and we meant no'.

Labour, meanwhile, has struggled to match the clarity and consistency of Conservative opposition to independence. Both its UK and Scottish leaders in 2017, Jeremy Corbyn and Kezia Dugdale, could be tied to equivocal statements on the issue. Moreover, while the Conservatives had focused almost exclusively on independence, Labour had sought to fight on a range of other fronts. This risked them seeming less committed to fighting independence, and it also moved them onto the ideological territory of the 'Yes' side. During the 2014 referendum campaign, tight rhetorical links were forged between independence and the kind of left-wing, anti-austerity politics espoused by Corbyn's Labour. It was no surprise that Labour in 2017 was able to pick up support from 'Yes' voters; but it was also no surprise that the party struggled to convince 'No' voters of its full commitment to their cause, and lost some of them to the Conservatives as a result.

There is no clearer indication of the continuing 2014 effect than its capacity to deliver votes from Labour to the Tories. Until relatively recently, the

Conservatives had seemed more or less a pariah party in Scotland. So toxic had the Tory brand become that ahead of the Scottish party's 2011 leadership contest, eventually won by Ruth Davidson, Murdo Fraser, one of her defeated rivals, proposed disbanding the Scottish party altogether.[28] Anti-Conservative sentiment was held to run too deep in the Scottish electorate to allow the kind of revival seen in 2017. The mass transfer of support from their long-standing enemies Labour was considered unthinkable. So how did these voters make the psychological journey? Admittedly, the Conservatives themselves smoothed the path by using the 'C-word' very sparingly in their election literature, giving it in full as the 'Scottish Conservative and Unionist Party' when mentioning names was deemed unavoidable. But there were deeper reasons than that.

First, voters who had stuck with Labour in 2015 were already a less anti-Tory subsection of the party's traditional base. They had just rejected a 'Yes' campaign that had equated the Union and a 'No' vote with Conservative governments and policies, both of which were characterised as being at odds with Scottish values and interests. Unlike the many Labour supporters who were converts to independence – and, later, to the SNP – these 'No' voters had indicated that their dislike for independence potentially trumped any strong anti-Conservative feelings. Second, there is the 'my enemy's enemy is my friend' logic, a pervasive feature of polarised politics. For 'No' voters in the 2014 referendum, the SNP has become the primary enemy, and the Conservatives had successfully positioned themselves as the Nationalists' enemy. That same logic is the engine of tactical voting and there were clear signs of this in the 2017 election: unionist voters tended to coalesce around the candidate most likely to defeat the SNP. Such calculations are not always straightforward, requiring voters to combine information about the previous local result with the latest nationwide polling information. In 2017, the Conservatives probably benefited a good deal from their well-publicised second place in Scottish polls throughout the campaign. While Labour and the Liberal Democrats won only in constituencies in which they had been first or second in 2015, six of the Conservatives' 13 seats were won from third place.

The 2016 Brexit referendum added a little extra thrust to the Conservative bandwagon. The 'Leave' side polled only 38.0 per cent in Scotland, but Leave voters constituted 60 per cent of those 'No' voters who switched to the Tories between 2015 and 2017, and 87 per cent of the 'Yes' voters who made the same switch.[29] Among the small group of voters who backed independence in 2014 and the Conservatives in 2017, almost all had supported Brexit. If the EU referendum was less important than the independence referendum in explaining the Tory resurgence, this was partly because Leave voters were thinner on the ground than 'No' voters, and partly because it was only after the Brexit vote that the Conservatives were in a position to win them over. During the 2016 campaign, all the mainstream parties, including the Scottish Conservatives, had been united behind Remain. Only after the referendum, when Theresa May committed the party to implementing the result, were the Tories in a position to win over Brexiteers. These voters were concentrated in the north-east of Scotland, where the Tories were often already in second place. The resulting Brexit effect, combined with tactical unionist voting, generated some startling Conservative victories. In Moray, Scotland's most Leave-friendly council area in the 2016 referendum, a dramatic 14-point swing enabled the Tories to unseat the SNP's Westminster leader, Angus Robertson.

While pursuing Brexit thus won the Tories some Leave voters in 2017, opposing Brexit won the SNP fewer votes than it had hoped. The party targeted voters so aggrieved at Scotland being dragged out of the EU against its will that they might be converted to the cause of self-determination. The problem was that there were very few such voters. As already noted, Scots' views on independence were already held with force and inflexibility. Not only did most voters in Scotland care much more about the independence issue than the EU issue, but the 2014 referendum was essentially about whether an outcome like that of 2016, when Scotland was outvoted within the United Kingdom, was legitimate. Those who felt passionately that it was not had already converted to independence and the SNP. Those who had voted 'No', by contrast, recognised the SNP's post-Brexit message as an argument that they had already rejected. They also dismissed the notion, put forward only half-heartedly by the SNP leadership, that the EU referendum result placed a second independence referendum on the agenda.

Another prevalent explanation for the Conservatives' revival was the popularity of its Scottish leader, Ruth Davidson. First elected in 2011, her popularity certainly extended beyond her own party's supporters: in the 2017 SES, she was rated the most likeable of all Scottish leaders on a standard 0–10 scale, with an average score above the midpoint of 5 even among Labour voters. But there are problems with attributing the Tory revival to her popularity. For one thing, voters are quite capable of liking a politician without being induced to vote for them. Davidson's predecessor as Scottish Conservative leader, Annabel Goldie, was another engaging personality who proved markedly more popular than her party.[30] Yet, Goldie's popularity did not translate into votes or do much to 'detoxify' the Conservative brand in Scotland. A more restrained reading of Davidson's electoral impact in 2017 is that she effectively exploited the opportunities offered in the wake of the 2014 and 2016 referendums by taking a staunchly anti-independence stance and by accepting Brexit, two positions that were key to the post-2015 Tory revival. But then again, it is hard to imagine any Scottish Conservative leader taking anything other than these positions. In that sense Davidson's strategic impact has been limited. But her personal appeal may have had an effect at the margins, helping hesitant voters to make the switch to the Tories.

Another leadership effect that has been overestimated is that of the declining popularity of SNP leader and first minister, Nicola Sturgeon. This had very little to do with SNP losses in 2017, let alone Conservative gains. Even in 2015, an election held at the peak of her honeymoon period, Sturgeon won grudging acclaim but never the votes of 'No' supporters. The reason should be familiar by now: attitudes to independence were strongly held and deeply entrenched. A popular Sturgeon could not persuade unionists to vote SNP in 2015, and a less popular Nicola Sturgeon would not lose 'Yes' voters to a 'No' party in 2017. In fact, Sturgeon retained very high approval ratings (an average of 8.7 out of 10 according to the standard SES measure) among those who voted 'Yes' in 2014 and SNP in 2015. Jeremy Corbyn was also strikingly popular among this group (an average approval score of 7.2), which may have helped Labour to win votes from the SNP. If so, it had little to do with any comparison with Sturgeon. This brings us back to the key point about the 2017 election: as with their English and Welsh counterparts, most Scottish voters saw it as a battle between Theresa May's Tories and Corbyn's Labour. Any drift in Nicola Sturgeon's ratings was largely irrelevant.

A final possible explanation for the SNP losses and Conservative resurgence deserves a similarly curt dismissal, and for similar reasons. This is the notion that the SNP's performance in government at Holyrood cost it support. It was certainly true that ratings of the SNP's record had been sliding, with criticisms in particular over the performance of Scottish schools. However, the fact that such criticisms intensified after the 2014 referendum was not a coincidence. For voters, like politicians, assessments of the Nationalists became even more deeply coloured by attitudes towards independence. In the 2011 SES, SNP performance in government was rated as 'very good' or 'fairly good' by 78 per cent of those who would go on to vote 'Yes', but by only 37 per cent of those who would go on to vote 'No' in 2014. In the 2016 survey, the corresponding figures were 77 per cent and 18 per cent. The perceived decline in performance thus existed largely in the minds of those whose real complaint about the SNP government was its constitutional position. When the Conservatives exhorted Sturgeon to 'focus on the day job' of governing Scotland, it was really a complaint about what she was getting up to in the evenings.

Conclusion

Based on the seminal early studies of voting behaviour, party loyalty was sometimes described as the 'unmoved mover': a highly stable attitude that could shift citizens' opinions on the other issues, personalities and events of the time. The electoral volatility of recent decades – not only in the UK but across Europe – shows that such deep loyalty is now much rarer. The 2017 general election was the second in a row in which more than half of Scotland's seats changed hands, an extraordinary testament to the 'easy come, easy go' nature of electoral change. In Scottish politics, however, there is a new unmoved mover: attitudes to independence. These are the new anchor. Referendum vote-intention polls show that they are largely unmoved in the aggregate, and panel data confirm that there is very little changing of individual minds.

In 2017, attitudes to independence were not just unmoved but also one of the big movers. They triggered an unprecedented shift of Scottish votes from Labour to the Conservatives. Many erstwhile Labour supporters found that their overriding enmity was now to independence and the SNP, and in turn found themselves on common ground with the Tories. It is hard to say how far this represents an enduring realignment on the 'No' side of Scottish politics; it is probably due in part to short-term factors such as tactical voting, the Conservatives' more popular leader, and the general disarray of Scottish Labour.

More broadly, attitudes to independence have reshaped the Scottish party system, or, more accurately, party systems. The SNP was able virtually to sweep the board in 2015 because the 'No' side was split both nationally and in many constituencies. In 2017, there was a more concerted attempt on the unionist side to unite around a single challenger to the SNP, and with some success: the SNP lost 26 per cent of its vote but 38 per cent of its seats. In most places the challenger was obvious: Labour in the urban central belt, the Conservatives in rural areas to the south and east, and the Liberal Democrats in isolated strongholds. Apart from the latter enclaves, Scotland appeared in 2017 to have two different two-party systems: SNP versus Labour in urban areas, and SNP versus Conservative in rural Scotland. Before its recent breakthrough, the SNP used to struggle to win seats because its vote was distributed fairly evenly across the country. If tactical coordination against the party tightens further, those days might return.

There were, of course, movers other than attitudes to independence. Brexit took some SNP voters across the constitutional divide into the Conservatives' hands; the Corbyn effect took some into Labour's. Yet, amid plenty of vote-switching, the independence referendum played a major anchoring role in 2017. For every Leave voter that defected from the SNP to the Conservatives, three more Leave voters stayed with the party. For every left-wing voter that defected from the SNP to Labour, six more stayed with the party.[31] This loyalty seems unlikely to be to the party per se, given that many of these voters had not voted SNP until 2015. Instead, it betokens the strength of commitments to the 'Yes' side, on which the SNP remains the overwhelmingly dominant force.

Ever since the 2014 independence referendum, it is natural to ask what each election means for Scotland's constitutional future. But the entrenching effect of that referendum means that the independence question is much more influential over elections than vice versa. The 2017 election saw a switch from 'Yes' parties to 'No' parties, but not from 'Yes' to 'No'. More importantly, the results have virtually no impact on the timing or outcome of any future 'Indyref 2' because both depend on what the opinion polls say about support for independence. Thus a second referendum seems unlikely now, just as it seemed so before June 2017, and for the same reason: there has been no sign of a sustained shift towards independence. The SNP, deeply fearful that its cause would not survive a second defeat, will only take the plunge once, or if, this shift has occurred. It was perhaps not surprising, then, that the 2017 general election had the air of a phoney war on the issue. The SNP insisted on its mandate to hold a referendum that it had no intention of holding; its opponents insisted that it should not hold a referendum that they knew it had no intention of holding. Independence remains on the horizon of Scottish politics, looming for some, gleaming for others, but it is still a distant horizon.

Notes

1   Ahead of the 2005 general election, the number of constituencies in Scotland was reduced from 72 to 59 to reflect the additional representation Scottish voters enjoyed as a result of devolution. Previously, Scotland had been over-represented at Westminster, in the sense that it had more seats relative to its population than did England. The reduction in constituencies meant that Scottish seats now contained broadly the same number of voters as English seats.

2   John Curtice and Ben Seyd (eds), *Has Devolution Worked? The Verdict from Policy Makers and the Public* (Manchester: Manchester University Press, 2009), p. 116.

3   Robert Johns and James Mitchell, *Takeover: Explaining the Extraordinary Rise of the SNP* (London: Biteback, 2016), ch. 6.

4   The term 'Nationalists' (with capital 'N') is sometimes used simply to avoid tiresome repetition of 'SNP'. The term 'nationalist' (with small 'n') applies of course both to Scottish nationalism and British unionism.

5   Lindsay Paterson, Alice Brown, John Curtice, Kerstin Hinds, David McCrone, Alison Parks, Kerry Sproston and Paula Surridge, *New Scotland, New Politics?* (Edinburgh: Polygon, 2001).

6   Ironically, as it turned out, MMP was chosen partly to avoid the danger of the SNP wining an outright victory and hustling Scotland into independence.

7   Peter Nannestad and Martin Paldam, 'The costs of ruling', in Han Dorussen and Michael Taylor (eds), *Economic Voting* (London: Routledge, 2002), pp. 17–44.

8   John Curtice, 'Is Holyrood accountable and representative?' in Catherine Bromley, John Curtice, David McCrone and Alison Park (eds), *Has Devolution Delivered?* (Edinburgh: Edinburgh University Press, 2006), pp. 90–122; Robert Johns, James Mitchell, David Denver and Charles Pattie, *Voting for a Scottish Government: The Scottish Parliament Elections of 2007* (Manchester: Manchester University Press, 2010), pp. 113–114.

9   See Alberto Panebianco, *Political Parties: Organization and Power* (Cambridge: Cambridge University Press, 1988). For an application to the SNP, see James Mitchell, Lynn Bennie and Robert Johns, *The Scottish National Party: Transition to Power* (Oxford: Oxford University Press, 2012), ch. 3.

10 The question wording changed in 2009 to reflect the SNP's renaming of the Scottish executive as the Scottish government. This is not just a methodological footnote: this change of name will have encouraged voters to think of Holyrood and Westminster as more equal players.

11 Karl-Heinz Reif and Hermann Schmit, 'Nine second-order national elections: A conceptual framework for the analysis of European election results', *European Journal of Political Research*, 8 (1980), 3–44. For a recent assessment of where Scottish Parliament elections fall within this framework, see Christopher Carman, Robert Johns and James Mitchell, *More Scottish than British: The 2011 Scottish Parliament Election* (Basingstoke: Palgrave Macmillan, 2014), ch. 5.

12 Curtice, 'Is Holyrood accountable and representative?'

13 Robert Johns, David Denver, James Mitchell and Charles Pattie, 'Valence politics in Scotland: Towards an explanation of the 2007 election', *Political Studies*, 57 (2009), 207–233.

14 See Anthony King, 'Ministerial autonomy in Britain', in Michael Laver and Kenneth A. Shepsle (eds), *Cabinet Ministers and Parliamentary Government* (Cambridge: Cambridge University Press, 1994), pp. 203–225, at pp. 218–219.

15 Jane Merrick, 'Johann Lamont resigns: Party has "no clue" on Scotland, says former Labour first minister', *Independent*, 25 October 2014, available at: www.independent. co.uk/news/uk/politics/johann-lamont-resigns-party-has-no-clue-on-scotland-says-former-labour-first-minister-9818656.html, last accessed 10 October 2017.

16 Johns *et al.*, *Voting for a Scottish Government.*

17 The 2011 majority was also based on well short of 50 per cent of the votes. The architects of devolution chose a proportional-but-not-very-proportional system for Scottish elections, presumably reasoning that this would be sufficient to prevent an SNP majority.

18 Carman *et al.*, *More Scottish than British.*

19 See, for example, Lynn Bennic, Jack Brand and James Mitchell, *How Scotland Votes* (Manchester: Manchester University Press, 1997); Peter Lynch, 'From social democracy back to no ideology? The Scottish National Party and ideological change in a multi-level electoral setting', *Regional and Federal Studies*, 19 (2009), 619–637.

20 For a more detailed discussion of these, see Johns and Mitchell, *Takeover*, ch. 1.

21 It should be said that the 'Scottish question' was already in the air following the report in November 1973 of the Kilbrandon Commission on the Constitution which, to the surprise of many, had recommended devolution.

22 At this and various points in the chapter, results are calculated from British Election Study (BES) and Scottish Election Study (SES) survey data. While these specific results are not necessarily published, the data are available at: www.britishelectionstudy. com/data/ and http://blogs.sps.ed.ac.uk/scottishreferendumstudy/, respectively, last accessed 10 October 2017.

23 See David Clegg, 'David Cameron, Ed Miliband and Nick Clegg sign joint historic promise', *Daily Record*, 16 September 2014.

24 Patrick Sturgis, Nick Baker, Mario Callegaro, Stephen Fisher, Jane Green, Will Jennings, Jouni Kuha, Ben Lauderdale and Patten Smith, *Report of the Inquiry into the 2015 British General Election Opinion Polls* (London: British Polling Council and Market Research Society, 2016).

25 Moreover, since the referendum also saw a surge in registration, this was 85 per cent of a much larger denominator than usual.

26 There was also a three-point drop in UK-wide turnout between the Brexit referendum and the general election a year later.

27 Heinz Brandenburg, Zachary Greene and Neil McGarvey, 'Explaining change in turnout with constituency level electoral data: The ephemeral effect of deprivation

in the Scottish Referendum', paper presented at EPOP Annual Conference, University of Kent, 9–11 September 2016.

28 Alan Cochrane, 'Scottish Conservative Party set to disband', *Daily Telegraph*, 3 September 2011.

29 For a detailed analysis of vote-switching and the Brexit referendum, see Chris Prosser and Ed Fieldhouse, 'A tale of two referendums: The 2017 election in Scotland', *British Election Study*, 2 August 2017, available at: www.britishelectionstudy. com/bes-findings/a-tale-of-two-referendums-the-2017-election-in-scotland/#. WdvAqEyQ1E4, last accessed 10 October 2017.

30 Carman *et al.*, *More Scottish than British*, ch. 3.

31 For this calculation, left-wing voters are those who placed themselves at 0, 1 or 2 on the BES's 0–10 left–right scale.

6

From Thatcher to May and beyond

Women in British politics

Meryl Kenny

The 1979 volume of *Britain at the Polls* described that year's general election as 'a stride forward and several small steps back for women'.[1] On the one hand, Margaret Thatcher was elected as Britain's first female prime minister, a position she would go on to hold for over 11 years. On the other hand, the 1979 election saw only 19 women elected to the House of Commons – the smallest number of female MPs since 1951 – no increase in the number of women appointed to the cabinet, and setbacks in the advocacy and representation of women's issues.

The 2017 general election was the first to be contested by Britain's second female prime minister, Theresa May, and provides a timely opportunity to reassess the place and progress of women in contemporary British politics. Heralded as a 'record-breaking' moment for women, media coverage of the 2017 election highlighted the fact that the '200 women' mark had been breached in the House of Commons for the first time, with more female MPs elected than ever before. Coverage also emphasised the wider diversity of the new House and championed the rise in the numbers of black, Asian and minority ethnic (BAME), LGBT, and disabled MPs. As the dust settled in the aftermath of the election result, many of the key power players left standing were women, including, in addition to Theresa May, the leader of Northern Ireland's Democratic Unionist Party (DUP) and 'queen-maker', Arlene Foster; Scotland's first minister and the leader of the Scottish National Party (SNP), Nicola Sturgeon; and the Scottish Conservative leader, Ruth Davidson.

Do the gains made by women in the 2017 election signal a potential fracturing of the political 'glass ceiling'? Looking past the headlines, the House of Commons was still obviously unrepresentative. Despite the increasingly female face of political leadership in the United Kingdom, the gains in women's numerical representation were modest, with significant differences across the political parties. Gender parity remains a very long way off. Meanwhile, the number of BAME MPs needed to have doubled in 2017 if they were to have reflected the

BAME presence in the population. Instead the number rose from 41 to 52 (or 8 per cent of all MPs), most of whom sit on the Labour benches. Five disabled MPs were also elected, including Labour's Marsha de Cordova in Battersea and Jared O'Mara, who memorably took Sheffield Hallam from the former Liberal Democrat leader Nick Clegg, yet they constituted less than 1 per cent of the House of Commons' membership. In comparison, about one in five of the population self-identify as disabled.[2]

This chapter investigates the dynamics of representation in the 2017 general election and evaluates the extent to which the 'promise' of the election for women in particular was fulfilled. It examines the numerical representation of women as candidates, MPs and party leaders in 2017, as well as the substantive representation of women's issues and policy concerns. In doing so, the chapter points to some progress made, while highlighting the distance yet to be travelled before the House of Commons can be characterised as truly representative. It concludes by evaluating the prospects for women's representation in British politics. Without statutory measures in the form of legal gender quotas, the prospect of achieving equal representation any time soon is slim.

Women's issues

Much like the election that preceded it, the 2017 campaign was full of women, but not necessarily about women. Despite the presence of Theresa May and other prominent female party leaders, as well as the entry of the new Women's Equality Party, which fielded candidates in seven constituencies, gender itself was not a significant political talking point in an election overshadowed by Brexit. However, since at least 1997, the main political parties in Britain have made concerted attempts to target women voters as a distinct group. Indeed, Tony Blair and New Labour's success in securing women's votes played a major role in the party's landslide election victories in 1997 and 2001. Yet, the prominence of women's issues has waxed and waned across election campaigns. For the Conservatives, David Cameron's election as leader in 2005 marked a step-change in the party's efforts to win women's votes. As part of a party feminisation strategy, Cameron called for more Conservative women MPs, promised to give one-third of senior ministerial jobs to women, and made repeated references to women's policy concerns.[3] Subsequent competition for women's votes has brought the main parties closer together on 'women's issues'. With the possible exception of the right-wing populist United Kingdom Independence Party (UKIP), most parties have shifted towards a more liberally feminist position.[4]

Ahead of the 2017 election, all of the parties made manifesto pledges 'to', 'for' and 'about' women. Some of these pledges explicitly targeted women as women – often as mothers – while other pledges addressed policy concerns prioritised by women voters or policies that more indirectly tend to affect women as a category.[5] For example, women, including Conservative-supporting women, often express greater support for increased taxation and spending on public services than men, and they are also generally more strongly opposed to cuts in public spending, particularly in the areas of health and education.[6] All of the party manifestos pledged increased resources for schools, as well as higher levels of spending on the NHS.

Meanwhile, the funding of social care proved to be an unexpectedly important election issue, marking out significant differences between the main parties and dominating the headlines. Since 2010, Conservative austerity and cuts to public spending had exacerbated the demands of caring for an ageing population. Women had borne the brunt of this social care crisis, as both the majority of those in need of care, and the majority of the (paid and unpaid) care workforce. Labour's manifesto had pledged to increase social care budgets by £8 billion over the next parliament, to 'lay the foundations' of a National Care Service for England, and to increase the Carer's Allowance – a benefit paid to unpaid full-time carers – to the same level as the Jobseekers' Allowance – the benefit paid to the unemployed. The Conservative manifesto, in contrast, proposed raising the threshold for free domiciliary social care and bringing it into line with the threshold for free residential care. Under these plans people receiving care services in their own homes would have to pay for it themselves until they reached their last £100,000. Dubbed a 'dementia tax' by the opposition parties, the policy triggered significant backlash and prompted a hasty U-turn. Within days, Theresa May promised that if the Tories were re-elected, the government would consult on an upper cap for social care costs (see Nicholas Allen in Chapter 1).

The various party manifestos also included a number of policy pledges aimed specifically at women *as women*. Labour's manifesto, for example, included a specific two-page section outlining the party's past record on women's rights and future policy commitments, including a pledge to conduct a gender impact assessment of all policy and legislation before their implementation. The Green Party, meanwhile, produced a separate 'gender equality' manifesto, which they pointedly unveiled outside Yarl's Wood Immigration Removal Centre, a controversial facility housing adult women and family groups awaiting deportation. This separate manifesto promised to shut down such detention centres, decriminalise sex work and 'save women's healthcare'. UKIP, meanwhile, proposed to introduce a 'social attitudes test' to stop migrants who believed in treating women or gay people as 'second-class citizens' from entering the country. In one of their most controversial manifesto commitments, UKIP also pledged to ban the wearing of the niqab and the burka from public places. These are common tactics used by populist anti-immigration parties, which often use the liberal feminist rhetoric of gender equality and women's rights to further denounce immigrant communities.[7]

To varying degrees, virtually all the parties' manifestos addressed the issue of violence against women. The Conservatives pledged to create a new domestic violence and abuse commissioner in law, in order to hold the police and criminal justice system to account. Labour promised to create a similar office of violence against women commissioner, as well as to estab-lish a National Refuge Fund. The Liberal Democrats, meanwhile, pledged to allocate government funding to a national rape crisis helpline; the Greens and Plaid Cymru would reverse cuts to domestic violence and legal aid ser-vices; while both the SNP and the Women's Equality Party promised to ratify the Istanbul Convention, a Council of Europe convention on preventing and combating violence against women and domestic violence. Many of the parties also pledged specific support for pregnant women and mothers, including protecting their rights as afforded under EU law (a promise made by the SNP, the Liberal Democrats, the Women's Equality Party, the Greens and Labour); introducing mandatory workplace risk assessments for pregnant women (Labour); improving mental health support for pregnant women, new mothers and those who have experienced miscarriage or stillbirth (the Liberal Democrats and UKIP); creating new entitlements to child bereavement leave (the Conservatives); reducing (the Greens) or reversing (Labour) employ-ment tribunal fees to ensure that women could raise complaints about mater-nity and pregnancy discrimination; ensuring that pregnant women seeking asylum or whose immigration status was uncertain could have free access to NHS prenatal, birth and postnatal care (the Women's Equality Party and the Greens); and introducing a legal right to breastfeed in the workplace (the Greens, the SNP and the Women's Equality Party).

All of the main parties except for UKIP and Plaid Cymru also made mani-festo pledges regarding women's representation. Labour committed itself to a gender-parity cabinet comprising at least 50 per cent women. Jeremy Corbyn, Labour's leader, had already made good on a prior commitment to appoint women to half the shadow-cabinet jobs, although he was criticised for initially appointing only men to the most prestigious posts (see Thomas Quinn in Chapter 2). The Conservative manifesto, meanwhile, committed the party to working towards parity in the number of public appointments going to women, to increasing the number of women sitting on company boards, and to diversifying civil service recruitment – but there was little detail of how these goals might be achieved. The Liberal Democrats committed to pushing for at least 40 per cent of board members of FTSE 350 companies being women, while the Greens proposed a requirement that at least 40 per cent of all public-company and public sector boards should be women. The Greens also committed to creating a '50/50 Parliament', although the party focused on measures like job-sharing to achieve this, rather than the introduc-tion of gender quotas. Meanwhile, the SNP called on the British government to legislate for gender balance in public sector boardrooms, following the lead of the Scottish government. Perhaps not surprisingly, the most comprehen-sive proposals on women's representation were to be found in the Women's Equality Party manifesto, which promised, among other things, to encourage parties to use 'all-women shortlists' (or other methods) to ensure that two-thirds of their candidates replacing retiring MPs, as well as two-thirds of all their other candidates, were women for the next two parliamentary terms or until gender parity has been achieved. The party also promised to give three-quarters of all new appointments to the House of Lords to women, to introduce gender-balanced boards for all listed companies by 2025, and to appoint women to half of all ministerial posts with immediate effect.

The final set of key policy commitments outlined in the party manifestos were redistributive policies seeking to reduce inequalities between men and women.[8] All of the main parties, for example, pledged to address the gender pay gap: Labour promised a civil enforcement system to ensure compliance with gender pay auditing; both the Conservatives and the Liberal Democrats would require companies with more than 250 employees to publish more data on their gender pay gaps; and the SNP would require the same but from companies with over 150 employees, backed up with sanctions for employers that failed to comply. Of the two main parties, however, Labour's 'offer' on gender equality policy was the strongest and most specific, with the Tories offering few commitments to reducing gendered economic inequalities.[9] For example, Labour's manifesto set out plans to extend maternity pay to 12 months, to double paid paternity leave to four weeks and to increase paternity pay, whereas the Conservatives promised to improve the take-up of shared parental leave and to help companies provide more flexible work environments. Similarly, on childcare, the Tories pledged 30 hours of free care to working parents of three- and four-year-olds, as well as the creation of a capital fund to help primary schools develop nurseries. Labour, meanwhile, pledged direct government subsidy for childcare, the extension of the current 30 hours of free childcare to all two-year-olds (and some one-year-olds), and more money for the threatened Sure Start centres, a New Labour initiative designed to support children and families in disadvantaged areas.

On the issue of social security, the Conservatives outlined that they had no plans for further radical welfare reform in the upcoming parliament and would instead focus on continuing the roll-out of Universal Credit, the new all-in-one benefit. Labour, in contrast, promised to scrap immediately the various caps on benefits and sanctions introduced in the Welfare Reform Act 2012 (see Nicholas Allen in Chapter 1), to reform and redesign Universal Credit and to end six-week delays in payments. Many of the opposition parties also made specific manifesto pledges to abolish the Conservative government's 'family cap' policy, which put a two-child limit on Universal Credit and Child Tax Credit. A particularly controversial element of this policy was the so-called 'rape clause', which allowed a woman to claim assistance for a third or subsequent child if they could prove that child was born as a result of rape. First raised as an issue by the SNP MP Alison Thewliss in 2015, the rape clause was especially prominent as an election issue in Scotland during the general election campaign, with the SNP, Scottish Labour, the Scottish Liberal Democrats and the Scottish Greens uniting in the Scottish Parliament chamber to condemn the policy.

Gender and voting

Since the 1970s in the United Kingdom, women's and men's voting patterns have been largely the same.[10] Historically, women tended to be slightly more pro-Conservative than men, a tendency that underpinned the 'traditional' gender gap. Tony Blair and New Labour reduced this gap by picking up younger women's votes, particularly those of middle- and higher-income mothers, creating a gender-generation gap.[11] However, this newer gap had largely disappeared by the 2010 general election, when the Conservatives were able to win back some of these younger women and middle- and high-income mothers, thanks in part to David Cameron's party-feminisation strategy.[12] In the run-up to the 2015 general election, meanwhile, newspapers devoted many column inches to discussing the Conservative problem with female voters, or Cameron's so-called 'woman problem', even though the overall differences in vote choice between men and women were rather modest.[13] However, aggregate figures hid differences between age groups: younger voters were more supportive of Labour overall in 2015, and young women were more supportive of Labour than young men, just as older women were much more likely to vote Conservative than older men.[14]

While there is no straightforward gender gap in vote choice in British politics, there is evidence of consistent sex differences in some political attitudes. For example, when asked directly, women are less likely to express an interest in politics than men, although the size of this gender gap varies depending on how the question is framed and whether or not respondents are asked about specific policy areas such as education and health.[15] When participants are asked to rank-order policy issues, there are differences in the priority given to particular topics by men and women.[16] In 2017, early polling suggested that women were less likely to say that Brexit was a key election issue than men, and were instead more likely to list the NHS, education, health or welfare as important election issues.[17]

Women are also more likely than men to say 'don't know', when pollsters ask them who they are going to vote for. Ahead of the 2015 general election, this tendency had prompted Labour's then deputy leader Harriet Harman to deploy a pink 'battle bus' in order to reach the '9.1 million missing women voters'. In the run-up to the 2017 general election, concerns were again expressed that turnout might be especially low among women, with the Fawcett Society warning of a 'missing 8 million women' voters on the basis that fewer women than men said they were certain to vote in the election or were registered to vote. However, such warnings should be taken with a large pinch of salt. While surveys generally show women to be more uncertain about their vote intentions than men, data from past British Election Studies shows that men and women have voted at roughly similar rates in recent general elections.[18]

Our knowledge of women's and men's voting behaviour in the 2017 general election necessarily reflects the available data at time of writing. Most of the polls published at the start of the campaign suggested that, as in 2015, younger women would be more likely than younger men to support Labour, whereas older women would be more supportive of the Conservatives than older men. Later polls also suggested that women were increasingly shifting towards Labour as the campaign drew on, and that this movement was a key driving force in the tightening of the race.[19] In particular, the Conservatives' lead among female respondents fell dramatically after their difficult manifesto launch, with women generally expressing more negative views about the party's social care policies than men.[20] Overall, available data suggest that women were more likely than men to vote Labour and less likely than men to vote Tory, as John Bartle describes in Chapter 8, and that the gender gap among younger people has grown, with women under 50, and particularly women in full-time work, especially likely to vote Labour.[21]

Women as candidates

The 2017 general election presented a favourable opportunity for increasing the number of women elected to Westminster. As an unexpected snap election, the various parties' central headquarters could be expected to play a more significant role in candidate selection. Centralised candidate selection procedures can have a positive impact on women's political presence, as they give party leaders who wish to implement and enforce gender-equality reforms, including measures like quotas, the opportunity and power to do so.[22] The election was also notable because of the presence of the Women's Equality Party, which, as noted, fielded candidates in seven constituencies, including Shipley in West Yorkshire, where party leader Sophie Walker challenged the high-profile 'anti-feminist' Tory incumbent Philip Davies. The party's presence, however, proved to be controversial. In Shipley, the party attracted criticism for potentially splitting the anti-Davies vote and for its failure to engage local feminists. The Women's Equality Party also attracted controversy for contesting the north London constituency of Hornsey and Wood Green, which was held by a sitting female MP, Labour's Catherine West.

A record proportion of female candidates were selected in 2017, 973 out of 3,304 (or 29 per cent of the total). Although the actual number of female candidates was lower than in the 2015 general election, fewer men stood as well, and thus the proportion of women increased. As ever, the overall numbers masked significant inter-party differences, as shown in Figure 6.1. In 2017, Labour selected 256 women, the highest number of any party, which equated to 41 per cent (compared to 34 per cent in 2015). Behind Labour, 35 per cent of the Green Party's candidates were women, as were 34 per cent of the SNP's candidates and 28 per cent of Plaid Cymru's candidates. The Conservatives and the Liberal Democrats, meanwhile, selected women in 29 per cent of the seats they contested. For the Tories, this amounted to a nine-point increase on the proportion of female candidates selected in 2015, and a record number

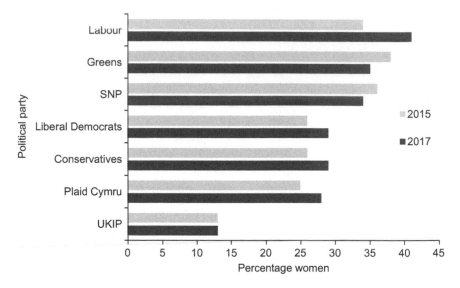

Figure 6.1 Proportion of female candidates by party, 2017
Source: House of Commons.

for the party. By contrast, only 13 per cent of UKIP candidates were women. The Women's Equality Party fielded an all-woman candidate slate, albeit in just seven constituencies.

There are three key strategies that political parties can use to increase women's political presence, all of which were employed in 2017.[23] *Equality rhetoric* involves the public acceptance of claims for women's representation and features in party platforms, manifestos and speeches. As already noted, few of the major parties' manifestos made explicit commitments to increasing women's representation in politics, with the exception of Labour's pledge to appoint a 50/50 cabinet. *Equality promotion* entails measures like training, mentoring and, in some cases, financial assistance, and is aimed at getting women to the starting line. The Conservatives' *Women2Win* campaign is a good example of such a strategy, and most of the parties had similar initiatives in place. Lastly, *equality guarantees* involve the use of measures such as legal or party gender quotas to secure places for aspiring women candidates. The evidence clearly suggests that strong measures like equality guarantees are the most likely to produce substantial improvements in women's representation. There is also evidence that the adoption of quotas by one political party means they may 'catch on' across the political spectrum, as other political parties respond by implementing similar measures.[24]

The use of gender quotas, however, has been largely one-sided in elections thus far to the House of Commons. The Conservatives have continued to reject equality guarantees, preferring instead to use equality rhetoric and equality promotion measures. The party under Cameron did experiment with an 'A List' in 2010, a priority list of approved parliamentary candidates that was 50 per cent women, but the initiative proved controversial and was quietly dropped before the 2015 general election.[25] Labour, on the other hand, has success-fully employed gender quotas in the form of all-women shortlists in all elections since 2005. As seen, the party had the highest proportion of female candidates overall in 2017, but it also had the highest proportion of female candidates in safe seats. Women were 70 per cent of Labour candidates in constituencies that the party had won in 2015 by a margin of 20 to 30 per cent, compared to only 26 per cent of Conservative candidates in similarly safe seats.[26] In con-trast, 43 per cent of Conservative candidates in the party's most winnable target seats – those where the majority to be overturned was 10 per cent or less – were women, compared with 33 per cent of Labour candidates in similarly winnable constituencies.

After years of resisting the arguments for gender quotas, the Liberal Democrats also implemented all-women shortlists in key seats for the first time, and over half their female candidates (56.3 per cent) stood in poten-tially winnable seats. Only the SNP fielded a higher proportion of female candidates in winnable seats, but this point is misleading: the party won all but three seats in Scotland in 2015, as Robert Johns details in Chapter 5, and fielded women in two of those seats it did not win – Orkney and Shetland, and Dumfriesshire, Clydesdale and Tweeddale – in 2017. Despite specula-tion that they would do so, the SNP did not implement all-women shortlists in Glasgow East and Edinburgh West, two seats they had won in 2015 and in which the sitting MPs, both women, had left the party in controversial circumstances. Male candidates were selected to contest both of these seats in 2017, with David Linden narrowly holding on to Glasgow East for the SNP, and Toni Giugliano losing to the Liberal Democrat Christine Jardine in Edinburgh West.

The use of gender quotas, then, has still not fully caught on across the polit-ical spectrum. Most of the other parties continue to lag behind Labour on the recruitment and selection of female candidates, and in translating that into MPs elected, as the following section makes clear. And although the proportion of female candidates did increase overall between 2015 and 2017, there were still 105 constituencies (16 per cent of the total) in which no women stood in 2017. This compares with just one constituency, Glasgow Central, where no men stood for election. While there were on average 5.1 candidates per constituency across the United Kingdom, the average number of female candidates per con-stituency was still only 1.5.[27]

Women as MPs

The last MP to be elected in 2017 was Labour's Emma Dent Coad, who was finally declared the winner of the once-safe Tory seat of Kensington after three recounts. Her victory took the total number of women in the House of

Commons to 208, up from the 196 in office immediately before the election. The 208 included some notable 'firsts' in British politics. Preet Gill became the first female Sikh MP, winning Birmingham Edgbaston for Labour. Marsha de Cordova, a disability rights campaigner, overturned a large Tory majority in Battersea to become the first black disabled female MP. Layla Moran's win in Oxford West and Abingdon made her the first British MP of Palestinian descent, and the first female Liberal Democrat MP from an ethnic minority background.

Ultimately, however, these women still only comprised 32 per cent of all MPs, a glacial two-point increase from before the election. Much was made in subsequent media coverage of passing the '200 women' mark, but this is an arbitrary threshold that is less than one-third of all MPs and far short of the 325 women MPs needed to achieve gender parity in the House of Commons. Within the United Kingdom, the Commons lags behind two of the three devolved legislatures when it comes to women's representation, including the National Assembly for Wales (42 per cent women) and the Scottish Parliament (35 per cent women). Globally, the United Kingdom ranks thirty-ninth in the league table of women's national representation at time of writing, and lags behind many of its European comparators.[28] A large number of the countries that have overtaken Britain in this area have done so through the use of 'fast track' equality guarantees: 18 of the top 20 countries for women's representation worldwide use some form of gender quota, whether voluntary party or legal quotas.[29]

The outcome of the 2017 general election highlights a number of classic issues around women's representation. The first is that progress cannot be assumed. The overall trend in recent years has been one of glacial progress with elements of stagnation and even fallback. Gains in women's representation continue to be slow and incremental, while aggregate trends conceal a great deal of regional and inter-party variation. In Scotland, for example, the proportion of female MPs fell between 2015 and 2017, from 34 to 29 per cent, largely as a result of Conservative gains. Only one of the 13 Scottish Tory MPs elected in 2017 was a woman. Although the Scottish Tories are led by the high-profile and charismatic Ruth Davidson, the party has adopted a laissez-faire approach to women's representation and continues to resist the use of gender quotas, with the result that fewer than one in five of Scottish Conservative MSPs and councillors are women. Meanwhile, the defeat of the SNP's Tasmina Ahmed-Sheikh in Ochil and Perthshire has left Scotland without any BAME MPs in the new parliament.

The second issue is that of party asymmetry, as reported in Table 6.1. The overall increase in the proportion of women MPs again masks significant differences between the parties. In 2017, Labour's use of gender quotas in the form of all-women shortlists continued to deliver. As already highlighted, Labour had the highest proportion of female candidates in safer seats, and the highest number of women MPs elected (119), 20 more than in 2015. Women are now 45 per cent of all Labour MPs in the House of Commons.

Table 6.1 Female MPs by party, 2015 and 2017

Party	2015 (N)	2015 (%)	2017 (N)	2017 (%)
Conservatives	68	21	67	21
Labour	99	43	119	45
SNP	20	36	12	34
DUP	0	0	1	10
Liberal Democrats	0	0	4	33
Sinn Féin	0	0	2	29
Plaid Cymru	1	33	1	25
Green	1	100	1	100
SDLP*	1	33	--	--
Independent	1	100	1	100
Total	191	29	208	32

Note: * The SDLP lost of all three of its Westminster seats in 2017.
Source: Author's calculations.

There was some speculation in the run-up to the election that the Conservatives would achieve a 'breakthrough moment' on women's representation, potentially catching up with Labour for the first time.[30] In the end, there was no such moment: in fact, the gap between the two main parties widened slightly. The Conservatives, in contrast to Labour, saw a fall in the total number of female MPs elected, dropping from 70 immediately before the election to 67 in 2017. However, in the context of an overall loss of seats, the percentage of female Tory MPs remained unchanged at 21 per cent.

Turning to the other parties, the Liberal Democrat went from being a men-only party after their coalition-induced electoral meltdown in 2015, to having four female MPs out of 12 in 2017. Of these, the most notable was former junior equalities minister, Jo Swinson, who re-took her old seat of East Dunbartonshire and subsequently became her party's deputy leader. Meanwhile, the 12 female SNP MPs – six less than in 2015 – comprised just over one-third of the party's reduced group at Westminster. Only one of the ten DUP MPs elected in 2017 – a crucial group that acted as political 'queen-makers' by supporting the minority Tory administration, as Rosie Campbell outlines in Chapter 9 – was a woman, Emma Little-Pengelly, who won Belfast South. Caroline Lucas retained her seat in Brighton Pavilion as the only Green MP, and Liz Saville Roberts returned as Plaid Cymru's only female MP. The remaining three women MPs were elected in Northern Ireland: Sylvia Hermon, an Independent, and Michelle Gildernew and Elisha McCallion, who, as Sinn Féin members, refuse to take their seats at Westminster. The Women's Equality Party failed to make an electoral impact and lost all seven of its deposits. The party faces significant obstacles going forward, particularly in a political context where all of the main British political parties have responded to demands for women's individual and collective representation in some form, even if they have not fully delivered on this front.

Women as leaders

The 2017 general election was the first since 1987 to be called by a female prime minister. Theresa May's ascent to the top in British politics prompted many (perhaps inevitable) comparisons between her and Margaret Thatcher. From the right of the Tory-leaning press, for example, both the *Daily Telegraph* and *Daily Mail* proclaimed the party had found another 'Iron Lady', the moniker first given to Thatcher by the Soviet newspaper *Red Star*. May's debut at Prime Minister's Questions in 2016 prompted the *Guardian*'s John Crace to declare that the 'Thatch is back ... close your eyes and it could have been the early 80s'.[31] There are, of course, many differences between May and Thatcher, whether in terms of their background, political positions, experience or ways of working. Indeed, back in the early 2000s when she had been party chairman, May had famously alighted on Thatcher's legacy as one of the reasons behind the Tories' reputation as the 'nasty party'. For many journalists and commentators, however, the logic seemed to be that May and Thatcher were women and therefore immediately comparable. May herself dismissed these comparisons between her and Thatcher as being 'lazy', stating that she'd never thought of herself 'like anybody else, or as doing the job like anybody else'.[32]

Like many female leaders, Theresa May came to power at a moment of crisis. Comparative research suggests that women are more likely to get the chance to lead in times of political upheaval or decline, usually when parties are out of power or losing favour with voters.[33] Margaret Thatcher became Conservative Party leader after the party had lost two successive elections. Angela Merkel took the helm of the Christian Democrats in Germany after a major electoral defeat and political corruption scandal.[34] In other words, women often come to power when the job at the top is least desirable, and are left to clean up someone else's mess. The reason is straightforward: periods of political or party crisis often result in the disgrace or removal of party leaders and their immediate teams, the vast majority of whom are likely to be men. This in turn opens up more opportunities for women to run for the top job.[35] Other male challengers may also decide not to throw their hats in the rings, waiting for a better opportunity further down the line, particularly in contexts where they are weak candidates running against more experienced women.[36] In the case of the Conservatives in 2016, David Cameron's failure to keep Britain inside the European Union led to his immediate resignation and terminally damaged the leadership aspirations of chancellor George Osborne. Meanwhile, as Nicholas Allen describes in Chapter 1, the assumed frontrunner Boris Johnson's leadership bid crashed before it had even started thanks to his last-minute betrayal by fellow Leave campaigner Michael Gove. The absence of Osborne and Johnson left the field clear for both May and junior minister Andrea Leadsom, who were due to contest a ballot of all party members before Leadsom pulled out.

The unfortunate flipside of crises favouring aspiring female leaders is that they can also leave them on the edge of a 'glass cliff': they are more likely to be elected to leadership posts when there is a high chance of failure. And women are more likely than men to be thrown out – and thrown out more quickly – if their parties continue to flounder.[37] In Theresa May's case, the cliff she found herself on was particularly sheer: she inherited a divided country, a divided party, and a deeply uncertain political and economic future. At times, however, it seemed that May was actively running towards the edge of her own glass cliff. 'Presidentialised' election campaigns can be particularly difficult for female leaders and politicians to navigate, in that they face an almost impossible task of having to live up the masculine expectations of political and executive office, while simultaneously maintaining and 'managing' their femininity.[38] Yet, by any measure, the Tories' 2017 election campaign was shambolic. May presented herself as a 'strong and stable' leader who would be a 'bloody difficult' woman in Brexit negotiations, but then refused to participate in televised leaders' debates. Her notable absence prompted the widespread use on social media of the hashtag #wherestheresa. She did, however, appear with her husband on the BBC's *One Show*, a supposedly relaxed magazine format, where she awkwardly said there were 'boys' and girls' jobs' in a discussion over who took out the bins at home.

While the election was undoubtedly a failed gamble for May, some post-election criticism went further and associated this failure specifically with her 'being prime minister while female'. Indeed, the media personality and broadcaster Janet Street-Porter argued that 'May's incompetence had set women in politics back decades', and that 2017 had 'been a disaster for women in politics'.[39] It is hard to conceive of such a headline being written about a male politician. In 2016, for example, no column inches were dedicated to how David Cameron's failed gamble in calling the Brexit referendum had set men in politics back decades.

Has May's premiership benefited women more generally? Some studies have found that having more women in leadership positions boosts the overall numbers of women candidates and parliamentarians.[40] May has made a number of high-profile female appointments during her premiership, including Amber Rudd as home secretary, Liz Truss as justice secretary (subsequently moved after the election) and Justine Greening as education secretary (though she later chose to leave office rather than be reshuffled). Yet, after her post-election reshuffle, there were only six female cabinet ministers, including the prime minister, or 26 per cent of the total. Four other women, Liz Truss, Andrea Leadsom, Claire Perry and Caroline Noakes, attended cabinet, as chief secretary to the Treasury, leader of the House of Commons, energy minister and immigration minister, respectively.[41] Meanwhile, the key ministerial portfolios responsible for managing Britain's withdrawal from the European Union continued to be occupied by men: David Davis as secretary of state for exiting the EU, Liam Fox as international trade secretary and Boris Johnson as foreign secretary. Their initial appointments owed much to their well-established leadership ambitions: Davis had run unsuccessfully in 2001 and 2005, Fox in 2005 and 2016, and Johnson not quite in 2016. By giving them these important offices, May had doubtless sought to protect her base, an instance of 'keep your friends close, and your enemies closer'. Had the Tories increased their parliamentary majority, an emboldened May might well have replaced one or more of them. In the circumstances she was unable to do so.[42]

Theresa May's record on the promotion of women's issues is also decidedly mixed. On the one hand, she once memorably associated herself with this agenda by donning a 'This is what a feminist looks like' t-shirt in support of a Fawcett Society campaign, and she also founded *Women2Win*, the equality-promotion initiative set up to encourage and help more Conservative women to run for office. Moreover, as home secretary, May introduced laws criminalising coercive control and ordered an inquiry into police treatment of domestic abuse cases. She also sponsored the Modern Slavery Act 2015, which sought to tackle human trafficking, an issue she continued to champion once in Downing Street. On the other hand, as home secretary she also presided over a draconian immigration regime and the indefinite detention of pregnant women at Yarl's Wood Immigration Removal Centre. Throughout her time in government, she also backed austerity policies which had had a disproportionately detrimental impact on women, particularly women of colour.[43] And as prime minister, she sought to forge a good relationship with Donald Trump – at one point holding his hand during a visit to the White House – despite the new American president's history of misogynistic remarks and discriminatory policies. Lastly, in the wake of the election's indecisive outcome, she reached out to the anti-abortion, anti-gay marriage DUP in order to secure a confidence-and-supply agreement in Parliament, as Rosie Campbell describes in Chapter 9.

Theresa May is not, of course, the only woman at the top in British politics. Going into the election, the DUP were led by former Northern Irish first minister, Arlene Foster; the SNP and Scottish government were led by Nicola Sturgeon; and the Scottish Tories and Scottish Labour were led by Ruth Davidson and Kezia Dugdale, respectively. Moreover, Plaid Cymru was led by Leanne Wood; Sinn Féin, at least in the Northern Ireland Assembly, was led by Michelle O'Neill; and the Greens were co-led by Caroline Lucas. UKIP was now led by a man, but it had briefly been led by be a woman in 2016, Diane James, who quit only 18 days after being elected.

Not surprisingly, female party leaders and MPs played a prominent role in the 2017 campaign and especially in the televised debates. During the *ITV Leaders' Debate*, the UKIP leader Paul Nuttall memorably referred to Plaid Cymru's Leanne Wood as 'Natalie', an apparent reference to the Green Party's former leader Natalie Bennett, which raised questions as to his ability to tell women apart. Yet, as in previous elections, media coverage in 2017 was dominated by men.[44] Indeed, a report by Loughborough University's Centre for Research in Communication and Culture found that 63 per cent of politicians that featured in election news were male, and that men dominated in all election media roles, whether as experts, spokespeople or pollsters.[45] In contrast to 2015, when minor parties received more column inches and higher levels of news presence, 2017 was a highly personalised campaign in which media coverage focused largely on the two main party leaders, May and the Labour leader Jeremy Corbyn. Although the prime minister was the most prominent politician in news coverage, followed by Corbyn, the next most prominent woman, the SNP's Nicola Sturgeon, was a long way behind them being the subject of just 3.7 per cent of news coverage.[46]

In 2017 women were also subject to the sexist stereotyping and objectification that characterises a great deal of the traditional and new British media. Shortly before she called the election, for instance, Theresa May had met with Nicola Sturgeon to discuss Brexit and the possibility of a second Scottish independence referendum. Despite the huge political significance of their meeting, the *Daily Mail's* front page had focused on their physical attributes with the headline: 'Never mind Brexit, who won Legs-it!' The 2017 election also brought into sharp focus the continuing abuse and threats faced by female politicians, particularly women of colour. In one particularly stark incident during the campaign, Women's Equality Party candidate Nimco Ali received a death threat signed 'Jo Cox', the name of the female Labour MP brutally murdered during the 2016 Brexit referendum. Meanwhile, research by Amnesty International found that almost half of all abusive tweets sent to female politicians in the six weeks before polling day were received by Labour's shadow home secretary, Diane Abbott, who was a frequent target for racial and sexist abuse.[47] In the previous six months, Abbott had received just under a third of all abusive tweets sent to female MPs.

Two steps forward, one step back?

While women made small gains in the 2017 general election, the results amounted to a scratching, rather than a shattering, of the political glass ceiling. There is still a long way to go before equal representation at Westminster is achieved. Patterns established in previous elections also persisted. Labour continued to lead the way on women's representation, while most of the other parties continued to lag behind. Without greater intervention by all of the parties across the political spectrum, gains in women's representation will continue to be slow and incremental at best.

All of this suggests, yet again, that the prospect of equal representation in British politics cannot rely solely on individual party champions and 'soft' equality measures like equality rhetoric or equality promotion. The next general election might be a few months away, or it might be in five years' time, but the evidence overwhelmingly suggests that stronger equality measures are needed to ensure real change in the representativeness of the House of Commons. Yet, the debate over gender quotas in Britain continues to be marginal – in that it has largely taken place within the parties – and parochial and non-scientific – in that it has largely disregarded the global evidence.[48] Pressure for a new approach is building, however. A number of recent inquiries have all recommended the introduction of legislative quotas, including a 2010 report by the Speaker's Conference on Parliamentary Representation, a 2014 report by the All Party Parliamentary Group for Women in Parliament, the 2016 *Good Parliament Report*, and a 2017 report by the House of Commons Women and Equalities Select Committee.[49]

Yet, the Conservative government has shown a distinct lack of enthusiasm for such recommendations, as well as a lack of ambition and political will. In responding to the recent Women and Equalities Select Committee report, for example, the government agreed that a 'gender-balanced Parliament is long overdue', but argued that legislative quotas were not the 'right approach' to the issue and preferred to leave responsibility in the hands of political parties.[50] The government also refused to commence Section 106 of the Equality Act 2010, which requires parties to publish candidate diversity data, on the grounds that this represented an excessive 'potential regulatory burden'. It also held off from extending further the time for which the Sex Discrimination (Election Candidates) Act 2002 – a piece of legislation that allows parties to discriminate positively and employ all-women shortlists – is in force, as well as allowing gender quotas to be used for electing local mayors and police and crime commissioners.

Meanwhile, in the wake of the 2017 general election, the unrepresentativeness of the House of Commons again hit the headlines over the issue of select committee memberships. Women formed a majority on just three committees – those dealing with women and equalities, education and health – and made up less than a quarter of the committees overseeing Brexit, transport, defence and foreign affairs. This reflects wider gendered patterns in politics, where women are often disproportionately represented in 'feminine', low-prestige committees and portfolios, whilst men are over-represented in 'masculine', high-prestige areas. Scorn was heaped on the membership of the Science and Technology Select Committee after it was revealed that it had no female members at all. Conservative MP Vicky Ford was subsequently elected to become the only woman on the committee. Another case, then, of *plus ça change, plus c'est la même chose*.[51]

Why does all this matter? While the link between women's political presence and the promotion of gender equality policies is far from straightforward, there is considerable evidence to suggest that female politicians 'make a difference', or more accurately, that more gender-balanced parliaments and councils do. Troubled times lie ahead. Britain faces the possibility of continuing austerity and economic recession. As a result of Brexit, it also faces the potential scrapping of various EU frameworks, including those offering certain legal protections for women, and the loss of the recourse provided by the European Court of Justice. The EU has been a crucial actor in promoting gender equality, particularly in the area of women's employment rights, yet there has been little substantive discussion of the consequences of Brexit for women and for gender equality. Even the United Kingdom's Brexit negotiating team initially included only one woman. The continuing exclusion of women from British politics is thus a serious democratic deficit that demands action. It is vitally important that women sit at the table as Britain negotiates its exit from Europe, as well as its own constitutional future. Leadership and vigilance are needed in order to keep women's representation and equality issues on the agenda; otherwise gendered inequalities are likely to widen. There is no room for complacency in the days ahead.

Notes

1   Monica Charlot, 'Women and elections in Britain', in Howard R. Penniman (ed.), *Britain at the Polls, 1979* (London: AEI Press, 1981), pp. 241–262, at p. 262.
2   Robert Booth, 'New intake brings number of disabled MPs in Commons to five', *Guardian*, 11 June 2017.
3   Sarah Childs and Paul Webb, *Sex, Gender and the Conservative Party* (Basingstoke: Palgrave Macmillan, 2012).
4   Rosie Campbell and Sarah Childs, 'All aboard the pink battle bus? Women voters, women's issues, candidates and party leaders', *Parliamentary Affairs*, 68 (2015), 206–223.
5   Sarah Childs, Paul Webb and Sally Marthaler, 'Constituting and substantively representing women: Applying new approaches to a UK case study', *Politics & Gender*, 6 (2010), 199–223; Claire Annesley, Isabelle Engeli and Francesca Gains, 'The profile of gender equality issue attention in Western Europe', *European Journal of Political Research*, 54 (2015), 525–542.
6   Rosie Campbell, 'What do we *really* know about women voters? Gender, elections and public opinion', *Political Quarterly*, 83 (2012), 703–710; Rosie Campbell and Sarah Childs, '"To the left, to the right": Representing Conservative women's interests', *Party Politics*, 21 (2015), 626–637.
7   See, for example, Birte Siim, 'Political intersectionality and democratic politics in the European political sphere', *Politics & Gender*, 10 (2014), 117–124.
8   What is referred to as 'class-based' gender equality issues in Annesley et al., 'The profile of gender equality issue attention in Western Europe'.
9   Research on previous elections points to similar findings. See for example Claire Annesley and Francesca Gains, 'Investigating the economic determinants of the UK gender equality policy agenda', *British Journal of Politics and International Relations*, 15 (2013), 125–146.
10 Rosie Campbell, *Gender and the Vote in Britain* (Colchester: ECPR Press, 2006).
11 Pippa Norris, 'A gender-generation gap?', in Geoffrey Evans and Pippa Norris (eds), *Critical Elections: Voters and Parties in Long-Term Perspective* (London: Sage, 1999), pp. 148–163.
12 Rosie Campbell and Sarah Childs, '"Wags", "wives" and "mothers" … but what about women politicians?', *Parliamentary Affairs*, 63 (2010), 760–777.
13 Campbell and Childs, 'All aboard the pink battle bus'; Rosalind Shorrocks, 'In what ways does gender matter for voting behavior in GE2017?', *LSE British Politics*

and Policy Blog, 31 May 2017, available at: http://blogs.lse.ac.uk/politicsandpolicy/gender-and-voting-behaviour-in-ge2017/, last accessed 18 August 2017.

14   See Campbell and Childs, 'All aboard the pink battle bus'. Age dynamics, however, have not been historically consistent between elections – on this point, see Rosalind Shorrocks, 'Modernisation and government socialisation: Considering explanations for gender differences in cohort trends in British voting behaviour', *Electoral Studies*, 42 (2016), 237–248.

15   Rosie Campbell and Kristi Winters, 'Understanding men's and women's political interests: Evidence from a study of gendered political attitudes', *Journal of Elections, Public Opinion and Parties*, 18 (2009), 53–74.

16   Campbell, 'What do we *really* know about women voters?'

17   Shorrocks, 'Modernisation and government socialisation'; Campbell, *Gender and the Vote in Britain*.

18   Campbell and Childs, '"To the left, to the right"'.

19   Ben Riley-Smith and Patrick Scott, 'Labour narrows gap to six points as women voters surge towards Jeremy Corbyn', *Daily Telegraph*, 28 May 2017.

20   Rosalind Shorrocks and Stephen Fisher, 'Labour poll surge mainly thanks to younger women, but also old', available at: https://electionsetc.com/2017/06/02/labour-poll-surge-mainly-thanks-to-younger-women-but-also-old/, last accessed 20 August 2017. See also, for example, Survation, 'General election 2017 poll, 19–20 May 2017', available at: http://survation.com/wp-content/uploads/2017/05/Final-MoS-Poll-190517GOCH-1c0d1h7.pdf, last accessed 20 August 2017.

21   See for example YouGov, 'How Britain voted at the 2017 general election', available at: https://yougov.co.uk/news/2017/06/13/how-britain-voted-2017-general-election, last accessed 20 August 2017; Peter Kellner, 'Why did so many voters switch parties between 2015 and 2017?', *New Statesman*, 29 September 2017.

22   See, for example, Miki Caul Kittilson, *Challenging Parties, Changing Parliaments* (Columbus: The Ohio State University Press, 2006); Meryl Kenny and Tània Verge, 'Decentralization, political parties and women's representation: Evidence from Spain and Britain', *Publius: The Journal of Federalism*, 43 (2013), 109–128.

23   See Joni Lovenduski, *Feminizing Politics* (Cambridge: Polity, 2005).

24   Lovenduski, *Feminizing Politics*; Meryl Kenny and Fiona Mackay, 'When is contagion not very contagious? Dynamics of women's political representation in Scotland', *Parliamentary Affairs*, 67 (2014), 866–886.

25   Rosie Campbell and Sarah Childs, 'Conservatism, feminization and the representation of women in UK politics', *British Politics*, 10 (2015), 148–168.

26   House of Commons Library, *General Election 2017: Results and Analysis* (London: House of Commons, 2017), p. 41.

27   House of Commons Library, *General Election 2017*.

28   Inter-Parliamentary Union, 'Women in national parliaments: Situation as of 1 August 2017', available at: www.ipu.org/wmn-e/classif.htm, last accessed 20 August 2017.

29   Global Database of Quotas for Women, available at: www.quotaproject.org, last accessed 20 August 2017.

30   Ben Riley-Smith, '"Theresa factor" credited with surge in women candidates as party looks set to make history by securing more women MPs than ever before', *Daily Telegraph*, 6 May 2017.

31   John Crace, 'Theresa could have reinvented herself as anyone – but she came as Maggie', *Guardian*, 20 July 2016.

32 George Parker and Lionel Barber, 'Theresa May on decision-making, Brexit and doing the job her way', *FT Magazine*, 8 December 2016.

33 Diana Z. O'Brien, 'Rising to the top: Gender, political performance, and party leadership in parliamentary democracies', *American Journal of Political Science*, 59 (2015), 1022–1039.

34 Karen Beckwith, 'Before prime minister: Margaret Thatcher, Angela Merkel, and gendered party leadership contests', *Politics & Gender*, 11 (2015), 718–745.

35 Beckwith, 'Before prime minister'.

36 Beckwith identifies these dynamics in the cases of Margaret Thatcher and Angela Merkel. See Beckwith 'Before prime minister', and Rikhil R. Bhavnani, 'Do electoral quotas work after they are withdrawn? Evidence from a natural experiment in India', *American Political Science Review*, 103 (2009), 23–35.

37 O'Brien, 'Rising to the top'.

38 Kathleen Jamieson, *Beyond the Double Bind: Women and Leadership* (Oxford: Oxford University Press, 1995); Rainbow Murray (ed.), *Cracking the Highest Glass Ceiling* (Oxford: Praeger, 2010).

39 Janet Street-Porter, 'Theresa May's incompetence has set women in politics back decades', *Independent*, 9 June 2017.

40 See, for example, Kittilson, *Challenging Parties*.

41 The nature of cabinet membership in Britain has been muddied in recent years by prime ministers inviting an increasing number of ministers to 'attend' cabinet, a strategy they have sometimes but not always used to 'make up the numbers' on women's representation. When measuring levels of women's political presence, the comparative literature on gender and cabinets generally focuses only on ministers who are formally recognised as having full cabinet status. In keeping with the comparative literature, this chapter counts only full members of cabinet, not attendees. Full-cabinet ministerial positions are comparable across contexts, while sub-cabinet positions or those who get to attend cabinet meetings vary considerably across contexts. On this point, see especially Claire Annesley, Karen Beckwith and Susan Franceschet, *Cabinets, Ministers and Gender*, unpublished manuscript, 2017.

42 All prime ministers have to manage the ambitions of those who seek to replace them. Since most challengers to female leaders are likely to be men, it is perhaps not surprising that female leaders trying to hold onto power are often especially vulnerable to male challengers and try to encourage loyalty by rewarding them with key government posts. On this point, see especially Diana Z. O'Brien, Matthew Mendez, Jordon Carr Peterson and Jihyun Shin, 'Letting down the ladder or shutting the door: Female prime ministers, party leaders, and cabinet ministers', *Politics & Gender*, 11 (2015), 689–717.

43 See for example, Women's Budget Group, 'A cumulative gender impact assessment of ten years of austerity policies', available at: https://wbg.org.uk/wp-content/uploads/2016/03/De_HenauReed_WBG_GIAtaxben_briefing_2016_03_06.pdf, last accessed 20 August 2017.

44 Emily Harmer, 'Pink buses, leader's wives and "The most dangerous woman in Britain": Women, the press and politics in the 2015 election', in Dominic Wring, Roger Mortimore and Simon Atkinson (eds), *Political Communication in Britain* (Basingstoke: Palgrave, 2017), pp. 259–272.

45 Centre for Research in Communication and Culture, 'Media coverage of the General Election campaign – Report 4', Loughborough University, 2017, available

at: https://blog.lboro.ac.uk/crcc/general-election/media-coverage-of-the-2017-general-election-campaign-report-4/, last accessed 20 August 2017.

46   Centre for Research in Communication and Culture, 'Media coverage of the General Election campaign'.

47   Amnesty International, 'Unsocial media: Tracking Twitter abuse against women MPs', available at: https://medium.com/@AmnestyInsights/unsocial-media-tracking-twitter-abuse-against-women-mps-fc28aeca498a, last accessed 6 September 2017.

48   Meryl Kenny, 'Who runs the world? Gender and politics in the UK and beyond', *Political Insight*, 8 (2017), 30–33.

49   Speaker's Conference (on Parliamentary Representation), *Final Report*, HC 239-I (London: The Stationery Office, 2010); APPG Women in Parliament, *Improving Parliament: Creating a Better and More Representative House* (London: House of Commons, 2014); Sarah Childs, *The Good Parliament* (2016), available at: www.bristol.ac.uk/media-library/sites/news/2016/july/20%20Jul%20Prof%20Sarah%20Childs%20The%20Good%20Parliament%20report.pdf, last accessed 6 September 2017; Women and Equalities Committee, *Women in the House of Commons after the 2020 Election*, HC650 (London: The Stationery Office, 2017).

50   HM Government, *The Government Response to the Women and Equalities Committee Report on Women in the House of Commons*, Cm 9492 (London: Cabinet Office, 2017).

51   Which translates as: 'the more things change, the more they stay the same'.

7

Electoral integrity and post-truth politics

Sarah Birch

Electoral integrity is a relatively new issue in relation to UK election campaigns. Between the end of the Second World War and the turn of the twenty-first century, there was a general elite consensus among politicians, academics and media commentators that elections were well conducted, and electoral administrators largely escaped journalistic attention except in rare cases of unintentional foul-ups.[1] Recent cases of electoral fraud, however, have caused trust in electoral administration to fall. Public confidence in the conduct of electoral campaigns by political parties has always been in greater doubt, but in the last several years the veracity of political communication and the propriety of campaign techniques have been subject to intense public scrutiny. At the same time, the integrity of the UK's electoral processes has come under threat from a new source entirely, digital technology, which has enabled the targeted dissemination of bespoke campaign messages. The honesty of campaign claims had been a major concern ahead of the 2016 referendum on leaving the European Union. Concerns about misinformation lingered a year later in the general election. There was also growing unease over the use of direct marketing techniques to identify voters' political sympathies and sway their choices. The result is that electoral integrity in Britain is no longer taken for granted. It has become an electoral issue in its own right. This chapter first provides an overview of recent developments in the regulatory framework governing UK elections and the rise of concern about electoral integrity over the course of the past two decades. It then analyses the role that electoral and political integrity played in the 2017 general election campaign and its aftermath.

Background and regulatory framework

The United Kingdom has long prided itself on being an exemplar of democratic electoral practice. The 'mother of parliaments' has provided a role model for representative government across the Commonwealth and beyond. Though electoral malpractice was a major problem before the nineteenth-century parliamentary reforms that ushered in current electoral arrangements, the regulation of elections and political parties took a light touch throughout the twentieth century, and concerns about electoral integrity were relatively muted during much of the post-war period (with the partial exception of elections in Northern Ireland).[2] Several recent developments changed this situation, however. The introduction of party-list voting for European Parliament elections in 1999 required the regulation of political parties and some of their campaign activities. Responsibility for enforcing these regulations was placed in the hands of the Electoral Commission, a new body created in 2001. This body was also tasked with overseeing electoral practices more generally.[3] The development of international law and best-practice standards in the area of elections, including the rise of election observation in the member states of the Organization of Security and Co-operation in Europe (OSCE) of which the UK is part, also required Britain to up its electoral game. The advent of devolution in 1999 and the consequent creation of new assemblies in Scotland, Wales and London, together with directly elected mayors in some municipalities, has also resulted in a rise in the opportunities for electoral misconduct. Finally, an alteration in electoral law to allow postal voting on demand greatly facilitated voter fraud, resulting in a spate of scandals and a decline in public confidence in elections.[4] The 'modernisation' of UK elections has thus not been without controversy.

Postal voting on demand was a child of the newly formed Electoral Commission. In its early years, the Commission was mainly focused on ensuring participation at elections, partly due to concerns about turnout, which had fallen below the psychologically significant 60 per cent mark in the 2001 general election. The Commission subsequently busied itself with inventing new ways to engage voters, and even proposed schemes such as voting at cashpoints, by text and via digital television. There was limited appetite to forge ahead with these innovations, however. Electoral experts expressed concerns about the security implications of these proposals.[5] Perhaps more importantly, trials suggested that such schemes did little to increase turnout. The only mechanisms that did appear to have a significant impact on electoral participation was postal voting, so the Commission proposed, and in 2001 the government duly enacted, postal voting on demand. Of all the recent developments, the introduction of postal voting on demand has probably done most to focus popular and journalistic attention on violations of electoral integrity. The inherently more limited opportunities for monitoring secrecy and the authenticity of postal voting made this institution ripe for manipulation, and it was not long before wily political actors began to take advantage of the opportunities afforded by this less transparent and less secure means of casting a ballot. These developments resulted in a tightening of the rules in 2007, but by this time popular confidence in electoral integrity had begun to fracture. Matters of electoral practice suddenly became newsworthy.

The turning point in public concern came in 2004 when a major postal-vote scandal in Birmingham prompted a rethink of the drive to increase participation. In his judgement on the case, Election Commissioner Richard Mawrey QC made the now infamous remark that he had heard 'evidence of electoral fraud that would disgrace a banana republic'.[6] A damning 2007 report by the Committee on Standards in Public Life chided the Electoral Commission for neglecting voting integrity. From that time the Commission's focus increasingly turned to tightening up the UK's regulatory framework.[7]

The result was a swerve in the direction of fraud-prevention, including a move from household to individual voter registration in 2011. In 2014 the Electoral Commission recommended further tightening of security provisions, including the introduction of ID at polling stations, which had never previously been required in the UK, outside of Northern Ireland.[8] A number of further problems prompted the Conservative government in 2015 to invite former minister and now 'Anti-Corruption Champion' Sir Eric Pickles to undertake a review of electoral fraud. In his report, Pickles echoed the Electoral Commission's call for requiring ID at polling stations and made a number of other recommendations designed to increase the penalties for fraud and to broaden the range of actors who could lodge electoral petitions.[9] The Conservatives duly included a manifesto commitment in 2017 to require formal identification at polling stations. This proposal caused alarm in some quarters due to its apparent effects on access to voting among mobile and marginalised groups. Electoral administration was once again front and centre stage.

But if the conduct of elections has come to occupy a larger role in the British public mind over recent years, it is also worth mentioning those aspects of elections that have *not* yet become contentious issues. The drawing of MPs' constituency boundaries, for example, is largely unpoliticised (though political parties and other groups contribute to the process), and the independent boundary commissions are known for their integrity. The one boundary-related issue that was relevant to the 2017 general election was the fact that a regular redrawing of parliamentary constituency seats had been scuppered by the Liberal Democrats when they were part of the 2010–15 coalition government. As a result, the boundaries on which the 2017 contest were fought were somewhat outdated. There was no question, however, of *administrative* malfeasance in the decision to postpone the introduction of the new boundaries.

The integrity of electoral administrators is also still largely taken for granted in the UK. Some may view the British electoral system as being open to abuse by voters and parties, but electoral staff are for the most part widely considered to be honest and non-partisan, being drawn from the ranks of local government officialdom. Their competence has been called into question on occasion in several places at the time of the 2017 election (see below), but their integrity is not generally an issue with most voters. Surveys have found that over the past decade, between two-thirds and three-quarters of citizens have confidence in the integrity of electoral administration in the UK.[10] This compares favourably with attitudes towards politicians, for instance, who are held to be honest by only between one-fifth and one-third of Britons.[11]

Electoral misconduct as an issue in 2017

Though Brexit, public services and the economy were undoubtedly the most important issues for politicians and voters in the 2017 general election, the integrity of the electoral process itself was a significant issue as well, and one that generated considerable news coverage. Electoral misconduct was a focus of public attention even before the campaign started as the shadow of malprac-tice allegations in elections past loomed over the 2017 poll. During the course of the campaign several electoral integrity news stories that had been bubbling along for some time broke the surface again. These included the fraught 2014 local election in the inner London borough of Tower Hamlets, allegations of the misuse of campaign funds at the 2015 general election, concern over the hon-esty of campaigning techniques used in the run-up to the 2016 EU referendum, and the prospect of photo identification being required at polling stations in future elections.

Tower Hamlets 2014: Following the 2014 local election in Tower Hamlets, the victorious mayoral candidate, Lutfur Rahman, was convicted of elect-oral fraud, undue influence and various other electoral offences. The London Metropolitan Police investigation into the episode was heavily criticised by the London Assembly in March of 2017. In April the police launched a criminal investigation into Rahman, who had previously been convicted of civil offences only.[12] The Tower Hamlets election had been one of the most egregious cases of electoral malpractice in the UK for several years, as it involved not only fraud but large-scale voter intimidation; on the night of the vote count, the crowds both within and outside the counting centre had been so aggressive and chaotic that the building was locked down and part of the count was suspended.[13] Such events are virtually unheard of in the UK and raised serious concerns about the fragility of electoral procedures in a limited number of geographic regions.[14] Renewed discussion of these events during the 2017 campaign is bound to have raised concern and primed many voters to be on the alert for improper electoral practices.

General election 2015 campaign spending: The UK operates a system whereby spending in individual parliamentary constituencies is strictly limited by the number of registered electors in each seat, whereas national spending by parties is less tightly regulated. It had been an open secret among politicos that con-stituency campaign spending regularly over-spilled the official limits imposed, but as virtually all political parties were guilty of peccadillos of this nature, they were understandably reluctant to grass each other up, and there long reigned an informal 'understanding' on this matter. Those parties too poor to overspend were also too poor to bring costly court cases against those that did exceed the limits, and police resources were sorely stretched, particularly after the public spending cuts introduced by the coalition government after 2010. All this changed after 2015, when the major political parties received serious slaps on the wrist, and fines, for breaching campaign-finance regulations. Several of these cases were ongoing at the time of the 2017 general election, prompting Scotland's first minister, Nicola Sturgeon – whose Scottish National Party had escaped censure – to claim that prime minister Theresa May was calling the general election early in order to have it out of the way before the most signifi-cant effluent arising from the Tories' spending in 2015 hit the proverbial fan.[15] If this was indeed the prime minister's motive, it backfired. On 1 June, a week before polling day, charges were brought against Thanet South Conservative candidate Craig Mackinlay for campaign spending excesses in the 2015 gen-eral election campaign.[16] The timing of the charges was criticised by the Tories, given that they were lodged only days before an election in which Mackinlay was again contesting the seat. These accusations were largely submerged in the hubbub of election coverage in most media outlets. Curiously, they were set out in huge letters across the front page of the 2 June issue of the *London Evening Standard* newspaper, now under the editorship of former Conservative chan-cellor George Osborne who had been sacked by Theresa May (see Nicholas Allen in Chapter 1). Since Thanet South seat is some 80 miles from London this editorial decision accentuated divisions within the Conservative Party.[17]

The EU referendum 2016: Debate about the conduct of the Brexit refer-endum campaign focused not so much on whether there had been maladmin-istration or a violation of electoral law, but rather on the claims made by those campaigning to leave the EU and those fighting for the UK to remain a member. The consequences of any proposed major constitutional change are by def-inition open to debate, so any predictions of what would happen in the event of one result or the other were not amenable to refutation on factual grounds. Some of the claims made by the two camps were disputed on the basis that they represented wilful mis-interpretations of the nature of the UK's link to the EU and how withdrawal would legally alter the UK. One of the arguments that engendered especial ire on the part of the Remain camp was a claim, emblazoned on the Leave campaign bus, that the UK would be £350 million a week better off if it did not have to make payments to the EU, and that this money could then be spent on other things, such as funding the cash-strapped National Health Service. On the other side of the Brexit fence, then prime min-ister David Cameron's claim that leaving the EU could trigger a third world war was widely criticised as irresponsible scare-mongering.[18]

Photo ID at polling stations: Most states in the world require voters to produce some kind of formal identification when they arrive at polling stations to vote. In many contexts, sophisticated biometrics are employed in order to ensure that voters are who they say they are. Great Britain is anomalous in this regard. Prospective voters are obliged simply to tell the polling clerk their name and address. Provided that name and address corresponds to an entry on the register, and provided that person is not already listed as having voted, the elector in question is handed a ballot. Even if the polling clerk has reason to sus-pect that an individual is not who they say they are, he or she only has powers to ask the person to confirm their identity verbally before voting. The situation in Northern Ireland is somewhat different, a consequence of its distinctive and troubled politics. There citizens must produce some form of identification in order to vote, and the Electoral Commission has recommended introducing the same system in mainland Britain, despite the fact that the UK has no national system of identification cards.[19] This idea was taken up by the Conservative government and included in their 2017 election manifesto, much to the consternation of many who held that this requirement would suppress voting, especially among younger and less affluent electors, who have traditionally been less likely to vote for the Tories. In short, the proposal was seen as a self-serving and blatantly partisan wheeze to inflate the vote of the incumbent government on the grounds of concerns about voter fraud that did not match the reality.[20] The Tory move and the reaction of other parties echoed the long-standing and highly politicised debate about 'voter suppression' in the United States, where a significant proportion of less advantaged citizens are disenfranchised on the basis of legal provisions.[21] The requirement to show ID at polling stations is not such a provision, but the parallel with the American debate was sufficient to raise alarm bells on the part of those who suspected the motives of the Conservatives in seeking to combat electoral fraud.

Thus in the run-up to the 2017 general election campaign, voters and commentators alike were primed to be suspicious of electoral conduct and on their guard against efforts to subvert the electoral process. Allegations of actual wrong-doing in 2017 fall into four broad categories: inappropriate campaigning practices by candidates, parties and their activists; supposedly biased and inaccurate media coverage; suspect campaign fundraising; and maladministration by election officials. The next four sections consider each of these topics in turn.

Election campaigns and digital technology: data mining and social media

The 1997 general election was the first major 'internet election' in Britain. Since then, the role of digital technology, including the online world and latterly data mining and social media, have grown with each successive poll.[22] By 2017, certain digital tools had been so finely honed and designed for political purposes as to begin to cause concern in certain quarters as to the appropriateness of their use. Two such techniques stand out: the mining of voter data for the purposes of targeting campaign messages via social media; and telephone 'push polling' involving the use of leading questions to change the behaviour – rather than simply record the opinions – of targeted voters.

Concerns about 'dark advertising', which appears on the social media feed of targeted individuals but is not publicly available to view, came to the fore ahead of the 2017 general election. Labour, the Conservatives and the Liberal Democrats all invested heavily in Facebook advertising during the campaign.[23]

The Tories even allegedly used their resources to inflate the cost of Facebook adverts and 'drown out' non-partisan get-out-the-vote messages aimed at younger – and Labour-leaning – voters.[24] A series of articles in the *Observer* and *Guardian* – newspapers that are sympathetic to Labour and hostile to the Tories – highlighted the issue.

Companies such as Cambridge Analytica and AggregateIQ had advanced the use of data mining and social media in the US presidential election campaign of 2016, and similar tools had also allegedly been employed in the EU referendum campaign.[25] The psycho-profiling algorithms used to mine social-media data via machine-learning techniques were of serious enough concern that in May 2017 the Information Commissioner's Office – an independent authority established to uphold information rights in the public interest – launched an investigation into possible legal violations associated with data uses of this sort.[26]

The second main way in which innovations in digital technology touched the 2017 general election campaign was through deliberately manipulative opinion polling. Push polling is not a new campaigning technique, but its combination with precise targeting on the basis of voter databases is something that is relatively new to the UK. An investigation by Channel 4 television following the general election suggested that deceptive push polling had been used by the Conservative Party in certain parts of Wales in advance of 8 June. The polls were allegedly carried out in the name of a fake market research company, which breached data protection rules.[27] Push polling had also been linked to the Tories in the 2015 general election campaign and to the Leave campaign in the EU referendum.[28]

A third significant use of digital technology in 2017 was possibly more empowering to citizens: the rise of vote-exchange websites through which voters in safe seats could pledge to swap votes with voters elsewhere in order to maximise the electoral fortunes of their favoured parties.[29] This type of collective tactical voting is a way of getting round the UK's first-past-the-post voting system, which leaves many electors in safe seats with the feeling that their votes are wasted. If such a person can find someone in a marginal seat who will promise to vote for their preferred party in exchange for their voting for the other person's preferred party in their seat, both voters will be better off. Since the agreements involve no exchange of funds and no coercion, they are not in violation of the prohibitions on 'undue influence' in electoral law. Vote-swapping systems are open to manipulation, of course, as they depend for their success on the voluntary cooperation and good faith of those who use them. So far, however, there is little to suggest that there has been widespread misuse of such systems in the UK context.

Developments in digital technology are so rapid that each successive election is affected by the possibilities of the online world in different ways. The experience of the 2017 general election demonstrates that these effects can be both positive and negative.

Media bias, 'fake news' and political facts

In a 2005 book written largely as a commentary on the New Labour era, journalist and author Peter Oborne identified systematic 'lying' as a new development in British politics. 'Britain now lives in a post-truth political environment',
Oborne declared.[30] In the intervening 12 years, this notion entered the political mainstream, boosted by recent popular concern in the United States about
'fake news'. The making of false claims by politicians and journalists is by no
means a new phenomenon. Yet several factors have converged in recent years
to heighten unease about the veracity of the factual information voters receive
during election campaigns.

First, the internet and the diversification of broadcast news sources have led
to an exponential increase in the number of 'news providers', including large
numbers of citizen journalists and bloggers, whose products are accessed as
easily as those of traditional news outlets – and even more easily than items
behind newspaper paywalls.

Second, the rise of social media as a dissemination device has gone a long
way towards overcoming the distribution advantage enjoyed by traditional news
providers in the early days of the internet. Over a third of Britons now access
news via social media.[31] Factual claims of dubious veracity can and do 'go viral'
in a matter of minutes. We know from social psychology that people are more
likely to believe views that accord with notions they already hold dear.[32] Even
news stories and other facts whose provenance is unclear if not dubious will
be accepted by large numbers of people if they accord with what the readers
want to be true. Psychologists have also shown that people are more likely
to believe information that is communicated to them by someone they trust,
such as a friend on social media.[33] This means that in the current age, news
stories no longer require the authority of an established or 'mainstream' media
outlet for large numbers of people to give them credence. Thus even barring an
actual increase in the number of fabricated news stories circulating online, the
inaccurate information that is available has the potential to play a larger role in
conditioning public opinion and shaping the news agenda. And this very fact
provides an incentive for the fabricators of false facts to generate more of them.

A third factor linked to the rise of inaccuracy in news reporting is the catastrophic recent fall in newspaper profits that has resulted from the migration
online of newspaper reading and advertising.[34] With many fewer people paying
for a daily paper and organisations like Facebook and Google sucking up an
increasing proportion of advertising revenue, newspapers have had to cut back
considerably on reporting costs. This has led to a huge reduction in their capacity to scrutinise public bodies effectively, investigate stories properly and fully
check facts. With their budgets cut, they are far more likely to fill their pages
with sponsored content and lightly re-written press releases sent to them by
organisations which typically have an interest in portraying an issue in a particular way. Moreover, many local titles in the UK have closed altogether in the

past decade, leaving only citizen journalists, bloggers and local authorities to disseminate information about what is happening in some areas.[35]

It is in this general context that we must consider the accuracy of information circulated in connection with the 2017 general election. Already at the time of the 2016 Brexit referendum, the topic of inaccurate claims and media-disseminated falsehoods had been widely aired, but in 2017 the profile of this issue was raised by political developments across the Atlantic. One of the major legacies of Donald Trump's victory in the 2016 US presidential election was the concept of 'fake news', and this term began to be widely used in the UK at this time also. Figure 7.1 depicts weekly data, drawn from Google Trends, on Google searches in the UK for the term 'fake news' between September 2016 and July 2017.[36] The numbers on the y-axis reflect not the actual count of searches, but rather the relative popularity of the term in any week, with 100 representing the maximum and 0 the minimum in the time period shown. As can be seen here, 'fake news' was little searched before the US election in November 2016, whereupon the British public suddenly picked up on the concept. Searches for the term then peaked shortly after Trump assumed power in Washington, DC in late January 2017. The term was later searched for frequently during Britain's own election campaign in April and May of 2017.

But how much lying and actual fake news was there in the general election campaign of 2017? It is first necessary to distinguish between news reporting that is factually and wilfully inaccurate – the most obvious understanding of the term 'fake news' – and media bias. In keeping with practice in most established

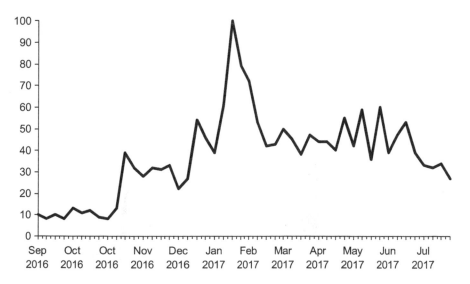

Figure 7.1 Google Trends searches for the term 'fake news' in the UK, September 2016–July 2017

Source: Google Trends.

liberal democracies, media law in the UK, as reflected in the Communications Act 2003, dictates that the broadcast media of television and radio are expected to remain politically neutral. Newspapers are free to be as partisan as their owners or editors wish. For example, the broadcast regulator Ofcom's code has this to say about elections and referendums:

> Due weight must be given to the coverage of parties and independent candidates during the election period. In determining the appropriate level of coverage to be given to parties and independent candidates broadcasters must take into account evidence of past electoral support and/or current support. Broadcasters must also consider giving appropriate coverage to parties and independent candidates with significant views and perspectives.[37]

By contrast, the Independent Press Standards Organisation's 'Editors Code of Practice' makes no explicit mention of elections or political reporting, noting simply that: 'The Press, while free to editorialise and campaign, must distinguish clearly between comment, conjecture and fact.'[38] The implicit flexibility does not, of course, mean that it is acceptable for British newspapers to print stories that are factually inaccurate – although sometimes they do – but it is widely accepted that the print media are entitled to be selective in choosing the stories they report, the facts they emphasise, and the interpretation they give to both stories and facts. Any oversight of editorial decisions has traditionally been the preserve of a collection of privately financed and scandal-prone self-regulatory bodies. The question for any consideration of electoral integrity is where that selectivity crosses the line into wilful deception.

On balance, major British newspapers played a constructive role in holding party politicians to account in the spring of 2017. For example, on 5 June, Theresa May made the claim that the Conservative government had 'increased the number of armed police officers', but the *Daily Mirror* newspaper questioned this claim, noting that the number of 'authorised firearms officers' had dropped 'by more than 1,300 under the Tories, from 6,976 in March 2010 to 5,639 in March 2016'.[39] Likewise, when shadow home secretary Diane Abbott said in a radio interview on 2 May that a Labour government would pay just £300,000 to put 10,000 more police officers on the streets, it was widely pointed out in the news media that this was a wildly implausible figure. The Labour party then issued a correction, saying that the true cost would be £300 million, though fact-checking organisation Full Fact – an independent fact-checking charity – noted that this would be insufficient to cover the costs of training and equipment.[40]

Much of the unchecked misinformation that floated around during the campaign took the form of 'news stories' posted online by people who were not trained journalists, and then circulated via discussion fora and Facebook groups (many of which were closed). Some voters thus created news ecologies for themselves in which they gleaned information from sympathetic sources, not all of which were backed up by sound journalism. An analysis by researchers at the Oxford Internet Institute of some 2.5 million tweets collected during the election campaign suggested that Labour supporters were far more avid users of Twitter than their Conservative counterparts. This striking difference was perhaps due to the younger age profile of the 2017 Labour Party, which Thomas Quinn describes in Chapter 2. The same study also found that most of the news shared on this social media platform was from professional news organisations. Worryingly, however, 'junk news' – a term the authors use to describe 'propaganda and ideologically extreme, hyper-partisan, or conspiratorial political news and information' – made up 11.4 per cent of the news content shared.[41]

The concern generated by media bias and fake news has led to discussion of means of curbing them. There have been calls for regulation to counter the threat of news inaccuracy and the fabrication of stories. In early 2017, the House of Commons Culture, Media and Sport Select Committee had launched an inquiry into 'fake news' that was ongoing – albeit temporarily suspended for the duration of the campaign – at the time of the general election. Some witnesses suggested that inaccurate campaign claims should be subject to the same legal test as claims made about candidates, who are currently protected from factual inaccuracy under laws governing libel and slander.[42] The legal precedent suggests that the courts do not have great difficulty in adjudicating such laws, and that they could therefore be extended in a relatively straightforward way to manifestly false claims made about topics other than individuals. Others objected that such regulation would be an unwarranted violation of freedom of speech and recommend a beefed-up system of press and internet regulation. Given that the UK has only recently revised its press regulatory infrastructure – which remains underpinned by a voluntary system of self-regulation – this proposal seems unlikely to be implemented.

At the time of the general election, a third possible remedy to fake news was already being implemented: systematic fact-checking. Specialist fact-checking organisations such as Full Fact and First Draft, funded by Google and Facebook, as well as traditional news outlets such as the BBC's 'Reality Check', scrutinised campaign claims in an effort to identify misinformation and increase public confidence in the quality of debate. The extent to which these services were successful is yet to be determined, but fact-checking does have the advantage of increasing transparency and providing ammunition for those keen to dismantle fallacious arguments.

With the media landscape becoming ever more diversified and the amount of information shared through digital devices increasing all the time, voters in contemporary elections are bombarded with a dizzying number of facts and figures, which they must try to make sense of in order to form a reasoned view of the options on the ballot. This is a daunting project at any time, but when the accuracy of the information received must also be assessed, the task becomes even more difficult. All in all, the British broadcasters and print media did a relatively good job of providing accurate electoral coverage in 2017. The strict regulation of television in the UK means that television news is subject to much more stringent impartiality requirements than is the case, for example, in the United States. And if many UK newspapers overtly favour one political party over the others, the amount of genuine misinformation they contain is limited. This is not the case with many of the other online sources from which voters increasingly harvest their news, however, and the rise of social media may pose a significant threat to the integrity of British election campaigns in years to come.

Campaign funding: the return of sleaze

Campaign finance has long been a contentious issue in British electoral politics. Party funding scandals in the 1990s involved both major parties and were an important factor in the establishment of the Electoral Commission, which now regularly publishes information on donations. Its creation marked a move towards greater transparency and accountability, but successive efforts to reform the funding system have foundered. The Conservatives have long benefited from donations from the business elite, whereas Labour has traditionally been able to rely on trade unions for financial support. Both alliances have provoked periodic disquiet; occasionally concern has been further increased by apparently egregious attempts to buy influence over policy-making. One such episode occurred on 18 May 2017, towards the end of the election campaign. On that day, two stories broke in the news: the first was that the Conservative Party had received a donation of £50,000 from oilman Ayman Asfari, a gift that was matched by his wife. Asfari, a member of the Conservative Leader's Group of large donors who are regularly invited to dinners with the prime minister, had recently been interviewed under caution by the Serious Fraud Office in connection with a bribery and money-laundering investigation. The second story that broke that day was of the Conservative government's intention to abolish the Serious Fraud Office if it won the election.[43] The timing of these events was presumably coincidental, but the association was not lost on commentators who alleged a connection between the two. In late May it also came to light that figures in the oil industry had together donated £390,000 to the Conservative Party in the ten months since Theresa May had assumed the leadership. When the Conservative Party manifesto pledged to provide 'unprecedented' government support for the oil and gas industries, eyebrows were raised.[44]

The Conservatives were not the only party to be beset by finance scandals, however. In mid-June it emerged that a Liberal Democrat donor, Sudhir Choudhrie, who also happened to be the party's adviser on India, had given £200,000 to the party to help fill its campaign war chest.[45] This would been a very large single donation from anyone, but Choudhrie was also a controversial figure. Claims had been made in India of his links to a Rolls Royce bribery scandal that had been investigated by the Serious Fraud Office.[46]

Meanwhile, it was revealed that donations to the Labour Party in the run-up to the 2017 contest had come almost entirely from the trade union movement, tightening the link between the two and leading to fears that the party was being 'taken over' by the unions, to which it might be beholden should it win power.[47]

A less explicitly partisan episode was the revelation that pro-Brexit asset manager Jeremy Hosking was spending lavishly to remove 138 pro-Remain MPs from their seats through his own personal Brexit Express campaign, which offered £5,000 each to candidates who had a chance of ousting them.[48]

Modern election campaigns are expensive, and in the absence of a continental European-style system of public funding, political parties must finance their own campaigns largely from private means. Despite their best efforts, parties struggle to raise sufficient funds through membership subscriptions or modest donations by ordinary citizens, leaving them dependent on people or organisations with substantial coffers. Claims then invariably arise about influence-peddling and cronyism. The role of money in politics is one of the weak points of British democracy.

The blunders of our returning officers

A general election is the largest peace-time logistical operation any state has to undertake. Providing for 46.8 million people – the size of the total registered electorate – to perform the same act in conditions of secrecy and security across the country is a huge undertaking, and some things are always bound to go wrong. Yet the conditions under which the 2017 general election were conducted meant that the production of the poll was more vulnerable than it had been in the past. The under-resourcing of local authorities in an era of government austerity (see Nicholas Allen in Chapter 1) had put considerable strain on the electoral offices of many town halls. Having to hold a second general election in two years on short notice put extreme pressure on some councils' ability to cope, compounded by the fact that they had also been obliged to administer a national referendum the previous year. Not surprisingly, difficulties revealed themselves on polling day. In Plymouth, Guildford, Hackney and Bristol there were problems with postal vote ballots going missing.[49] The difficulties in Plymouth were particularly acute: over 6,100 votes were omitted from the total reported at the vote count.[50]

The administrative issue that led to the greatest outcry was not the result of a blunder, however. Concerns were raised about returning officers' apparent inability to prevent students from voting twice, once in the constituency where they were studying and once in the seat of their family home. UK electoral law allows students legally to be entered on both voter lists, but the general political disinterest and penury of undergraduates has meant that few have traditionally abused this rule and illegally cast more than one vote. All eligible electors are required to provide officials in Britain with the information necessary to include them on the voter roll, making electoral registration effectively compulsory. Yet a significant proportion of young people had typically been reluctant registrants in recent years, due to apathy or a general aversion to official systems, and registration figures had been falling in the run-up to 2017. A new system of online voter registration, combined with concerted drives by many groups to promote it, was designed to attain the goal of full registration. The success of the Labour Party and voluntary groups such as the National Union of Students in mobilising young people thus brought into the electorate a surge of students.

In the event, a record 2.9 million people applied to be included on the roll between 18 April, when the election was called, and 22 May, the last possible day. Of these, 69 per cent were under the age of 34.[51] This was a major achievement for electoral registration officers around the land. At the same time, the unexpected success of these efforts raised concerns that the system of double registration was not robust enough.[52] The Electoral Commission received 1,028 emails and telephone calls from concerned members of the public together with representations from 38 MPs following admissions made on social media by some electors that they had voted twice. Though the Commission maintained that there was 'a lack of evidence of widespread abuse', it accepted in a post-election report that 'tools to prevent double voting at general elections should be explored quickly'.[53] One of the difficulties with the current system is that there is no easy way of checking for illicit multiple registrations by people who are not entitled to be on the roll in more than one locality. Though the UK has toyed with the idea of introducing a single national election register for decades, there are still 381 separate voter lists. As noted above, attention was focused in the 2000s on voter apathy and measures to improve turnout; electoral security now appears to be under threat from the excessive enthusiasm of some voters, and systems in place to ensure 'vote facilitation' have come back to bite.

All in all, the 2017 general election was well run and there were no serious concerns of widespread malpractice or mismanagement. There were isolated problems, to be sure, and there were aspects of the UK electoral infrastructure that could be improved. However, there is no indication that any of these difficulties affected the overall outcome of the electoral contest.[54] The populace is currently more attuned to electoral integrity than was previously the case, and though this may have magnified the perception of impropriety, heightened popular sensitivity to electoral abuse most likely had the effect of deterring malpractice. Vigilant citizens are an important part of the armoury that defends a country against electoral fraud.

Conclusion

The integrity of the electoral process was a prominent feature of the 2017 general election campaign, and the issue of electoral integrity is now firmly fixed in the landscape of UK electoral politics. Yet despite the popular suspicions that have been aroused concerning the conduct of elections, there is very little evidence that the mechanics of preparing for and conducting polls is subject to systematic manipulation or partisan interference. All in all, the UK's still largely analogue electoral processes work well, even following bungled attempts to modernise them. This is not to say that there are no aspects of democratic contestation that could be improved in the British context, however. Certainly campaign spending and the funding of political parties is an area that is long overdue for reform, even if there is little prospect of change being introduced in the near future. The regulations governing election campaigning also require updating in order to take account of the realities of a networked age where all citizens can broadcast anything to all in a matter of seconds. Evidence suggests that discursive integrity is the aspect of political ethics that most irks the British public.[55] If the United Kingdom is to prevent a further erosion of public confidence in the claims made by political campaigners, some further regulation of the veracity of campaign speech is sorely needed.

With growing levels of polarisation in British politics, it is not surprising that some voters should be reluctant to accept election results. 'Losers' consent' has been fraying at the edges in a number of democracies in recent years.[56] There are signs that this is now beginning to happen in the UK. Following the 2014 Scottish independence referendum, there was a Twitter storm of disappointed pro-independence voters expressing scepticism at the integrity of the voting process, despite the absence of any evidence of serious problems.[57] But though shadow chancellor John McDonnell called for a peaceful 'day of rage' in the wake of Labour's 2017 election defeat, the losing parties did not question the result. If British voters no longer take electoral integrity for granted, there is no sign of any crisis of confidence in the electoral process. Britons have instead become more 'critical citizens' with respect to the administration of elections: their criticisms are at times wide of the mark, but vigilance in the electoral sphere can only be good for democracy.[58] Whether the cynical manipulation of voters by campaign activists and irresponsible media outlets serves the needs of democracy is another matter entirely.

Notes

1 See Toby S. James, *Elite Statecraft and Election Administration: Bending the Rules of the Game?* (Basingstoke: Palgrave Macmillan, 2012).

2 James, *Elite Statecraft and Election Administration*; Alistair Clarke, 'Investing in electoral management', in Pippa Norris, Richard W. Frank and Ferran Martínez i Coma (eds), *Advancing Electoral Integrity* (Oxford: Oxford University Press, 2014), pp. 165–188; Alistair Clarke, 'Public administration and the integrity of the electoral process in Britain', *Public Administration*, 93 (2015), 86–102; Alistair Clarke, 'Identifying the determinants of electoral integrity and administration in advanced democracies: The case of Britain', *European Political Science Review*, 9 (2017), 471–492 and Bob Watt, *UK Election Law: A Critical Examination* (London: Routledge-Cavendish, 2006).

3   The Electoral Commission was set up on the recommendation of the Committee on Standards in Public Life, of which Anthony King, long-time editor of the *Britain at the Polls* series, was originally a member.

4   Stuart Wilks-Heeg, *Purity of Elections in the UK: Causes of Concern* (York: Joseph Rowntree Trust, 2008).

5   Bob Watt, *Implementing Electronic Voting: A Report Addressing the Legal Issues Raised by the Implementation of Electronic Voting* (London: Electoral Commission, 2002); Lawrence Pratchett, *The Implementation of Electronic Voting in the UK* (London: Local Government Association, 2002).

6   Richard Mawrey, *Fraud at the Elections: Judgment of Commissioner Mawrey QC* (Nottingham: Spokesman, 2005).

7   Committee on Standards in Public Life, *Review of the Electoral Commission*, Cm 7006 (London: HMSO, 2007).

8   Electoral Commission, *Electoral Fraud in the UK: Final Report and Recommendations* (London: Electoral Commission, 2014).

9   Eric Pickles, *Securing the Ballot: Report of Sir Eric Pickles's Review into Electoral Fraud* (London: Cabinet Office, 2016).

10 Electoral Commission, *Winter Tracker 2016* (London: Electoral Commission, 2016).

11 Nicholas Allen and Sarah Birch, *Ethics and Integrity in British Politics: How Citizens Judge Their Politicians' Conduct and Why It Matters* (Cambridge: Cambridge University Press, 2015).

12 ITV News, 'Police launch new probe into Tower Hamlets electoral fraud claims', 26 April 2017, available at: www.itv.com/news/london/2017–04–26/police-launch-new-probe-into-tower-hamlets-electoral-fraud-claims/, last accessed 29 October 2017.

13 Robin De Peyer, 'Lutfur Rahman re-elected as mayor of Tower Hamlets after chaotic vote count', *Evening Standard*, 24 May 2014.

14 Electoral Commission, *Electoral Fraud in the UK*.

15 Ashley Cowburn, 'Nicola Sturgeon: Theresa May called a snap election before expenses fraud allegations "caught up" with party', *Independent*, 24 April 2017.

16 BBC News, 'South Thanet election expense police inquiry extended', 1 June 2017, available at: www.bbc.co.uk/news/uk-england-kent-36429681, last accessed 29 October 2017.

17 Martin Bentham, Joe Murphy and Kate Proctor, 'Senior Tories' fury at expenses charges for candidate Craig Mackinlay', *Evening Standard*, 2 June 2017.

18 Steven Swinford, 'David Cameron: Brexit could lead to Europe descending into war', *Daily Telegraph*, 9 May 2016.

19 Electoral Commission, *Electoral Fraud in the UK*; See Michael Clarke and Kyran Dale, 'Estimating what proportion of the public will be able to use GOV.UK Verify', 25 January 2016, available at: https://identityassurance.blog.gov.uk/2016/01/25/estimating-what-proportion-of-the-public-will-be-able-to-use-gov-uk-verify, last accessed 29 October 2017. According to official government figures, approximately 78 per cent of the over-18 population holds a driving licence, and 80 per cent holds a passport. Both these documents contain photographs. These figures vary considerably by socio-economic and age group, however, suggesting that there would be demographic differentials in ease of access to the polls if a photographic identification requirement was introduced.

20 May Goodfellow, 'No photo ID, no vote: Why this cynical Tory plan will suffocate democracy', *Guardian*, 19 May 2017; Andrew Griffin, 'Conservatives will

force people to use photo ID to vote, stopping millions from taking part in future elections', *Independent*, 18 May 2017.

21 Organisation for Security and Cooperation in Europe, *United States of America General Elections 8 November 2016: Needs Assessment Mission Report* (Warsaw: OSCE, 2016), available at: www.osce.org/odihr/elections/usa/246351?download=true, last accessed 29 October 2017.

22 Stephen Ward and Rachel Gibson 'The first Internet election? UK political parties and campaigning in cyberspace', in Ivor Crewe, Brian Gosschalk and John Bartle (eds), *Political Communications 1997: Why Labour Won the General Election of 1997* (London: Frank Cass, 1998), pp. 93–114.

23 Robert Booth, 'Conservatives launch online offensive against Corbyn', *Guardian*, 15 May 2017; Robert Booth, 'Inquiry launched into targeting of UK voters through social media', *Guardian*, 17 May 2017.

24 Carole Cadwalladr, 'Revealed: Tory "dark" ads targeted voters' Facebook feeds in Welsh marginal seat', *Observer*, 27 May 2017.

25 Booth, 'Conservatives launch online offensive against Corbyn'; Jamie Doward and Alice Gibbs, 'Did Cambridge Analytica influence the Brexit vote and the US election?', *Observer*, 4 March 2017; Luke Harding, 'MP calls for inquiry into Arron Banks and "dark money" in EU referendum', *Guardian*, 19 October 2017; Jane Mayer, 'Trump's money man', *New Yorker*, 27 March 2017, 34–45; Holly Watt, 'Leave.EU under investigation over EU referendum spending', *Guardian*, 21 April 2017.

26 Booth, 'Inquiry launched into targeting of UK voters'.

27 Channel 4 News, 'Revealed: Inside the secretive Tory election call centre', 22 June 2017, available at: www.channel4.com/news/revealed-inside-the-secretive-tory-election-call-centre, last accessed 29 October 2017.

28 Ben Gelblum, 'Tories embroiled in new election law breach scandal', *The London Economic*, 23 June 2017, available at: www.thelondoneconomic.com/news/tories-embroiled-new-potential-election-fraud-scandal/23/06/, last accessed 29 October 2017.

29 Vanessa Barford, 'Election 2015: Does "vote swapping" work?', *BBC News*, 23 April 2017, available at: www.bbc.co.uk/news/magazine-32410531, last accessed 29 October 2017; Jon Stone, 'Think your vote won't count at the general election? Here's how to swap it', *Independent*, 27 May 2017.

30 Peter Oborne, *The Rise of Political Lying* (London: Free Press, 2005), p. 2.

31 Nic Newman, Richard Fletcher, David A.L. Levy and Rasmus Kleis Nielsen, *Digital News Report 2016* (Oxford: Reuters Institute for the Study of Journalism, 2016), p. 9.

32 Ziva Kunda, 'The case for motivated reasoning', *Psychological Bulletin*, 108 (1990), 480–498; Milton Lodge and Charles Taber, *The Rationalizing Voter* (Cambridge: Cambridge University Press, 2013).

33 W. Lance Bennett and Alexandra Segerberg, *The Logic of Connective Action: Digital Media and the Personalization of Contentious Politics* (Cambridge: Cambridge University Press, 2013).

34 Julia Kollewe, 'Google and Facebook bring in one-fifth of global ad revenue', *Guardian*, 2 May 2017; Dominic Ponsford, 'Small businesses in communities now spend more with Facebook than local press, Journalism Summit told', *Press Gazette*, 24 October 2017.

35 Jasper Cox, 'New research: Some 198 UK local newspapers have closed since 2005', *Press Gazette*, 19 December 2016.

36 Google Tends is available at: https://trends.google.co.uk, last accessed 29 October 2017.

37 Ofcom, *The Ofcom Broadcast Code* (London: Ofcom, 2017), p. 34

38 Independent Press Standards Organization, *The Editors' Code of Practice* (London: IPSO, 2016).

39 Mikey Smith and Dan Bloom, 'Fake news! Tories have said all these things in the general election campaign and they're not true', *Mirror*, 5 June 2017.

40 Full Fact, 'Can £300 million pay for 10,000 police officers?', 11 May 2017, available at: https://fullfact.org/crime/can-300-million-pay-10000-police-officers/, last accessed 29 October 2017.

41 Moica Kaminska, John D. Gallacher, Bence Kollanyi, Taha Yasseri and Philip N. Howard, 'Social media and news sources during the 2017 UK general election', *Oxford Internet Institute*, 2017, available at: http://comprop.oii.ox.ac.uk/wp-content/uploads/sites/89/2017/06/Social-Media-and-News-Sources-during-the-2017-UK-General-Election.pdf, last accessed 29 October 2017.

42 Mark Hanna and Mike Dodd, *McNae's Essential Law for Journalists*, 23rd edn (Oxford: Oxford University Press, 2016); K.P.E. Lasok, 'Written evidence submitted by K. P. E. Lasok QC', House of Commons Culture, Media and Sport Select Committee Inquiry into Fake News, 2017, available at: www.parliament.uk/business/committees/committees-a-z/commons-select/culture-media-and-sport-committee/inquiries/parliament-2015/inquiry2/, last accessed 29 October 2017.

43 Caroline Binham and Kate Croft, 'Tories plan to abolish serious fraud office – manifesto', *Financial Times*, 18 May 2017; Holly Watt and Rajeev Syal, 'Tories receive £50,000 from man questioned by Serious Fraud Office', *Guardian*, 18 May 2017.

44 Rajeev Syal, 'Oil bosses have given £390,000 to Tories under Theresa May', *Guardian*, 23 May 2017.

45 Rajeev Syal and Holly Watt, 'Controversial Lib Dem donor gave £200,000 to election campaign', *Guardian*, 15 June 2017.

46 BBC News, 'Rolls-Royce apologises after £671m bribery settlement', 18 January 2017, available at: www.bbc.co.uk/news/business-38644114, last accessed 29 October 2017.

47 Electoral Commission, 'Donations and loans reported every quarter by political parties, Q2 2017', available at: www.electoralcommission.org.uk/find-information-by-subject/political-parties-campaigning-and-donations/donations-and-loans-to-political-parties/quarterly-donations-and-loans, last accessed 29 October 2017; Jack Maidment, 'Labour election campaign "funded almost entirely by union donations"', *Daily Telegraph*, 18 May 2017.

48 Lucy Fisher, 'City financier sets sights on Remain MPs', *The Times*, 15 May 2017.

49 Sarah Marsh and Caroline Bannock, 'Plymouth blames loss of 1,500 postal voting packs on computer problem', *Guardian*, 8 June 2017.

50 BBC News, 'Labour MP Luke Pollard's fury as votes left out of result', 10 June 2017, available at: www.bbc.co.uk/news/uk-england-devon-40232776, last accessed 29 October 2017.

51 Electoral Commission, *Electoral Registration at the June 2017 UK General Election: Report on the UK Parliamentary General Election held on 8 June 2017* (London: Electoral Commission, 2017), p. 1.

52 BBC News, 'Students boasted of voting twice, MP says', 5 July 2017, available at: www.bbc.co.uk/news/uk-politics-40509178, last accessed 29 October 2017.

53 Electoral Commission, *Electoral Registration at the June 2017 UK General Election*, pp. 1, 12.

54 In addition to the incidents already mentioned, other integrity issues raised during the election included a hastily withdrawn offer by graffiti artist Banksy of free artwork in exchange for an anti-Conservative vote in Bristol (an illegal gift under electoral law). See Steven Morris, 'Banksy forced to withdraw offer to send free artwork to non-Tory voters', *Guardian*, 6 June 2017. In another case police were called into investigate possible voter fraud amid reports of 18 people arriving at polling stations only to be told they had already voted in the Northern Irish constituency of Foyle. See BBC News, 'General election 2017: Investigation into alleged voter fraud', 14 June 2017, available at: www.bbc.co.uk/news/uk-northern-ireland-foyle-west-40257949, last accessed 29 October 2017.

55 Allen and Birch, *Ethics and Integrity in British Politics*.

56 Christopher J. Anderson, André Blais, Shaun Bowler, Todd Donovan and Ola Listhaug, *Losers' Consent: Elections and Democratic Legitimacy* (Oxford: Oxford University Press, 2005); Francisco Cantu and Omar Garcia Ponce, 'Partisan losers' effects: Perceptions of electoral integrity in Mexico', *Electoral Studies*, 39 (2015), 1–14.

57 Sarah Birch and Fatma ElSafoury, 'Fraud, plot or collective delusion? Social media and perceptions of electoral misconduct in the 2014 Scottish independence referendum', *Election Law Journal*, 16 (2017), 470–484.

58 Pippa Norris (ed.), *Critical Citizens: Global Support for Democratic Government* (Oxford: Oxford University Press, 1999).

8

Why the Conservatives lost their majority – but still won

John Bartle

When Theresa May stepped into the glare of the television lights in Downing Street on 18 April to announce a 'snap' general election, there was almost universal agreement that she had made an astute if not brilliant call. It was widely assumed that the forthcoming campaign would centre on Brexit and Britain's future outside of the European Union. It was even more widely assumed that the Conservatives would win.

The first assumption, that the 2017 election would be the 'Brexit election', seemed unimpeachable. Britain's relations with Europe had long consumed the attention of its political elite. David Cameron's attempts to renegotiate the terms of Britain's membership of the EU had absorbed the prime minister's energies during his brief second term. Britain had then undergone the national trauma of a referendum campaign that resulted in a vote to leave, defeat for Cameron and his replacement with Theresa May. The complex process of withdrawal had then dominated the new government's agenda. Announcing the election the new prime minister characterised the choice as one between:

> strong and stable leadership in the national interest, with me as your Prime Minister, or weak and unstable coalition government, led by Jeremy Corbyn, propped up by the Liberal Democrats – who want to reopen the divisions of the referendum – and Nicola Sturgeon and the SNP.[1]

The second assumption, that the election would result in an easy Tory victory, seemed even more of a 'no-brainer' as the Americans say. Having just voted to leave the EU, it was hard to believe that the electorate would replace the Conservatives with Labour, a party largely devoted to the EU. The Tories had entered January 2017 with a 16-point opinion-poll lead over their main rivals. By April 2017 this lead had stretched to 20 points. May's decision also caught everyone on the hop. Labour under Jeremy Corbyn seemed singularly unprepared to fight the election, the Liberal Democrats were still a 'toxic' brand after their five years in coalition with the Tories between 2010 and 2015, and the United Kingdom Independence Party (UKIP) were in disarray having secured and effectively won the recent referendum. The Scottish National Party (SNP) posed no obvious threat to the Conservatives, whose 2015 majority was based almost entirely on English and Welsh MPs. For these reasons a Tory victory seemed inevitable. A survey of experts for the United Kingdom's Political Studies Association produced an average forecast vote of 43 per cent for the Conservatives and 29 per cent for Labour, and an average Tory majority of 92 seats.[2] A review published in the *Washington Post* produced a similar consensus.[3] Martin Boon of ICM Research declared that 'the result is going to be a foregone conclusion'.[4]

In the event, neither the campaign nor the outcome conformed to expectations. Labour's decision to accept that Britain was leaving the EU sucked much of the oxygen from the issue. Europe dominated the campaign's early skirmishes, but the publication of the manifestos shifted attention to the perennial issues of public spending, the economy and defence. The 2017 general election campaign was not, therefore, a replay of the 2016 referendum: attitudes towards Brexit were merely an additional influence on top of other enduring influences. And once votes were counted, it was clear that there would be no landslide Tory victory. The Conservatives scraped home as the largest party but fell just short of a majority in the new House of Commons.

The aggregate outcome

Before analysing why the election resulted in a hung parliament, it is worth establishing the 'facts' about the 2017 general election. The most important fact is that the Conservative Party 'won' the election, in that it gained more votes and seats than any other party (see Table 8.1), and Theresa May continued as prime minister.[5] The party's share of the vote was higher than under Cameron in either 2010 or 2015, and saw the largest increase (5.5 percentage points) achieved by any governing party since 1945. Viewed in isolation this was a remarkable achievement.

But the Conservative performance cannot be viewed in isolation. Pre-election expectations were so high that the party's victory felt like an emotional defeat. For similar reasons, Labour's defeat felt like an emotional – even euphoric – victory. Labour's share of the vote rocketed by 9.6 points to 40 per cent, exceeding its supporters' wildest dreams and bolstering Jeremy Corbyn's personal authority, as Thomas Quinn describes in Chapter 2. This performance represented the largest percentage-point increase achieved by either of the two major parties since 1945.[6] The net effect was that the Conservatives' lead over Labour fell from 6.4 points in 2015 to 2.3 points in 2017.

Table 8.1 The outcome of the 2017 United Kingdom general election

	Votes (%)		Seats	
	2017	Change	2017	Change
Con	42.4	+5.5	317	-13
Lab	40.0	+9.5	262	+30
SNP	3.0	-1.7	35	-21
Lib Dem	7.4	-0.5	12	+4
DUP	0.9	+0.3	10	+2
Sinn Féin	0.7	+0.1	7	+3
Plaid Cymru	0.5	-0.1	4	+1
UKIP	1.8	-10.8	0	-1
Green	1.6	-1.8	1	0
Others	1.7	-0.5	2	-6

Source: House of Commons library.

As the fortunes of the major parties improved, those of the smaller parties waned. UKIP received just 1.8 per cent of the vote, down 10.8 points compared with 2015. The party also lost its only seat in Clacton on the Essex coast. The Liberal Democrat vote fell to 7.4 per cent, down 0.5 points on its already low 2015 vote. Bizarrely, the electoral system translated this loss into a net gain of four seats. In Scotland, the SNP suffered a rebuff. Its share of the UK vote fell from 4.7 to 3.0 per cent and its share of the Scottish vote fell from 50.0 to 36.9 per cent. The party lost a total of 21 seats, 12 to the Tories, six to Labour and three to the Liberal Democrats. In Wales, Plaid Cymru failed to make headway in the face of a Labour revival. The Green Party's share fell from 3.8 per cent to 1.6 per cent, though Caroline Lucas retained her seat in Brighton Pavilion.

The flow of the vote

The aggregate election outcome provides an indication of the net changes that occurred between 2015 and 2017. Underneath the surface, however, were millions of individual changes, some of which cancelled out others. Table 8.2 illustrates these complex movements by displaying how individual respondents to the British Election Study (BES) reported having voted immediately after both the 2015 and 2017 general elections.[7] Table 8.2 suggests that around 84 per cent of all 2015 Tory voters voted for that party again in 2017. Similarly, 81 per cent of 2015 Labour voters voted Labour in 2017. The aggregate-level evidence from the constituencies confirms the impression of stability: the major parties' vote in 2015 was a powerful predictor of their vote in 2017. Nevertheless, Table 8.2 also shows that there was considerable switching. One in ten 2015

Table 8.2 The flow of the vote, 2015–17

Vote in 2015	Vote in 2017 general election						
	Con	Lab	Lib Dem	SNP	Plaid Cymru	UKIP	Green
Con	83.8	8.3	5.4	0.2	0.2	0.4	0.6
Lab	9.4	80.9	5.9	0.8	0.2	0.7	1.3
Lib Dem	17.7	22.8	54.6	0.5	0.5	1.1	1.5
SNP	8.5	16.3	2.0	71.8	0.0	0.5	0.0
Plaid Cymru	5.8	38.4	1.2	0.0	52.3	0.0	1.2
UKIP	56.1	17.0	3.6	0.1	0.8	18.2	1.8
Green	4.7	58.2	13.2	2.6	0.3	0.6	16.5
Did not vote	30.8	51.1	8.6	2.0	0.7	1.3	2.7

Source: British Election Internet Panel 2015–17, post-election waves 6 and 13.

Labour voters defected to the Tories in 2017, and one in 12 former Tory voters made the opposite journey.[8]

The behaviour of 2015 minor-party voters, relatively few of whom remained loyal, provides further clues about the forces shaping the 2017 general election. One of the most striking findings in Table 8.2 is that 56 per cent of 2015 UKIP voters switched to the Conservatives. This matches the aggregate-level evidence: at the constituency level, the UKIP vote in 2015 strongly predicts the Conservative vote in 2017. It appears that the referendum vote and Theresa May's increasingly hard-line on Brexit helped produce a realignment on the right. Nevertheless, some 17 per cent of 2015 UKIP voters switched to Labour in 2017. Brexit was far from the whole story.

There is also some evidence of a realignment on the left. Fully 58 per cent of 2015 Green Party voters switched to Labour, and the Greens' vote share in 2015 was strongly associated with Labour's vote share in 2017 at the constituency level. The impact of this realignment was limited, however, because there were few 2015 Green party voters. Finally, some 23 per cent of 2015 Liberal Democrat voters switched to Labour and 18 per cent to the Tories. This slight tendency among centrist voters to switch to Labour suggests the tide was moving leftwards.

Table 8.2 also illustrates some of the political dynamics in Scotland and Wales. Fully 16 per cent, or one in six, of 2015 SNP voters switched to Labour, and nearly 9 per cent or one in ten turned to the Conservatives. In Wales Plaid Cymru failed to hold onto many of its former voters. Some 38 per cent defected to Labour. Both sets of movements are consistent with Robert Johns' argument in Chapter 5 that the anticipated Tory landslide encouraged Nationalist voters to engage more closely with Westminster politics and take sides accordingly.

One final intriguing thing to note about the data in Table 8.2 is the behaviour of former non-voters. Most (54 per cent) of 2015 non-voters again did not vote in 2017, but of those who voted, 51 per cent chose Labour and 31 per cent Conservative.[9] The aggregate-level evidence suggests that Labour's vote share increased and the Conservatives' decreased as turnout increased.[10] In the run up to the election, many experts expressed doubts whether non-voters could make a difference. The experts, as with their predictions of the outcome, were wrong. Nevertheless, the substantial conversion of non-voters to the Tories suggests that pledges to reassert national sovereignty and to 'take back control' could mobilise voters almost as well as pledges to 'end austerity'.

The dealigned electorate

The 2017 general election witnessed a significant exodus of voters from the smaller to the larger parties. Just 64 per cent of those who voted cast their ballot for the same party in elections just two years apart. Clearly, the electorate was changeable. A clue about the source of this volatility is provided by Figure 8.1, which shows growing levels of party non-identification as measured by successive BES surveys.[11] Over time, the proportion of non-identifiers – those saying they do *not* think of themselves as 'Conservative', 'Labour', 'Liberal Democrat' or 'Nationalist' – has greatly increased, from 5 per cent in 1964 to 19 per cent in 2015. Since voters who identify with a party are more likely to remain loyal to that party and turn out, any increase in the number

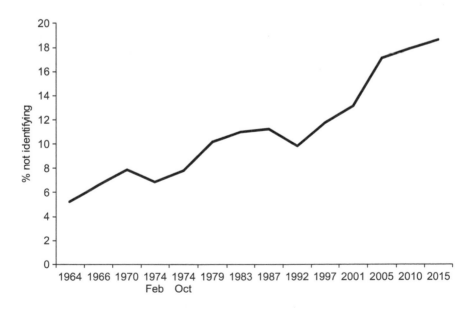

Figure 8.1 Non-identification with political parties, 1964–2015
Source: British Election Study, Information System.

of non-identifiers increases the pool of floating voters. At the same time, the strength of identification among the smaller pool of partisans has waned. In 1964, some 47 per cent of all identifiers thought of themselves as 'very strong' partisans and a mere 11 per cent thought of themselves as 'not very strong' identifiers. By 2015, a mere 21 per cent of respondents described themselves as 'very strong' identifiers and 25 per cent described themselves as 'not very strong' partisans.

Weakened party loyalties are partly a product of long-term social changes such as the expansion of education and exposure to non-partisan broadcast media that reduced individuals' dependence on social groups for information. They are also a product of past ideological movements by the parties towards the extremes, which loosened voters' psychological bonds.[12] The same ties have weakened further as parties have failed to deliver in office. By 2015, the Liberal Democrats as well as the Conservatives and Labour had gained experience of governing, and all were judged to have 'failed' the public in one way or another. They had also done things to cast doubt on their integrity. The 'cash for questions' scandal in the 1990s, the Iraq War of 2003, the financial crisis of 2007–08 and the MPs expenses scandal of 2009 all stimulated anti-system sentiment.[13] These sentiments were amplified by a cynical media.[14]

The weakening of partisan loyalties means that, other things being equal, short-term factors have a stronger impact on voting behaviour. Voters can be swayed by policy, the state of the economy or the populist appeals of anti-system parties. In the past, the Liberal Democrats were a convenient vehicle for protest votes. In 2015 UKIP successfully appealed to those who felt ignored by the 'Westminster elites', particularly on the issues of European integration and immigration. In 2017 both major party leaders tried to position themselves as anti-system. Theresa May, for example, claimed to represent the 'mainstream of the British public' that had been ignored by 'elites in Westminster'. Jeremy Corbyn spoke on behalf of 'the many, not the few' and argued that the poor should not be punished for the failures of the bankers that caused the 'great recession'.[15]

The social basis of the vote

Voting behaviour is rooted in people's social experiences. Voters' age, race, sex, education, social class and neighbourhood can profoundly shape their identities, perceptions of self-interest and exposure to information.[16] The same characteristics shape their policy preferences, evaluations of national or personal conditions and assessments of which party or leader is most likely to deliver.

In 2017 age emerged as *the* fault line in British electoral politics: younger voters were far more likely to vote Labour than the old. These differences were not entirely new. In 2015, the Labour vote among 18–24-year-olds was 43 per cent, compared with 23 per cent among those aged 65 and above. Conversely,

Table 8.3 How Britain voted in 2017, Ipsos MORI

	Con	Lab	Lib Dem	Con lead
Age				
18–24	27	62	5	−35
25–34	27	56	9	−29
35–44	33	49	10	−16
45–54	43	40	7	+3
44–64	51	34	7	+17
65+	61	25	7	+36
Gender				
Female	43	42	8	+1
Male	44	40	7	+4
Ethnic group				
White	45	39	8	+6
BAME	19	73	6	−54
Education				
No qualifications	52	35	4	+17
Other qualifications	46	39	6	+7
Degree and above	33	48	12	−15
Class				
AB	47	37	10	+10
C1	44	40	7	+4
C2	45	41	6	+4
DE	38	47	5	−9
Tenure				
Owned	55	30	7	+25
Mortgage	43	40	9	+3
Social renter	26	57	4	−31
Private renter	31	54	7	−23

Source. Ipsos MORI.

the Conservative vote was just 27 per cent among 18–24-year-olds and 47 per cent among those aged 65 and above. These differences reflected the old adages about youthful radicalism being replaced by conservatism in old age.[17] In 2015 they also had more immediate sources. Labour, under Ed Miliband's leadership, made a pitch for the youth vote, promising to reduce university tuition fees from £9,000 to £6,000 per year. This strategy had limited success, yielding just a six-point lead among 18–29-year-olds, and aroused little enthusiasm.

Table 8.3 shows how existing differences between the young and old widened considerably in 2017. Labour's lead over the Tories was fully 35 points among 18–24-year-olds, 29 points among 25–34-year-olds and 16 points among those aged 35–45. In contrast, the Tories enjoyed a three-point lead over Labour among those aged 45–54, which jumped to 17 points among 55–64-year-olds and 36 points among those aged 65 and above. Similarly, at a constituency level, Labour's share of the vote was associated with the proportion of the population aged 18–29.[18] In 2017 discussion about the causes and consequences of this new inter-generational politics, in which 'millennials' were seemingly set against 'baby boomers', moved from the seminar to public spaces such as television and radio phone-ins.

The reasons for this widening gap in 2017 are necessarily speculative. Some relate to the immediate political context. Young voters were more likely to vote Remain in the 2016 referendum, and Theresa May's subsequent commitment to a 'hard' Brexit alienated them. The Liberal Democrats, despite their pro-Europeanism, remained toxic after their acquiescence in raising tuition fees, as John Curtice explains in Chapter 3. The young, therefore, naturally gravitated towards Labour. The sharper generational divide also reflected political interests. Younger voters were more vulnerable to changes in the workplace and zero-hours contracts. Many welfare reforms, such as restrictions on housing benefit, affected the young most. Students entering higher education in 2017 from the poorest 40 per cent of families were forecast to graduate with debts of £57,000.[19] They increasingly found it difficult to find 'graduate' jobs or get a foot on the housing ladder. For 'generation rent' the dream of owning a property remained just that – a dream. Labour's promise to abolish tuition fees and re-introduce grants in 2017 appealed to younger voters' self-interest. So did their promise to regulate rents in the private sector. Older voters, on the other hand, were less likely to work, more likely to own their own homes, and were protected by the 'triple lock' on pensions. The Tories' proposals to change the rules on social care and winter-fuel payments tested their loyalties. In the zero-sum game of inter-generational politics, however, Labour's pull on the young may have also pushed the old towards the Tories.

Another factor driving young voters to Labour was undoubtedly a 'Corbyn effect'. Most politicians paid little attention to the young. They doubted whether young people could be induced to vote and whether it would make a difference if they did. Instead, most politicians 'wisely' focused on the 'grey vote' that could be relied on to turn out. Here, as elsewhere, Corbyn went against the conventional wisdom and focused on youth. The scale of Labour's pledge to abolish tuition fees was breath-taking. It was estimated to cost £11 billion per year. Young people responded to this attention with enthusiasm. Such was Corbyn's personal appeal that those aspects of his record that raised questions among older voters counted in his favour among the young. His rebelliousness on the Iraq War was taken to illustrate his commitment to principle. His reluctance to sing the national anthem demonstrated his unwillingness to conform. His dull speaking style and failure to deliver carefully prepared soundbites were evidence of his authenticity. Remarkably, he was generally absolved of charges of 'careerism', despite being an MP for over 30 years. Endorsements by musicians – for instance, the 'Grime4Corbyn' movement – and organs such as the *New Musical Express* (*NME*) music magazine, created a sense of excitement. Labour's unexpected gains in constituencies like Canterbury, Reading West and Kensington owed much to the efforts of students in particular.

The 2017 campaign was notable for efforts to mobilise young voters. As Sarah Birch notes in Chapter 7, the campaign witnessed a surge in voter-registration applications, driven in part by a campaign by the National Union of Students. There were 2.9 million applications to register between the announcement of the snap election on 19 April and the deadline on 22 May. Fully 96 per cent of these applications were made online and 69 per cent of these online applications were made by voters below the age of 34. The impact of all this was limited, however, since many were duplicate applications. And while initial estimates produced by pollsters suggested that turnout among 18–24-year-olds increased by about 11 points, the more reliable British Election Study (BES) suggests that turnout among this group may not have increased at all.[20] To be sure, the BES data suggests that turnout did increase more among 24–40-year-olds, a group still young enough to sing 'oh Jeremy Corbyn' at Glastonbury without embarrassing their children. Overall, however, the 2017 'youthquake' amounted to politically engaged young voters swinging heavily to Labour rather than previously unengaged young voters turning out to vote. Even more significantly, turnout appears to have declined among those aged above 70, perhaps as a result of Conservative confusion over social care and the retreat from the pensions 'triple lock'.

While the impact of age increased, that of social class declined. For much of the post-war period voting behaviour was rooted in social class. The middle class – those in non-manual occupations – tended to think of themselves as Conservative, while the working class – those in manual occupations – tended to think of themselves as Labour. Over time, the relationship between class and party declined. Nevertheless, in 2015 there were still significant differences. The Conservatives received 44 per cent of the vote from the ABs (those in managerial and professional occupations), 41 per cent from the C1s (clerical occupations, administrators and salespersons), 34 per cent among the C2s (skilled manual workers) and just 28 per cent from the DEs (semi- or unskilled manual workers). Labour received 28 per cent from the ABs, 30 per cent from the C1s, 33 per cent from the C2s and 42 per cent from the DEs.

By historical standards, the relationship between class and party was already weak in 2015, but as Table 8.3 shows, it was even weaker in 2017. The Tory vote among the ABs was just nine points higher than among the DEs, compared with 16 points in 2015. The Labour vote among the DEs was just ten points higher than the ABs, compared with 14 points in 2015. The Tories, moreover, enjoyed a four-point lead among the C2s, the skilled working class.

The most obvious reason for the further weakening of the association between class and vote between 2015 and 2017 was undoubtedly Europe. Working-class voters were far more likely to think that European immigration depressed their incomes and imposed burdens on the public services, as discussed by Paul

Whiteley, Matthew Goodwin and Harold Clarke in Chapter 4. They tended to vote Leave. In 2017 Labour reduced the salience of Brexit by accepting the result of the referendum but Brexit gave the Conservatives an opportunity to claim that Labour had abandoned the working class for a metropolitan elite. This strategy appealed as much to the social conservatism of parts of the working class as anti-immigration feeling, and was partly successful. The Tories gained five seats with high Leave votes: Mansfield, North East Derbyshire, Middlesbrough South and East Cleveland, Stoke-on-Trent South and Walsall North.[21] These gains, however, were far fewer than the Tories had hoped and entirely offset by losses in the southern middle-class seats that had voted Remain. Seats like Battersea and Bristol North West swung to Labour as a result of middle-class Remainers switching from the Tories. Labour's pledge to abolish tuition fees may have also reduced class voting since it was most likely to benefit middle-class children and middle-class parents.

As the association between class and vote waned, that between education and vote increased. As Table 8.3 shows, the Conservative vote peaked at 52 per cent among those with no qualifications, fell to 46 per cent among those with some qualifications and fell to just 33 per cent among graduates. The profile for Labour voters was a mirror image, rising from 35 per cent among the least educated to 39 per cent among those with some qualifications, and peaking at 48 per cent among graduates. These differences in part reflect the fact that older voters were less likely to be educated. They also reflect the fact that the educated were far more likely to vote Remain and were more supportive of an 'open' UK.

Housing continued to play a role in shaping party preferences. The Tories have generally favoured a 'property owning democracy' and Labour has supported social housing. Not surprisingly, therefore, fully 55 per cent of those who owned their own home voted Conservative compared to 30 per cent who voted Labour. Those with a mortgage divided 43 to 40 per cent in the Tories' favour, while social and private renters plumped for Labour. These differences again reflect age and education. Older and better educated people are more likely to own their home. The young are more geographically mobile and likely to rent. Labour's share among private renters leapt from 39 per cent in 2015 to 54 per cent in 2017. Labour's promises to control rents clearly proved attractive to hard-pressed tenants.

Table 8.3 suggests that Labour received slightly more support from women than men. The Tories had a lead of four points among men but were just one point ahead among women. Since women tend to live longer and older voters are more likely to vote Tory, gender-based differences are larger than they first appear. As Meryl Kenny notes in Chapter 6 there was also a striking relationship between gender, age and vote. Labour's support among men aged 18–24 was 16 points, nowhere near as large as its 55-point lead among women of the same age.

Ethnicity also played a visible role in vote choice in 2017. The Conservatives' share of the 'white' vote increased from 39 per cent in 2015 to 45 per cent in 2017.

Labour's share increased from 28 per cent to 39 per cent. The Conservatives' share of the BAME vote, on the other hand, fell from 23 to 19 per cent, while Labour's rose from 65 to 73 per cent. Both groups swung to Labour, though BAMEs swung more. Jeremy Corbyn's reputation as a campaigner on equality may have drawn ethnic minority voters back to Labour. The Conservatives' rhetoric on Europe and immigration may have had the opposite impact.

Austerity and the policy mood

Austerity defined both the Conservative–Liberal Democrat coalition and the post-2015 Conservative governments. The Coalition Agreement promised to reduce the deficit primarily by reducing spending.[22] While the health and overseas aid budgets were protected, all others were subject to cuts. Between 2011 and 2016 the Departmental Expenditure Limits (DELs) for local government were reduced by 51 per cent.[23] The impact of cuts was mitigated by efficiency drives, new working practices and technology. Nevertheless, the scale of the savings meant that frontline services were affected. Many Sure Start centres, designed to support parents back into work, were closed. Other cuts hurt the elderly poor. By 2014, 150,000 pensioners had lost access to help with washing and dressing.[24] The cuts even affected areas traditionally favoured by the Conservatives. The DELs for the Ministry of Justice and Ministry of Defence were cut by 34 and 14 per cent, respectively between 2011 and 2016.[25]

Britons generally support a 'cradle to the grave' welfare state. The British Social Attitudes (BSA) survey has regularly invited people to 'agree' or 'disagree' with the proposition that 'the creation of the welfare state is one of Britain's proudest achievements'. Responses in 2015 were typical: around 57 per cent agreed and a mere 11 per cent disagreed.[26] Those who receive no welfare still benefit from public services.[27] Few people have private health insurance and most rely on the NHS, especially for GP and accident and emergency services. Most people send their children to state-funded schools. Those living in urban areas rely on public transport. Not surprisingly, Britons prefer more spending on these things. The same people, however, pay taxes. Equally unsurprisingly, they prefer lower taxes.

In short, most Britons are ambivalent about the state.[28] They want it to act, to do something about unemployment and to provide high-quality public services and a safety net. They also worry about the consequences of the state doing too much and about high taxes, regulation, bureaucracy and the sapping of incentives and personal responsibility.[29] This ambivalence implies that their preferences about government activity depend, at least in part, on current policy. When policy moves left and governments increase spending and taxes, people come to want less activity than before. When policy moves right and governments reduce spending and taxes, people come to want more activity than before. Policy preferences respond 'thermostatically', moving in the opposite direction to policy.[30]

Between 2010 and 2017 the government's tax and spending policies shifted to the right. Total managed expenditure fell from 45.3 per cent of GDP in 2009–10, to 39.4 per cent of GDP in 2016–17 (see Figure 1.2). Even in those areas where spending was protected, such as the NHS, there was a growing sense that the public services were in crisis. Above-average inflation in the health sector, rising expectations and increased demands resulting from the failure to fund social care added to concerns. A Kings Fund survey in June 2017 reported that 43 per cent of all NHS Trust finance directors were forecasting a deficit.[31] The BSA has regularly asked respondents whether the NHS was getting better or worse over the last five years. In 2009, during Labour's last full year in office, 41 per cent said it was getting better and 19 per cent said it was getting worse, a net score of +21. By 2016, 25 per cent said it was getting better and 36 per cent worse, a net score of -11.[32] Just as in the 1990s, the Tories were associated with social decay. Just as in the 1990s, this cost the party at the polls.[33]

The Conservatives combined public sector spending restraint with cuts in direct taxation.[34] The coalition had adopted the Liberal Democrat policy of progressively raising the personal threshold for income tax from £6,475 in 2009–10 to £10,000 by 2014–15 and then £11,000 by 2017–18.[35] It had also scrapped Labour's top rate of income tax of 50 per cent and introduced a new rate of 45 per cent for those earning above £150,000. Tax cuts simultaneously reduced public concerns about taxation and waste, and raised concerns about public services and inequality.

This 'thermostatic' effect of the Conservative government's policies is clear in the public's changing responses to the same survey questions. From 1983 to 2016, for instance, the BSA has asked respondents whether they preferred to increase or decrease taxes and spending. In 2010, 34 per cent of respondents wanted to increase taxes and spending. This increased year by year until in 2016 support for higher taxes and spending stood at 48 per cent.[36] There were parallel movements on welfare. In 2010 only 30 per cent agreed that the government should spend more on welfare and 64 per cent disagreed, a net score of -34. By 2016, 35 per cent agreed and some 30 per cent disagreed, a net score of +5. There were also movements on attitudes to equality. In 2010 36 per cent agreed that the government should redistribute from the rich to the poor and 36 per cent disagreed, a net score of 0. By 2016 the same figures were 42 per cent and 28 per cent, producing a net score of +14. In each and every case, opinion had clearly moved leftwards.

Movements in public opinion such as these can be aggregated to infer the public's general left–right preferences or 'policy mood'.[37] Figure 8.2 displays the estimated policy mood from 1979 to 2017, using *all* the available data, from *all* sources. Scores above 50 indicate that there are more left than right preferences, and scores below 50 indicate that there are more right than left preferences. A score of 50 represents a perfect balance. From 2010 to 2017 the

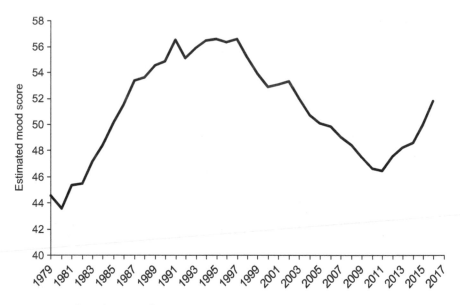

Figure 8.2 The policy mood, 1979–2017
Source: Author's estimates.

mood in Britain clearly shifted leftwards. Moreover, statistical modelling in previous studies suggests the electorate moves left as unemployment increases and
right as spending and direct taxation increases.[38] Had unemployment not fallen
between 2010 and 2017 (see Table 1.2) austerity would almost certainly have
driven the mood even further to the left.

By 2014 the mood was roughly where it had been in 2005, the year of Labour's
third successive election victory. By 2017, it was roughly where it had been in 1999,
just two years after New Labour's triumph. It is, of course, necessary to put these
developments in context. Britain had not become a radically left-wing nation. The
public remained ambivalent about government activity. Aggregate public opinion
evolves slowly. Nevertheless, on issue after issue and year after year, there were
incremental movements in opinion that cumulated to produce a leftwards shift
in mood. This movement directly shifted votes towards Labour, and it indirectly
shifted more by ensuring that Labour's messages on austerity, the public services,
welfare, housing and inequality cut through. By contrast, Conservative arguments
about the need for fiscal discipline had less traction. Not everyone was tired of
austerity but the balance of opinion had shifted in Labour's favour.

Brexit

Although the 2017 general election was not a re-run of the 2016 referendum,
Brexit continued to arouse strong feelings and the parties were sufficiently

Table 8.4 Brexit referendum vote and general election vote, 2017

	Con	Lab	Lib Dem	UKIP	Other	Total
Remain	25.1	49.7	15.2	0.3	9.7	100
Leave	60.9	24.0	3.6	5.5	6.0	100

Source: British Election Study Internet Panel.

distinctive for it to influence individual vote decisions.[39] Of the three major parties, the Conservatives and the Liberal Democrats had the clearest positions. Theresa May repeated her mantra that 'Brexit means Brexit' throughout the campaign. The Liberal Democrats promised a second referendum on any deal. Labour's policy was ambiguous. It accepted the vote for Brexit and that 'freedom of movement will end when Britain leaves the European Union'.[40] It also wanted to retain the benefits of the single market but was wholly vague on whether it wanted to remain inside the single market. Its manifesto simply stated that any deal would 'put jobs and the economy first'.[41]

Table 8.4 shows that support for Brexit divided Conservative and Labour voters. Fully 61 per cent of Leavers voted Conservative in 2017. Almost as strikingly, some 50 per cent of Remainers voted Labour and 15 per cent Liberal Democrat. Nevertheless, large portions of voters cast general election votes at odds with their 2016 referendum vote. One-quarter of Remainers still voted Conservative and one-quarter of Leavers still voted Labour in 2017.

In order to gauge the impact of referendum voting on vote choice in 2017, Table 8.5 uses evidence gathered immediately after the 2015 election, the 2016 referendum and 2017 election. Where referendum voting was aligned with the 2015 vote, voters tended to stay loyal in 2017. Fully 87 per cent of 2015 Conservative voters who voted Leave in 2016 voted Tory again in 2017. Equally, 85 per cent of 2015 Labour voters who voted Remain in 2016 voted Labour in 2017. Where the referendum vote was misaligned with the 2015 vote, people were less loyal. Only 69 per cent of 2015 Tory voters who voted Remain in 2016 stayed loyal in 2017 and only 72 per cent of 2015 Labour voters who voted Leave voted Labour in 2017. Fully 12 per cent of 2015 Conservatives who voted Remain defected to Labour and 12 per cent went to the Liberal Democrats. Among 2015 Labour voters who voted Leave some 18 per cent voted Conservative in 2017 and 2 per cent voted UKIP. The Liberal Democrats picked up a small portion of Labour Remainers, who may have voted for tactical reasons or out of disappointment with Labour's policies. On the whole, however, Labour's ambiguous position on Brexit seems to have been enough to keep potential defectors on board.

The aggregate-level evidence tells a similar story. The estimated Brexit vote in the referendum in 2016 is a powerful predictor of Conservative and Labour vote at the constituency level in 2017 even controlling for previous vote share.[42] The higher the Leave vote in 2016, the higher the Tory vote share

Table 8.5 The impact of Brexit on vote switching, 2015–17

2015 vote	Con	Lab	Lib Dem	UKIP	(N)
Conservative					
Leave	87.4	9.3	1.1	0.8	1,198
Remain	69.4	16.2	11.6	0.2	844
Labour					
Leave	18.3	72.0	3.0	3.7	629
Remain	4.0	85.4	7.4	0.0	1069
Liberal Democrat					
Leave	28.2	21.9	56.3	0.0	124
Remain	9.1	30.2	58.1	0.3	298
UKIP					
Leave	58.5	13.2	2.6	21.4	646
Remain	41.2	8.8	2.9	26.5	34

Source: British Election Study Internet Panel.

a year later and the lower the Labour vote. Although Brexit was less visible in the campaign than many expected, its impact on election night was still clear in the results.

The economy

Elections are shaped by the economic context. Governments are generally re-elected when times are good and ejected when times are bad. Britain's economic performance in 2017 was neither good nor bad. Unemployment had fallen from 8.5 per cent in 2011 to just 4.7 per cent in the first quarter of 2017, a 43-year low (see Table 1.2). Inflation, moreover, was at 2 per cent and interest rates, which had been stuck at 0.5 per cent since March 2009, were cut to just 0.25 per cent in August 2016. Growth and productivity, however, were disappointing.

The economic numbers in 2017 were mixed at best. But whatever the numbers indicated, most people did not feel the economy was getting better. Real earnings remained stubbornly below pre-2007 levels.[43] The headline indicators, moreover, masked changes that made workers feel insecure. The new 'gig economy' left many workers feeling stressed and uncertain. As Britain prepared for Brexit, its labour markets appeared to be moving away from European protectionist models and towards US-style flexibility.

The lingering impacts of the 2007–08 financial crisis and austerity were compounded by the fallout from European referendum. The pound depreciated from 1.45 euros in June 2016 to 1.26 in April 2017, partly as a result of the

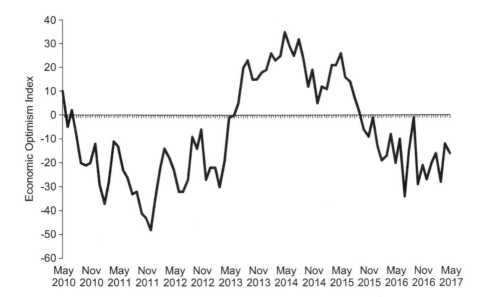

Figure 8.3 Economic Optimism Index, 2010–17
Source: Ipsos MORI.

cut in interest rates and partly because the markets downgraded the country's future worth. Inflation nudged upwards, raising the prospect of interest-rate rises that would further erode real standards of living. Public sector workers had been subject to pay restraint for seven years. They grumbled loudly.

Figure 8.3 displays Ipsos MORI's monthly Economic Optimism Index (EOI) from 2010 to 2017.[44] The index is the difference between the percentage of respondents who expect national economic conditions to get better and the percentage who expect things to get worse. The EOI had dipped below zero under the coalition government but tracked upwards from 2013. The 2015 general election had been fought against the backdrop of improving economic confidence. In April 2015 the EOI stood at +26. The Conservatives' 2015 campaign had made much of their 'long-term economic plan'. This claim, together with the memory that the economy had crashed under Labour, gave the Tories a clear lead over Labour on economic competence in 2015 according to YouGov. The 2017 election, by contrast, was fought against the backdrop of post-referendum uncertainty. In June 2016 the EOI stood at -10 but in July fell to -36. Theresa May's arrival initially led to a burst of economic optimism. The EOI in September 2016 was still negative (-1) but heading upwards. As uncertainty increased, however, optimism declined. In January 2017 the index dipped to -20. Although it rose to -16 in April, it was 42 points below its 2015 level. These developments eroded confidence in the government's economic policies. In March 2015 Ipsos MORI found that 53 per cent of respondents agreed that 'In the long term, this government's policies will improve the state of Britain's economy' and 39 per cent disagreed, a net score of +14. By March 2017 the equivalent figures were 44 per cent and 50 per cent, producing a net score of -6.[45]

The costs of ruling

The general election gave the public the opportunity to pass judgement on the government's record. The Conservatives had been in power from May 2010 until June 2017. They had presided over austerity and had been responsible for their fair share of policy blunders and U-turns. They had reorganised the NHS despite complaining loudly about previous 'pointless' reorganisations.[46] They had introduced the so-called 'bedroom tax' that was said to be responsible for splitting up families. The government found that almost every policy decision – let alone blunder – created a grievance among one group of voters or another. Like all governments everywhere and at all times, it was vulnerable to 'the costs of ruling', the tendency to lose support net of all other factors because it was blamed for everything.[47] In 2015 the Tories had been protected from judgement on its record by its junior coalition partner. In 2015 the Liberal Democrats bore the electoral brunt of public anger and were all but wiped out. By 2017 the Conservatives had to take all the blame themselves.

Figure 8.4 displays net satisfaction with the government – the percentage of respondents saying they were satisfied minus the percentage saying they were dissatisfied – from June 2010 right through to June 2017 as measured

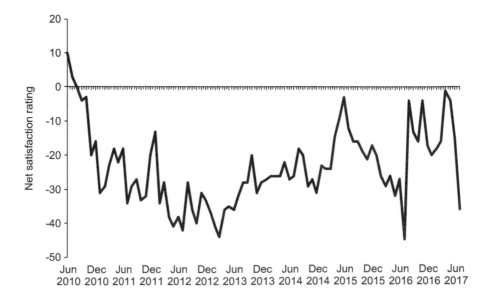

Figure 8.4 Net satisfaction with the government, 2010–17
Source: Ipsos MORI.

by Ipsos MORI.[48] Between 2010 and 2015 levels of net satisfaction broadly corresponded to a well-established pattern: a brief electoral honeymoon, followed by a long trough with consistently low satisfaction and a rally before the general election. The short 2015 parliament displays some of the same U-shaped features. Net satisfaction was relatively high in late 2015 but declined in the spring of 2016 when it averaged -30. This was followed by a sharp fall after the referendum. Satisfaction leaped upwards in August following May's elevation to prime minister. By the time that she had called her snap election net satisfaction was -1. As the government's record came under scrutiny in the campaign, it fell to -15, some four points lower than it had been in May 2015.

It is still possible for governments with negative net levels of satisfaction to win re-election, however. It was no impediment to the Conservatives in 1983, 1987 and 1992. It was no impediment to Labour in 2001 and 2005. Figure 8.5 displays the association between net satisfaction and the government's share of the Labour–Conservative vote – the votes secured by the two main parties of government – in 13 general elections from 1970.[49] Net satisfaction is positively correlated with vote for the governing party: the higher the satisfaction, the higher the expected vote.[50] Figure 8.5 suggests that the Tories' share of the two-party vote in 2017 is pretty much what one might expect given net satisfaction. From this perspective, the Conservatives' share of the two-party vote in 2017 should have come as no surprise.

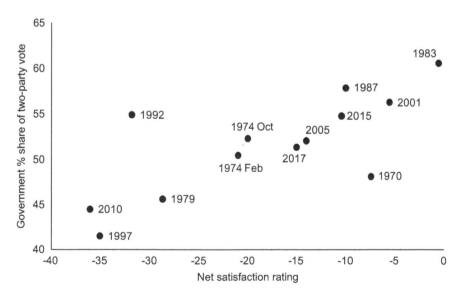

Figure 8.5 Net satisfaction and government's share of the Conservative–Labour vote, 1970–2017

Source: Author's calculations.

Competence and trust

Elections do not simply provide voters with a chance to cast judgements on incumbents – they also provide voters with a choice between competing futures. Both the policies offered to voters and prospective evaluations of competence matter. By April 2017 large portions of the electorate thought that the Tories had a poor record but were still more competent than Labour. This can be simply illustrated by responses to YouGov's regular questions about which party was best able to handle certain problems, such as the NHS, economy and Brexit, and which are reported by Nicholas Allen in Table 1.3.[51] The evidence shows that Labour was generally advantaged on the issues of the NHS and housing, while the Conservatives were advantaged on security issues like law and order, immigration and the economy. Indeed, the Conservatives' lead on the economy actually grew in early 2017, which is striking given the deterioration in the economy. In early January 2017 their lead on this issue was 16 points. By mid-April it had increased to 24 points. Doubts about Labour clearly represented a major source of Tory advantage.

Since the issue of immigration has attracted a lot of attention it is worth noting that the Conservatives were effective in persuading the electorate that they would 'take back control' of the borders. One indicator of the Tories' progress on the issue is provided by responses to a question posed by the BES: 'Would any of the following political parties be successful … in reducing the level of immigration?' Figure 8.6 (below) displays the net score – the percentage saying the party would reduce immigration minus the percentage saying they would not reduce – for both the Conservative and Labour parties over time. The Tories initially struggled to convince on immigration. In April/May 2016 their net score was -51. It was still negative by November/December 2016 but had risen to -33. By April/May 2017 it had risen to -15. Both their embrace of the referendum result and the prime minister's rhetoric about taking back control reduced this negative. Evaluations of Labour, by contrast, did not improve.

Ironically, the Conservative achievement in reassuring more voters that they could control the borders had a less positive effect than it might have. In the run-up to the 2017 election, there was no repeat of the European-wide migration crisis of previous summers and the issue was less visible. Fewer voters thought immigration was 'the most important issue' by the time the Tories had persuaded the electorate that they were taking back control. Their advantage over Labour thus counted for less.

A campaign that mattered

When the prime minister announced she would seek an early election, the Tories were around 20 points ahead in the polls. Labour appeared to be floundering. In the first couple of weeks of the campaign Conservative

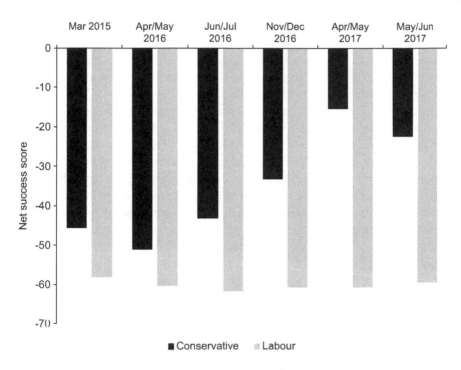

Figure 8.6 Evaluations of Conservative and Labour ability to reduce immigration, 2015–17
Source: British Election Study.

support fluctuated around 46 per cent. From around 14 May it drifted down a little but rallied to around 44 per cent on the eve of the election. Support for Labour, by contrast, started in the mid-20s and trended upwards remorselessly, as shown in Figure 1.5. By late May it had increased to the mid-30s as former Greens, Liberal Democrats, abstainers and Tory Remainers coalesced around Labour. By early June Labour appeared almost to have closed the gap, although the final pre-election polls gave the Tories a lead of eight points. In the event, these final polls understated Labour's share by four points and overstated the Tories' by about two points, massively overestimating the actual 2.4-point lead.

The improvement in Labour's standing over the course of the campaign was the largest ever observed ahead of any general election since polling began in 1945. There does not appear to be any obvious turning point, such as that which was observed in 2010 after the first ever televised prime ministerial debate.[52] The almost if not quite linear trends in both major parties' poll ratings suggest that their vote shares were returning to their long-term levels based on the policy mood, economic conditions and satisfaction with the government's record. There are good reasons for thinking that the campaign had an almost catalytic effect on vote choice.

From 'strong and stable' to 'weak and wobbly'

A great deal of the Conservative campaign was carried on the shoulders of Theresa May. Her elevation to the prime ministership less than a year before had appeared to represent a break with the past, as described by Nicholas Allen in Chapter 1. David Cameron, George Osborne and Michael Gove, the modernising members of the 'Notting Hill set', all left the cabinet, and May pointedly distanced herself government from the 'privileged few'. She promised to protect workers' rights after Brexit and have workers serve on the boards of companies. She even proposed to impose controls on energy prices. The 2017 manifesto declared: 'We must reject the ideological templates provided by the socialist left and the libertarian right and instead embrace the mainstream view that recognises the good that government can do.'[53]

May promised a different style of leadership appropriate to a national emergency. She was described, and liked to think of herself, as a 'bloody difficult woman'.[54] Her pledge to provide 'strong and stable government in the national interest' was repeated *ad nauseam*. The implicit claim was that she was a leader in the mould of Margaret Thatcher, who would bring the warring factions in her own party together, win an election and use her enhanced authority to get the best deal from the EU. This idea was appealing to many worried about Britain's post-Brexit future.

Although May promised change it was slow to materialise. The shift in the policy mood required a loosening of the purse strings. Revealingly, the Tories' most popular manifesto proposal was to increase spending on the NHS by at least £8 billion. This secured 79 per cent support.[55] Nevertheless, the Tories continued to emphasise fiscal prudence. She told a nurse who had not had a pay rise in seven years: 'there's no magic money tree'.[56]

Other polices raised questions about whether the prime minister offered change. Her commitment to lift the ban on new grammar schools was straight out of the Thatcher playbook, offering opportunity to a few gifted children from less advantaged backgrounds. Her promise to allow a 'free vote' on hunting foxes with dogs – an issue that animated a small minority of the landed wealthy – seemed incompatible with the pledge not to govern in the interests of the privileged few. 'Stability' was reassuring if you thought that the country was going in the right direction. It was *not* reassuring if you thought that it was not.

In 2007, following a series of political calamities and policy failures, the Liberal Democrat Vince Cable produced one of the most famous put-downs in British parliamentary history. He said of Gordon Brown, the then prime minister: 'The house has noticed [his] remarkable transformation in the past few weeks from Stalin to Mr Bean, creating chaos out of order, rather than order out of chaos.'[57] Brown's reputation never recovered. Theresa May underwent a similar transformation from April to June 2017, from being 'strong and stable' to 'weak and wobbly'. The immediate cause of her fall in public esteem related to policy. The Conservative manifesto made bold proposals to fund social care that alarmed pensioners. After a few days of token resistance the prime minister announced a U-turn right in the middle of the campaign. This may have not been quite so damaging if it had not followed two other U-turns. The government had backed down on proposals to reform national insurance in the March budget. The prime minister then performed the mother of all U-turns and announced the election. This new U-turn was part of an emerging pattern – and it was at odds with the prime minister's self-image.

Theresa May might have been less damaged by these changes had she admitted to her mistakes. Instead, she tried to maintain her reputation by repeating 'Nothing has changed. Nothing has changed'. A YouGov poll found that while 33 per cent said that U-turns are 'a good sign – showing they [politicians] are willing to listen and change their minds', 37 per cent said that 'U-turns are normally a bad sign – showing they are incompetent, weak, or have not thought their policies through properly in advance'.[58] The week before the manifesto launch a YouGov poll had suggested that 25 per cent thought the Conservative Party had 'lots of policies that seem well thought through' and just 20 per cent thought that they 'have lots of policies, but they don't seem very well thought through'. One week later 12 per cent thought that they had well thought through policies and 32 per cent thought that they did not.

May had promised new policies and a new style of leadership. The new policies were constrained by ideology and inertia. Her leadership was undermined by a tendency to change her mind under pressure. Her preference for carefully controlled media events and her refusal to take part in the televised debates sealed her growing reputation for insecurity. The Conservative Party's advantage on competence nose-dived across every issue from mid-May onwards. So did assessments of May as the 'best prime minister'. Conservative support was shallow indeed.

Despite the failures of her campaign, Theresa May still enjoyed a lead of 12 points over Jeremy Corbyn on the question of who would make the best prime minister (see Figure 1.4). This was lower than the 14-point lead that David Cameron had enjoyed over Ed Miliband two years earlier and far smaller than May's apparent lead in April. The movement in the polls and outcome confirmed that she was not the awesome electoral weapon that she or her advisers assumed. Nevertheless, comparisons of the two leaders in 2017 still probably benefited the Conservatives. Some 93 per cent of Tory voters thought that she would make the best prime minister, compared with just 55 per cent of Labour voters who thought the same of Corbyn.

'Jez we can'

The Labour election campaign began with low expectations. Labour MPs trooped back to their constituencies convinced that they would be hammered at the polls. Some decided to ignore the national campaign and fight on their own records. Many did not extend the customary invitations to their leader to visit their constituency. Jeremy Corbyn was thought to be a handicap rather than a source of appeal.[59]

Despite these forebodings, the first few days of the campaign witnessed a rise of around four points in support for Labour in the YouGov polls.[60] This was simply the result of former Labour voters returning home or anti-Conservative voters shifting to Labour when they realised that their preferred candidate could not win in their constituency. As the campaign wore on the election came to be seen as a two-horse race between the Conservative and Labour parties outside Northern Ireland, including, to some extent, in Scotland. Labour's share in the polls trended upwards. Even campaign gaffes, such as Diane Abbott's inability to cost Labour's policies on policing on 27 April, had no visible impact.

Ironically, given Corbyn's reciprocated antipathy towards Tony Blair, Labour's campaign slogan 'For the many, not the few' was drawn from the new Clause IV of Labour's constitution that Blair had penned. There may have been something of a whiff of New Labour in the central proposition of the party's manifesto that there could be improvements in public services by raising levels of corporation tax and income tax levels on the wealthiest 5 per cent. The pro-posal that corporations and the rich should pay more tax matched the leftward drift in the policy mood. Between 18 and 19 May, YouGov found that 58 per cent supported increasing the top rate of income tax.[61] Another proposal to cap rent rises in line with inflation was supported by 65 per cent. The party's commitments to nationalise the railways, the national grid and water companies were not quite as popular, but still secured the approval of 46 per cent. Proposals to abolish tuition fees were wildly popular with young people and 49 per cent of the public in total supported this proposal.

The manifesto helped to reassure voters abut Labour. At the start of May only 10 per cent of YouGov respondents thought that Labour had 'lots of policies that seem well thought through' and 20 per cent thought they 'don't have many pol-icies and those they do have are not well thought through'. By the end of May these figures had changed to 24 per cent and 10 per cent respectively. This did not represent a transformation but it suggested that Labour was being given a hearing. The popularity of Labour's policies contributed to the reduction in the Conservatives' advantage on competence from mid-May onwards across all issues.

Both the Conservatives and Labour were hampered by their associations with past failures, which made them vulnerable to populist appeals. Theresa May tried to put distance between her and Cameron by claiming to govern on behalf of the 'mainstream' but was hampered by the fact that she had served for seven years in his cabinet. Jeremy Corbyn, on the other hand, was a genuine out-sider. As Thomas Quinn describes in Chapter 2, his elevation to the leadership and the refusal of long-serving Labour MPs to serve in his shadow cabinet resulted in wholesale changes on Labour's frontbench, promoting many people who were neither associated with Blair and New Labour or with the financial crash under Gordon Brown. The public did notice the splits in Labour but these developments enhanced Corbyn's status as an outsider.

Labour's manifesto energised its members. Corbyn's election as leader had presaged a significant boost in Labour's membership to over 500,000 compared with the Tories' 180,000. These new members brought energy and commitment to the business of campaigning. Many had learned how to use social media to mobilise support for Corbyn in the two Labour leadership contests of 2015 and 2016. They now applied these methods to campaign on behalf of Labour in the country. Blogs such as the *Canary* and *Another Angry Voice* churned out arguments to support Labour and rebuttals to counter the pro-Conservative bias of the national press. Younger voters in particular relied on social media for their news and opinions. Those who relied on these sources were, in turn, more likely to vote Labour.[62]

The influx of new members undoubtedly had another positive effect on Labour's campaign: it meant that there were more people to deliver leaflets, canvass potential voters and mobilise the vote. In some places the official Labour campaign was supplemented by contributions from Momentum, the grassroots movement that was formed to support Corbyn. Some of this activity may have duplicated the official Labour campaign so it is difficult to establish its unique impact. For the first two or three weeks of the campaign, moreover, Labour appeared to be on the defensive and focused on consolidating its safe seats. Some Labour MPs ran a campaign that emphasised their constituency service and distanced themselves from the national campaign and their leader. There is tantalising evidence that such MPs fared better when the votes were counted.[63]

The leftward shift of the electorate, the deteriorating economy and the low esteem in which the government was held, together with Labour's policy appeal and the energetic campaigns waged by Labour, led to a rise in evaluations of Labour's competence and Corbyn's personal standing during the campaign. Yet, as noted above, only just over a half of Labour voters reported that he would make the best prime minister. Around one in ten Labour voters reported that Theresa May would make the best prime minister, and around one-third reported either that neither would or that they didn't know. The euphoria that followed the election outcome cannot obscure the fact that evaluations of Corbyn as a potential prime minister held Labour back in 2017.

The electoral system: the other national lottery

The electoral system mechanically translates votes into seats by applying the plurality rule in all the UK's 650 constituencies. This simple rule states that the candidate with the most votes wins. Nevertheless, the way in which it transforms votes into seats at the national level is difficult to predict because so much depends on the geographical distribution of the vote.

The plurality electoral system has been described as 'Britain's other national lottery'.[64] The simplest way to illustrate the weird and wonderful way that it operates is to examine the seats-to-votes (s/v) ratios, i.e. the percentage of seats won by party X divided by the percentage of votes won by the same party. These ratios vary across parties and time. The system penalises parties that have wide but geographically dispersed support. The s/v ratio for the Liberal Democrats, for example, has varied between 0.2 and 0.4. The system generally favours parties that have either geographically concentrated or high levels of support. The s/v ratios for the Tories and Labour, for example, usually exceed 1. The governing party always enjoys a winner's bonus so that its s/v exceeds that of the opposition. In 2017 the s/v ratio was 1.2 for the Conservatives and 1.0 for Labour.

One of the reasons why the s/v ratio was higher for the Tories in 2017 was that the average plurality was 13,423 for seats won by Labour and 12,481 for seats won by the Conservatives. In places like Liverpool and London, Labour piled up massive pluralities in some constituencies. This may be related to Labour's campaign, which initially focused on consolidating their core seats. To be sure, the Conservatives piled up impressive majorities in more rural or gentrified places, such as North East Hampshire, Maidenhead, East Hampshire, North Dorset and Meon Valley. On average, however, the Tory vote was more efficiently distributed than Labour. Other factors such as the number of voters in a constituency and differences in turnout can also influence the s/v, since – other things being equal – it takes fewer votes to win a constituency with fewer voters.[65]

The unpredictable operation of the electoral system in 2017 can be illustrated by comparing it with previous general elections. Figure 8.7 displays the s/v ratio for the party that went on to form the government between 1945 and 2017. The ratio has varied from a low of 1.07 in 1951, to a high of 1.56 in 2005. In principle, therefore, the system could translate 42.3 per cent of the vote into anything from (42.3 × 1.07 =) 45.3 per cent of the seats in the 'worst' year for the governing party to (42.3 × 1.56 =) 66.0 per cent in the 'best' year. In 2017 the s/v ratio was only 1.14 and the Conservatives only obtained 48.5 per cent of seats. In 2015, a Labour lead of 2.8 points in 2005 translated into 355 seats and a majority of 66. In 2017 a similar Tory lead of 2.4 points translated into 317 seats, some nine seats short of an absolute majority.

In short, Theresa May gambled the Conservative Party's 2015 majority on her personal appeal, the weakness of the opposition and the lottery that is the electoral system – and she lost.

The 2017 general election also resulted in the re-establishment of traditional patterns of party competition at the constituency level.[66] Table 8.6 shows which two parties were in first or second place at selected general elections. The traditional pattern is illustrated by 1966. In that election the Conservatives and Labour occupied the top two positions in 574 constituencies. By 2010 this figure had fallen to just 286 seats. From the 1970s onwards, the Liberals and their successors became the second placed competitors in many seats held by the major parties. By 2010 the Liberal Democrats came second in 245 seats held by the Conservatives or Labour. They also won 58 seats. The post-coalition backlash in 2015 left the Liberal Democrats in second place in just 46 seats to the major parties. Labour's revival in 2017 meant that the Liberal Democrat retreat of 2015 was carried forward another two years. The Liberal Democrats

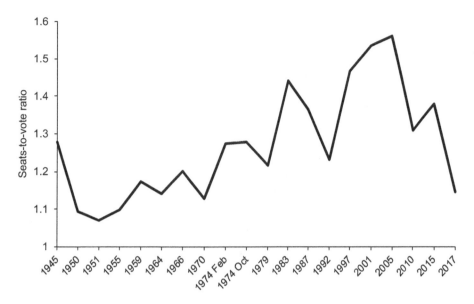

Figure 8.7 The seats-to-votes ratio for the governing party, 1945–2017
Source: Author's calculations.

Table 8.6 The shifting battlegrounds, 1966–2017

First place	Second place	1966	2010	2015	2017
Con	Lab	222	139	207	273
Lab	Con	352	147	169	246
Con	Lib Dem	19	167	46	29
Lib Dem	Con	10	38	4	8
Lab	Lib Dem	7	78	0	7
Lib Dem	Lab	2	16	2	0
Other		18	65	222	87

Note: 'Other' includes both Northern Irish constituencies and the seat won by the Speaker of the House of Commons, traditionally not contested by the main parties.
Source: Based on Ron Johnston, David Rossiter, David Manley, Charles Pattie, Todd Hartman and Kelvyn Jones, 'Coming full circle: The 2017 UK general election and the changing electoral map', *Geographical Journal*, 184 (2018), 100–108. Updated with data from the House of Commons.

came second in just 36 major party seats (29 Tory-held and seven Labour seats). The collapse of UKIP, however, meant that two major parties filled the top two places in 519 seats. Had Scotland not been dominated by competition between unionist parties and the SNP, the circle from 1966 to 2017 would have been complete. Superficially at least, Britain had returned to two-party politics. Future electoral contests look likely to be framed in a different way from now on.

Conclusions

This chapter has sought to explain why the Conservatives lost their majority but still won. Important parts of the story have been covered in other chapters. As John Curtice has shown in Chapter 3 and as Paul Whiteley, Matthew Goodwin and Harold Clarke have shown in Chapter 4, the collapse of the Liberal Democrats from 2010 and UKIP after 2016 meant that that, across most of the UK, the choice effectively boiled down to that of either a Conservative or Labour government. This chapter has showed that the electorate was volatile and up for grabs and that the policy mood had shifted leftwards in response to austerity and tax cuts. The post-referendum economy was subject to uncertainty and the Conservative government had a weak record. The Tories fought a dull and uninspiring campaign, while Labour caught both the policy and anti-system *moods* of the times. The electoral system funnelled this mess of motivations and causes into choices. A broad but shallow electoral coalition was formed out of traditional Labour voters, former non-voters, former Greens, former Conservative Remainers, former Liberal Democrats and Unionist social democrats in Scotland. The electoral system transformed these changes into a hung parliament.

At this point it is perhaps worth remembering that it is always easier to explain (or rationalise) than to predict. All but one of the brave forecasters who put their reputations on the line in 2017 had their fingers burnt.[67] Curiously, none felt the need to incorporate either the policy mood or policy into their forecasting models. Nor did they factor in the impact of the party campaigns. It may well be that the 2017 election is a one-off with little to teach us about elections in general. Yet, if the 2017 election has any lesson for students of British politics, it is surely that policy and unpredictable campaigns can matter. That being so, would-be forecasters are well-advised to heed Winston Churchill's advice to politicians: those seeking to predict election results need 'the ability to foretell what is going to happen, tomorrow, next week, next month and next year. And to have the ability afterwards to explain why it didn't'.[68]

Notes

1　'Statement from Downing Street', 18 April 2017, available at: http://press.conservatives.com/post/159746418610/theresa-may-statement-from-downing-street-18th, last accessed 20 October 2017.

2　Political Studies Association, 'Expert predictions of the 2017 general election: A survey by Stephen Fisher, Chris Hanretty and Will Jennings on behalf of the U.K. Political Studies Association', available at: www.psa.ac.uk/psa/news/expert-predictions-2017-general-election-survey-stephen-fisher-chris-hanretty-and-will, last accessed 24 October 2017.

3　Andreas Murr, Mary Stegmaier and Michael S. Lewis-Beck, 'How did the U.K. election forecasts do?' *Washington Post*, 12 June 2017.

4   Alan Travis, 'Pollsters believe general election is "foregone conclusion"', *Guardian* 18 April 2017.
5   Lukas Audickas, Oliver Hawkins and Richard Cracknell, *UK Election Statistics: 1918–2017*, Briefing Paper CBP7529 (London: House of Commons, 2017).
6   Indeed, it was only exceeded by the performance of the Liberals between 1970 and February 1974.
7   This panel data evidence provides a more reliable indication of the flows than those based on recollections of past vote recorded two years after the first election.
8   Since there were more 2015 Tory voters these cross-currents cancelled each other out.
9   In the referendum campaign by contrast, former non-voters appeared to vote Leave.
10   See Oliver Heath and Matthew Goodwin, 'The 2017 general election, Brexit and the return to two-party politics: An aggregate-level analysis of the result', *Political Quarterly*, 88 (2016), 345–358.
11   Some analysts treat partisan dealignment as a consequence rather than a cause of volatility. See Anthony Heath, Roger Jowell and John Curtice, *How Britain Votes* (Oxford: Pergamon Press, 1985).
12   Ivor Crewe, Bo Sarlvik and James Alt, 'Partisan dealignment in Britain, 1964–74', *British Journal of Political Science*, 7 (1977), 129–190.
13   Nicholas Allen, 'The restless electorate', in John Bartle and Anthony King (eds), *Britain at the Polls 2005* (Washington, DC: CQ Press, 2005).
14   John Lloyd, *What the Media are Doing to our Politics* (London: Constable, 2004).
15   'Statement from Downing Street', 18 April 2017.
16   See Angus Campbell, Philip E. Converse, Warren E. Miller and Donald Stokes, *The American Voter* (New York: Wiley, 1960).
17   David Butler and Donald Stokes, *Political Change in Britain: The Evolution of Electoral Preference* (Basingstoke: Macmillan, 1974).
18   Heath and Goodwin, 'The 2017 general election, Brexit and the return to two-party politics', table 2.
19   Richard Adams, 'Poorest students will finish university with £57,000 debt, says IFS', *Guardian*, 5 July 2017.
20   Heath and Goodwin, 'The 2017 general election, Brexit and the return to two-party politics'.
21   The Leave votes were estimated by Chris Hanretty.
22   HM Government, *The Coalition: Our Programme for Government* (London: Cabinet Office, 2010), p. 15.
23   See Institute for Fiscal Studies, *Recent Cuts to Public Spending*, 1 October 2015.
24   Sally Gainsbury and Sarah Neville, 'Austerity's £18bn impact on local services', *Financial Times*, 19 July 2015.
25   See Institute for Fiscal Studies, *Recent Cuts to Public Spending*.
26   See British Social Attitudes Information System, available at: www.britsocat.com/Home, last accessed 24 October 2017.
27   Anthony King, 'Why Labour won – at last', in Anthony King (ed.), *New Labour Triumphs: Britain at the Polls* (New York: Chatham House, 1998), pp. 177–208.
28   John R. Zaller, *The Nature and Origins of Mass Opinion* (Cambridge: Cambridge University Press, 1992).
29   John Bartle, Sebastian Dellepiane-Avalleneda and James A. Stimson, 'The policy mood and the moving centre', in Nicholas J. Allen and John Bartle (eds), *Britain at the Polls 2010* (London: Sage Publications, 2011), pp. 147–174.

30 Stuart Soroka and Christopher Wlezien, *Degrees of Democracy* (Cambridge: Cambridge University Press, 2009).

31 The Kings Fund, *Quarterly Monitoring Report*, June 2017.

32 British Social Attitudes, 2016.

33 King, 'Why Labour won – at last', p. 197.

34 VAT was increased from 17.5 to 20 per cent in George Osborne's first 'emergency' budget in 2010.

35 HMRC, 'Income tax rates and allowances: Current and past', available at: www.gov. uk/government/publications/rates-and-allowances-income-tax/income-tax-rates-and-allowances-current-and-past, last accessed 24 October 2017.

36 See National Centre for Social Research, *British Social Attitudes 34*, available at: www.bsa.natcen.ac.uk/latest-report/british-social-attitudes-34/key-findings/a-backlash-against-austerity.aspx, last accessed 24 October 2017.

37 James A. Stimson, *Public Opinion in America: Moods, Cycles and Swings* (Boulder: Westview Press, 1999).

38 John Bartle, Sebastian Dellepiane-Avalleneda and James A. Stimson, 'The moving centre: Preferences for government activity in Britain, 1950–2005', *British Journal of Political Science*, 41 (2011), 259–285.

39 John Bartle and Ben Clements, 'The European issue and party choice at British general elections, 1974–2005', *Journal of Elections Public Opinion and Parties*, 19 (2009), 377–411.

40 Labour Party, *For the Many Not the Few* (London: Labour Party, 2017), p. 28.

41 Labour Party, *For the Many Not the Few*, p. 24.

42 Heath and Goodwin, 'The 2017 general election, Brexit and the return to two-party politics'.

43 Larry Elliott, 'Unemployment is at its lowest since 1975, so why do people feel worse off?' *Guardian*, 17 May 2017.

44 Ipsos MORI, 'Economic Optimism Index (EOI): State of the economy 1997 – present', available at: www.ipsos.com/ipsos-mori/en-uk/economic-optimism-index-eoi-state-economy-1997-present, last accessed 24 October 2017.

45 Ipsos MORI, 'Ipsos MORI March 2017 political monitor', available at: www.ipsos. com/sites/default/files/migrations/en-uk/files/Assets/Docs/Polls/pm-mar-2017-topline.pdf, last accessed 24 October 2017.

46 Anthony King and Ivor Crewe, *The Blunders of Our Governments* (London: Oneworld Books, 2013).

47 See Peter Naanstead and Martin Paldam, 'The costs of ruling', in Han Dorussen and Michael Taylor (eds), *Economic Voting* (London: Routledge, 2002), pp. 17–44.

48 Ipsos MORI, 'Political monitor: Satisfaction ratings 1997-present', available at: www.ipsos.com/ipsos-mori/en-uk/political-monitor-satisfaction-ratings-1997-present, last accessed 24 October 2017.

49 The data from 1970 to 2001 are from Gallup and relate to approval. This wording tends to produce very similar results to 'satisfaction'.

50 The two outliers that don't quite fit the general pattern are 1970 and 1992, two elections that are associated with polling errors when the satisfaction ratings may have been biased. I am grateful to Will Jennings for this suggestion.

51 See YouGov, 'Best party on issues (GB)', available at: https://d25d2506sfb94s. cloudfront.net/cumulus_uploads/document/dggt8iprh5/YG%20Trackers%20-%20Best%20Party%20On%20Issues_W.pdf, last accessed 20 October 2017.

52 Bartle *et al.*, 'The policy mood and the moving centre'.
53 Conservative Party, *Forward Together: Our Plan for a Stronger Britain and a Prosperous Future* (London: Conservative Party, 2017), p. 7.
54 On 5 July 2016, Kenneth Clarke and Malcolm Riftkind, two senior Tory MPs, were recorded describing the prime minister in these terms.
55 Matthew Smith, 'How popular are the parties' policies?', *YouGov*, 22 May 2017, available at: https://yougov.co.uk/news/2017/05/22/how-popular-are-parties-manifesto-policies/, last accessed 24 October 2017.
56 Lizzie Dearden, 'Theresa May prompts anger after telling nurse who hasn't had pay rise for eight years: "There's no magic money tree"', *Independent*, 3 June 2017.
57 House of Commons Debates, volume 468, 20 February 2016, col. 275.
58 YouGov, 'YouGov survey results, 22–23 May 2017', available at: https://d25d2506sfb94s.cloudfront.net/cumulus_uploads/document/tv10mdfqm9/InternalResults_170523_Manifestos_W.pdf, last accessed 5 November 2017.
59 Kate McCann, 'Labour MPs reject Jeremy Corbyn's manifesto as Theresa May warns the party has "abandoned" working class', *Daily Telegraph*, 12 May 2017.
60 Labour support rose from 24 points on 19 April to 29 points by 26 April.
61 Smith, 'How popular are the parties' policies?'
62 Harold Clarke, Matt Goodwin, Paul Whiteley and Marianne Stewart, 'How the internet helped Labour at the general election', *BBC News*, 23 September 2017, available at: www.bbc.co.uk/news/uk-politics-41349409, last accessed 5 November 2017.
63 See Justin Fisher, *The Impact of Constituency Campaigning on the 2017 General Election* (London: Brunel University, 2017).
64 Stuart Weir and David Beetham, *Power and Democratic Control in Britain* (London: Routledge, 1999).
65 See David Rossiter, Ron Johnston, Charles Pattie, Danny Dorling, Iain Mcallister and Helen Tunstall, 'Changing biases in the operation of the UK's electoral system, 1950–97', *British Journal of Politics and International Relations*, 1 (1999), 133–164.
66 Ron Johnston, David Rossiter, David Manley, Charles Pattie, Todd Hartman and Kelvyn Jones, 'Coming full circle: The 2017 UK general election and the changing electoral map', *Geographical Journal*, 184 (2018), 100–108.
67 The exception is YouGov. Its model forecast the election outcome accurately from about two weeks out. Whether this was because its methods were correct or it was lucky is not yet clear.
68 Samuel Brittan, 'The irresistible folly of crystal gazing', *Financial Times*, 4 January 2001.

9

A coalition of chaos

Where next?

Rosie Campbell

Pity the author of the final chapter of *Britain at the Polls, 2017*! When the invitation to write the 'what next' chapter was first extended and accepted in early May 2017, it seemed as if such a chapter could almost write itself. At the time the Conservatives looked set for a landslide victory. Theresa May's decision to call an early general election was then thought to be a splendid idea by her party, and a cunning plan by almost everyone else. There was little need for the author to waste time thinking about how a government would be formed or the implications of any post-election deal for the Northern Irish peace process. Instead, it was necessary only to consider how the seemingly inevitable victory would enhance the prime minister's authority and enable her to mould her party more in her image, and further to reflect on how the election might strengthen the UK's position in the forthcoming Brexit negotiations. After all, the general election was supposed to be about producing 'strong and stable government', overcoming the 'division in Westminster' and making 'a success of Brexit'. That, at least, was the prime minister's idea.[1]

The country, it appears, had other ideas. The electorate – with the assistance of the electoral system – produced an outcome that no one had anticipated or – with the exception of the ever-vigilant civil service – seriously prepared for. In one of the most astonishing turnarounds in British political history, the Conservatives ended up falling just short of an overall majority, as John Bartle explains in Chapter 8. Having earlier warned against the prospects of a hung parliament – one in which no party has an overall majority of MPs – and a Labour-led 'coalition of chaos', Theresa May was now compelled to make arrangements for leading a minority government. Initial plans for this chapter had to be set aside: they had no more relevance than the Conservative manifesto.

The indecisive outcome of the election meant that the chapter would now have to pay considerable attention to the business of how the new government cobbled together a deal to ensure its survival and to the prime minister's immediate prospects. Would she even last a month in office? It would also have to examine how a severely weakened government would deal with, and be affected by, two difficult issues that loom so large they are not so much elephants in the room, but extremely unpleasant and hairy mammoths squashing everyone so severely that it is impossible for the room's inhabitants to think of anything else. How they are resolved will shape British politics for decades to come; they are austerity and Brexit.

The first of these mammoth issues, the future of austerity, would probably not have concerned Theresa May had she won the election with an enlarged majority. Although the Conservative Party had tried to attract working-class support by promising, among other things, to 'make Britain a country that works for everyone', the prime minister would probably have continued broadly with the economic strategy laid down under George Osborne and continued under Philip Hammond.[2] The second mammoth challenge, negotiating and implementing Brexit, would have confronted the prime minister even if she had won an emphatic victory, but she could still have faced it from a position of greater strength. There is little doubt that a resounding victory would have greatly enhanced her personal standing and ability to negotiate a deal.

Another initial plan for the chapter also fell by the wayside: how, if at all, a routed Labour Party would move on from its electoral humiliation. So great was the anticipated Tory landslide that it was not unreasonable to think that Britain might come to resemble a dominant-party system, at least in England. Instead, the outcome of the 2017 general election – in which both the Conservatives and Labour increased their shares of the vote – seemed to represent some-thing of a return to the 'traditional' two-party system associated with British politics in the 1950s and 1960s.[3] Yet, there are good reasons for thinking this apparent return to the old system is illusory. If recent experience is any guide – as reflected in the 'shock' outcomes of the 2015 and 2017 general elections, the 2016 Brexit referendum and even the election of Donald Trump in the United States – forecasting the future is extremely hazardous.[4] The road to the next election is likely to be treacherous for all the players. Indeed, the post-election landscape has not looked so uncertain since 1974, when two elections produced a hung parliament and then a Labour government with a wafer-thin majority.[5] Foolhardy indeed would be the author who sought to predict the future with any air of certainty. Set against this backdrop, the present chapter seeks simply to take stock of where we are now. It offers a broad overview of the complicated and changing post-election landscape, the options open to the various actors, particularly the incumbents, and the multiple challenges they face.

Forming the new government

The 'first-past-the-post' electoral system is justified in part on the basis that it usually manufactures single-party majority governments from plurality vote shares. In 2017, however, the Conservatives won only 317 out of 650 seats,

while Labour won 262 seats, the Scottish National Party (SNP) 35 and the
Liberal Democrats 12. Among the minor parties, the Northern Irish Democratic
Unionist Party (DUP) won ten seats and its Republican counterpart Sinn Féin
seven, while Plaid Cymru won four seats in Wales and the Green Party retained
one seat in Brighton. To add further complexity, one Independent Unionist was
elected in Northern Ireland. Finally, the election also saw the re-election of John
Bercow, the Speaker of the House of Commons, whose seat is traditionally not
contested by the main parties.

Formally, any party seeking to form a government needed at least 326 seats
to secure an overall majority. The Conservatives were comfortably the largest
party but fell nine seats short of this total. In practice the Tories were closer
to the finishing line than that because Sinn Féin, which refuses to recognise Westminster's sovereignty over Northern Ireland, would not take its seats
in the Commons. Their seven MPs could thus be removed from the parliamentary arithmetic, as could the Speaker and also three Deputy Speakers, who are
expected to withdraw from a party-political role.[6] All of this meant that, in effect,
the Tories needed 320 votes to ensure a working majority in the Commons.[7] It
was not altogether obvious how this number could be reached. Hung parliaments
and coalition governments are rare at Westminster. By convention and custom,
whenever there is a hung parliament the incumbent government remains in
office until the prime minister tenders his or her resignation, which means, in
practice, if or when it is clear that there is an alternative government ready to
take its place.[8] The last hung parliament in Britain occurred as recently as 2010,
when Gordon Brown continued in office as prime minister until it was clear that
the then Conservative David Cameron leader would almost certainly be able to
command the confidence of the Commons through a deal with Nick Clegg's
Liberal Democrats. Only then did Brown step down. Otherwise there were few
recent precedents. From 1945 until 2010, only one other general election, the
February 1974 contest, resulted in a hung parliament – and this ushered in a
brief period of minority Labour rule until Harold Wilson called another election
in the autumn.

The outcome of the 2010 election was somewhat different to that of February
1974. The opposition Conservatives had won 306 seats, making them comfortably the largest party, while the incumbent Labour government won just 258
and the Liberal Democrats 57. The remaining 29 seats were shared across several other parties. The prospect of a full-blown coalition government was now
very much on the cards, and it was one that was likely to involve the Liberal
Democrats: they could either form a majority two-party coalition with the
Conservatives or a minority coalition with Labour. Of these, the first option was
always more likely, partly because of the contemporary economic uncertainty
and need for a stable government, partly because Labour was discredited as the
losing party, partly because of the partial policy convergence between the Tories
and the Liberal Democrats, and partly because of the personal preferences of
the parties' respective leaders.[9]

After several days of negotiations, including some tentative discussions with Labour, the Liberal Democrats agreed to join a Conservative-led coalition. A formal agreement was soon drawn up, which detailed their shared programme for government.[10] Five Liberal Democrat ministers entered the cabinet, including Clegg as deputy prime minister, and all parties would be bound by the normal rules of collective cabinet responsibility. The Liberal Democrats seemingly did rather well in terms of policy. The coalition was committed to its policies of increasing the personal allowance for income tax, the pupil premium for spending on schools and a referendum on the Additional Vote.[11] In electoral terms, however, joining the coalition proved catastrophic for the Liberal Democrats, as John Curtice explains in Chapter 3. The party lost 49 of its 57 seats in the 2015 general election, and the Tories went on to win a majority. The whole experience was a poor advertisement for smaller parties thinking about joining any future coalition government. Indeed, at the start of the 2017 campaign, Tim Farron, Clegg's successor as leader of the Liberal Democrats, pledged that his party would not be a part of any coalition; although, given the shrunken size of his parliamentary party and the anticipated Tory landslide, his promise did not cause anyone to lose much sleep.

On Friday 9 June 2017, once all the results had been declared, it was clear that only the Conservatives were in a realistic position to form a government. With the Liberal Democrats recusing themselves, Labour could not have matched the Conservatives' numbers even if Jeremy Corbyn had been able to strike an almost impossible deal with all other parties. Theresa May immediately confirmed her intention of remaining in office, as was her right, but the Conservatives would still need to find some way of guaranteeing a majority for crucial parliamentary votes, especially on any confidence motions. The prime minister would need to assemble something approximating her own 'coalition of chaos'.

With all other parties either programmatically or politically out of bounds – including Labour and the SNP – or arithmetically unhelpful – everyone else – all eyes turned immediately to Northern Ireland and the DUP, the UK's other centre-right party.[12] Its ten votes would be just enough to guarantee an absolute majority in the Commons and enable the Tories to govern. This tiny party – previously ignored by most of the British media – found itself unexpectedly the subject of Conservative advances.

At this point, a brief description of Northern Irish politics and its distinctive party system is probably in order.[13] Northern Ireland was formed in 1921 after the island of Ireland was partitioned by the Government of Ireland Act 1920. For the next 50 years, Northern Ireland enjoyed a large amount of political autonomy – what today is called 'devolution' – until direct rule was re-imposed by London in response to the 'troubles' and mounting sectarian violence. A combination of Northern Ireland's history, politics and semi-detached status cultivated the emergence of a party system that was dissimilar to that in the rest of the United Kingdom.[14] Although Britain's Conservative, Labour and Liberal Democratic parties effectively had sister parties in Northern Ireland – the

Ulster Unionist Party (UUP), the Social and Democratic Labour Party (SDLP) and the Alliance Party respectively – they were always separate organisations. Moreover, the return of devolution to Northern Ireland after the 1998 Good Friday Agreement fuelled a shake-up in Northern Irish party politics. The SDLP, the moderate voice of the largely Catholic Nationalist community, was gradually supplanted by the more hardline Sinn Féin, while the UUP was gradually supplanted as the voice of the largely Protestant Unionist community by the more hardline DUP. Against expectations, the DUP and Sinn Féin were able to govern together in a power-sharing executive from 2007 until 2017.

The relationship between the Conservatives and the DUP is interesting, to say the least. Historically the Tories were allied to the UUP, who lost their last Westminster seats in 2017. Being on the centre right, the Conservatives and the DUP share some values, especially their strong commitment to unionism and the maintenance of the United Kingdom of Great Britain *and* Northern Ireland. But they also have strikingly different positions on many social issues.[15] To be sure, many Tories support 'traditional' values and are socially conservative when it comes to women's rights and gay rights, but the party leadership is now firmly on the liberal side of these debates. The DUP, on the other hand, continues to oppose same-sex marriage and the extension of the Abortion Act 1967 – which legalised abortions elsewhere – to Northern Ireland. Because of the its social conservatism, a number of equality rights groups expressed serious concerns that the DUP would demand retrogressive legislation that would seek to impose its values on England and Wales. However, Arlene Foster, the leader of the DUP, gave early assurances that the party would make no demands relating to these matters of conscience.

The Conservatives eventually concluded what is known as a 'confidence and supply' deal with the DUP. A similar arrangement, the so-called 'Lib-Lab pact', had sustained the Labour Party in power from March 1977 to September 1978, and it had then carried on as minority government until March 1979, when it lost a vote of confidence.[16] The DUP would not enter into government, in the way the Liberal Democrats had done so in 2010, and would not be bound by the doctrine of collective responsibility. Instead, they committed themselves only to supporting the government in key parliamentary votes: on explicit motions of confidence, as defined by the Fixed-term Parliaments Act 2011; on the Queen's speech and government's legislative programme; on the budget, as well as finance and money bills; on legislation necessary for national security; and, crucially, on legislation pertaining to Brexit.[17] Otherwise, the DUP made no commitment to voting with the government. Support for other votes would need to be brokered as and when necessary.

The deal took nearly three weeks to agree. Its specific form – a confidence and supply arrangement – can be explained by several factors. For a start, the Tories had no particular wish to share seats around the cabinet table with another party. The prime minister was a tribal politician with limited knowledge or understanding of parties beyond her own, and was known to have been unenthusiastic about working with the Liberal Democrats after 2010. Second, and related, the Northern-Ireland focused DUP had no particular wish to have a seat in government and share responsibility for UK government; and their small numbers gave them limited bargaining power in any event. Third, entering into government would probably have wrecked the Good Friday Agreement, which neither party particularly wanted. At the same time, the Tories wanted a formal agreement, rather than a more informal understanding, in order to maximise the government's stability; the alternative, negotiating a series of ad hoc deals or informal compromises of the kind that John Major's government struck with the UUP in the 1990s, would have been unstable and potentially distracting.[18]

In other jurisdictions, such as in Germany and the Netherlands, the process of government formation can take months. To many Britons, accustomed to rapid changes of power and the drama of removal vans lining up in Downing Street, three weeks seemed like an eternity.[19] Questions were inevitably asked about why it was taking so long and if some shoddy deal was being cooked up behind voters' backs. In the event, the DUP did very well in financial terms. The deal that was hammered out entailed £1.5 billon in transfers to Northern Ireland to support various infrastructure projects.[20] During the election campaign, when Theresa May had been asked by a nurse about ending the public sector pay cap, she had replied: 'there is no magic money tree'. This phrase, like her warnings of a 'coalition of chaos', rebounded on her in the media coverage of the DUP deal with the tree's apparent unearthing, many were quick to point out that the magic money tree had been found alive and well, and had bestowed its bounty on those living in Northern Ireland. For their part, the Tories were obliged to abandon their manifesto plans to introduce means-testing for the winter fuel allowance and to downgrade the 'triple lock' that protected state pensions (see Nicholas Allen in Chapter 1).

The deal with the DUP allowed Theresa May to stagger on as prime minister. She could claim, not unreasonably, that while she had lost her party's majority, she had nonetheless presided over a dramatic increase in its share of the vote. She could also claim, perhaps a little less reasonably, that she still possessed the experience and skills required to negotiate Brexit. She could also have claimed – but she did not, at least not explicitly – that she was responsible for the mess and had to own it. More generally, May owed her continued occupation of 10 Downing Street to the fact that there was no obvious successor in her party. Potential challengers like the foreign secretary, Boris Johnson, were mindful of the aphorism 'he who wields the knife never wears the crown'. For as long as there was no agreed-upon candidate to replace her, May was safe. In this sense the gravely weakened prime minister resembled the hole in the roof of Rome's Pantheon: like that empty space, she could still stop the rest of the dome, her government, from collapsing. However, while her party had no wish for a costly and divisive leadership election, May's weakened position meant a challenge could never be ruled out. Her ability to reshuffle her cabinet – and thus discipline her ministers and promote her allies – was severely constrained, and she would ever after be forced to balance carefully the Leavers and Remainers in her government. In short, she was left extremely vulnerable: any resignations could well undermine her ability to continue in post.

The deal with the DUP also came with political costs. At one level, almost everyone in her party was furious that she had had to strike such a deal in the first place. At another level, she risked alienating voters in other parts of the UK. The financial benefits delivered to the people of Northern Ireland would not be matched by support to people in the other devolved regions. This inconsistency could cause significant political tensions, not least in Scotland where the SNP could be relied upon to use it as another grievance against the Westminster government. At yet another level, the deal also angered those who felt aggrieved by the government apparently buying itself a lifeline. Almost inevitably, such feelings were particularly strong among those still smarting against the outcome of the 2016 referendum and the Conservatives' embrace of a 'hard' Brexit. In the wake of the deal, Gina Miller, the campaigner who had successfully initiated the court case requiring the government to secure parliamentary approval before triggering Article 50 of the Lisbon Treaty – the formal notification that Britain would leave the EU – wrote to the government threatening legal action.[21] Government lawyers rejected her complaint but conceded that any increase in spending in Northern Ireland – like all spending commitments – would require parliamentary approval.

The deal also had implications for the Northern Ireland peace process, which, since 1993, has been predicated on the British government's declaration that it had 'no selfish strategic or economic interest in Northern Ireland'.[22] One of the authors of the 'Downing Street Declaration', former Conservative prime minister, John Major, subsequently went public with his fears about what might happen if the government were seen to be taking sides in Northern Irish politics.[23] Two former Labour Northern Irish secretaries, Paul Murphy and Peter Hain, also expressed concerns that the deal would undermine the British government's ability to sustain its claim to impartiality.[24] It was certainly a bad time in Northern Irish politics to be doing anything that might compromise that claim. Since January 2017, the Northern Irish power-sharing executive had been in suspension following an environmental-subsidy scandal involving the DUP leader Arlene Foster and a breakdown in the relationship between her party and Sinn Féin. Fresh elections in March had failed to break the deadlock.

One specific commitment in the deal, the full implementation of the largely symbolic Armed Forces Covenant to Northern Ireland, was particularly problematic. In the rest of the UK, this covenant is a relatively uncontroversial pledge. Formalised in 2011, it asserts that both government and wider society should support former members of the armed forces and treat them fairly and consistently. In Northern Ireland, however, the armed forces are viewed somewhat differently by the Unionist and Nationalist communities.[25] In the past, those on the Unionist side tended to see the army as their protector from Republican terrorists, while those on the Nationalist side, and especially those on its Republican wing, tended to see it as the enemy. Some Republicans had even fought against – and had friends and family killed by – the armed forces. The DUP, representing the Unionist community, had long argued that the covenant was not being fully implemented in Northern Ireland and were in favour of its full extension. Sinn Féin, representing Republican and Nationalist sentiment, were not in favour. By re-emphasising their commitment to the covenant, the UK government took a clear side on what is a sensitive issue for both communities.

It is clear that even though the Conservatives' deal with the DUP was largely based on raising public expenditure in Northern Ireland, it has at least the potential to undermine an already precarious political situation there. It remains to be seen, of course, how long the deal holds. For the time being, it is in the DUP's interests to prop up the Conservative government – but circumstances back in Belfast could change and potentially require a rethink. More generally, the DUP's interests and support for the government are likely to be shaped by wider circumstances, not least the two mammoth challenges of austerity and Brexit. Both of these will have a significant impact on the government's immediate prospects. It is to the first of these challenges that we now turn.

The austerity mammoth

Austerity is the first of our two mammoths that the new government and the other parties must confront. Austerity was the Conservative's prescription for the British economy in the aftermath of the 2007–08 financial crisis and subsequent 'great recession'. The crisis was triggered by the discovery of high-risk or 'sub-prime' mortgages wrapped up in American financial products marketed as low risk.[26] The trouble soon spread to Britain, where there was a run on a number of banks that were exposed to these risks, most notably Northern Rock. The Labour government responded with effective but costly bailouts – including taking some institutions, such as the Royal Bank of Scotland and Lloyds TSB, into public ownership.[27] The financial crisis caused a massive contraction in lending and a 'credit crunch'. With the government stumping up so much cash, Britain was confronted with a massive structural deficit, where public spending commitments would continue to outstrip tax receipts well into the future.

The Conservatives under David Cameron and George Osborne responded to the crisis by arguing that the Labour government had failed to 'fix the roof whilst the sun was shining' (conveniently forgetting that they had, to that point, promised to match Labour's spending plans). Cameron and Osborne advocated a series of swingeing cuts to public spending. They were not, however, the only ones to respond in this way. Despite their subsequent anti-austerity rhetoric, neither Labour nor the Liberal Democrats promised lollipops and ice cream for everyone. The authoritative Institute for Fiscal Studies described Labour's

2010 spending promises as amounting to the biggest retrenchment in govern-ment expenditure since the IMF crisis of the 1970s.[28] The Liberal Democrats also accepted the need for cuts and became full parties to austerity after joining the coalition in May 2010.

Whether Tony Blair and Gordon Brown's governments could have done more to protect Britain from the crash by restricting public spending has been the subject of fierce debate. Certainly, their government's light-touch regulation of the banking sector was criticised by a broad range of commentators.[29] In political terms, however, what mattered was that the mud stuck to Labour. The Tory-led coalition initially escaped censure. A 2011 ICM poll for the *Guardian* showed that 30 per cent of respondents blamed the economic slow-down on 'debts Labour racked up' compared to 24 per cent who blamed coalition cuts.[30]

The policy of austerity had a severe impact on many Britons' quality of life. By 2017 many public sector workers had effectively gone without a pay increase for nine years, and some welfare benefits had been cut substantially. Before the financial crisis foodbanks were almost unheard of in Britain. By 2017 there were over 2,000.[31] Moreover, while key public services, such as the NHS and schools, were protected from cuts, investment was still insufficient to meet rising demands. Consequently, many services were struggling, while those areas left unprotected, such as social care, were very badly hit.

The 2017 Conservative manifesto continued to support austerity, alongside sev-eral policies aimed at struggling families. Labour's 2017 manifesto, *For the Many, Not the Few*, no longer advocated moderating the cuts, as it had done in previous elections, but challenged austerity head on and promised greater investment in public services.[32] Labour's success, relative both to prior expectations and its perform-ance in the 2010 and 2015 elections, intensified the pressure on the Conservatives to moderate their plans. Many commentators and politicians interpreted Labour's appeal in 2017 as a belated reaction to ten years of cuts and misery.[33]

There is evidence that the public's attitudes to austerity have changed. Since 1983 the British Social Attitudes survey has regularly asked respondents to choose from among three courses of action open to the government: 'Reduce taxes and spend less on health, education and social benefits', 'Keep taxes and spending on these services at the same level as now' or 'Increase taxes and spend more on health, education and social benefits'. Responses to this question are displayed in Figure 9.1. The pattern of responses reveal a clear 'social desir-ability bias': few select the option of reducing taxes and spending. The balance of support for increasing taxes and spending and keeping taxes and spending at the same level is more informative. Under the Conservatives from 1983 to 1997, the public were more likely to choose increased taxes and spending over the status quo. Then, under Labour from 1997 to 2010, preferences began to shift. From 2006 to 2015 the proportion favouring the status quo exceeded the pro-portion wanting taxes and spending to be increased. The gap steadily narrowed until, by 2016, more people (48 per cent) wanted tax and spending increases than wanted them to stay as they were (44 per cent).

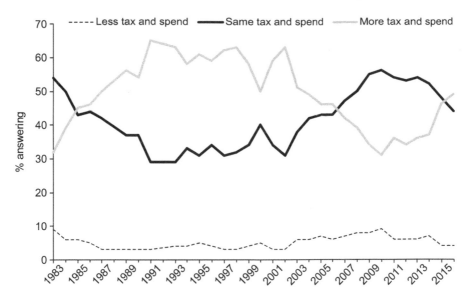

Figure 9.1 Public attitudes to taxes versus public spending, 1983–2016
Source: British Social Attitudes.

For reasons explained by John Bartle in Chapter 8, this shift is likely to continue unless there is a change of policy. It also adds to the pressure on the
Tories to loosen the purse strings. Less than a week after polling day, opposition to austerity found a new impetus in the public response to the Grenfell
Tower tragedy: a fire ripped through a London high-rise block, killing around
80 people and injuring over 70. At least some of the blame was soon focused
on cuts to local housing authorities' budgets. A more immediate pressure on
the Tories to loosen the purse strings comes from the DUP, which is opposed
to some austerity measures. A number of DUP figures have hinted that they
would act as a 'brace against hard austerity'.[34] Several other factors also make
the Conservatives' continued commitment to austerity look shaky. Labour's
unexpectedly good electoral performance led some Conservatives to question
whether persisting with severe spending cuts is either in Britain's economic or
their party's electoral interests. Theresa May's precarious position also makes
the government vulnerable to demands from 'big beasts' within the cabinet,
such as Boris Johnson, who have an eye on the leadership and are willing to
spend in order to curry favour with others.

Just two months after the election, the government announced the partial
lifting of the 1 per cent cap on public sector pay rises, including for the police
and prison officers.[35] While the chancellor of the exchequer, Philip Hammond,
conceded that the public was 'weary' of austerity, he remained adamant that
increasing public borrowing was not the solution.[36] Public sector net borrowing
in 2017–18 was forecast to be £58 billion or 2.9 per cent of GDP.[37] It was
forecast to fall to £17 billion or 0.9 per cent of GDP by 2021–22. Free-market

Conservatives undoubtedly view taxation and spending as too high. It is an article of faith for them that left to their own devices, markets will deliver prosperity. More pragmatic Tories, on the other hand, view the evidence for this assertion more sceptically and may be rather more willing to trim policy.

The Tories' internal debate about the size of the state, like Brexit, represents a fault line that threatens the government's stability. If continuing with cuts produces growth, the government may receive an electoral boost. If cuts produce sluggish growth of the kind observed since 2010, the Tories may be punished for both failing to improve the public services and presiding over a deteriorating economy. The government's fate will depend on this key economic judgement. It will also depend on luck. As the financial crash and credit crunch proved, governments are extremely vulnerable to developments in the global economy. And, if many economists are right, the other mammoth challenge presently facing the government – Brexit – may flatten the economy.

The Brexit mammoth

To say that Brexit is the second mammoth issue facing the government, parties and the country is something of an understatement; it is certainly the biggest and heaviest beast. The ramifications of extricating Britain from the EU are colossal.

On 29 March 2017 Theresa May triggered Article 50 of the Lisbon Treaty, signalling Britain's intention to leave the European Union. Article 50 sets out how member states can quit the EU and provides for a two-year process. Unless there is massive pressure to halt the process from the public, Britain will leave the EU on 29 March 2019.[38] Such a change of opinion by voters seems highly unlikely: there is little evidence of widespread 'Bregret'. Opinion polls suggest that a majority of voters continue to believe that the outcome of the referendum should be honoured.[39] Although the occasional poll provides a small glimmer of hope for Remainers, any shift in public opinion would need to be far larger and sustained over a prolonged period if it were to induce the government to halt Britain's departure from the EU.

Masses of legislation will need to be passed as a result of Brexit, and new bodies created to take the place of EU regulators. But before the task of building the post-EU legislative infrastructure can be completed, a deal with the EU needs to be thrashed out. The EU has so far resisted negotiations on any post-Brexit deal until a 'divorce settlement' is agreed to cover the UK's share of ongoing liabilities. This is likely to be costly and thus politically sensitive. Moreover, negotiating with an organisation made up of 27 member states is not straightforward. It took Canada seven years to conclude a free-trade agreement with the EU.[40] The UK hoped to complete the same task, along with many others – such as negotiating common security policies and agreeing immigration procedures – in just two years.

Given the breadth and complexity of negotiating Brexit, it is probable that there will need to be a transition period in which EU rules continue to apply to the UK. Theresa May has described such a period as an 'implementation phase' and has suggested that two years should suffice.[41] Any whiff of delay involves risks, however. Hard Brexiteers in her own party and elements of the right-wing press are ready to cry 'betrayal' at the mention of transition arrangements. The election was almost certainly meant to free her from the influence of such groups, but it has made her more vulnerable to their machinations. If there is no deal, Britain risks a 'cliff edge' departure from the EU in 2019. In these circumstances, it would have to revert to World Trade Organization (WTO) tariffs in its trade with the EU, and some travel agreements could cease to operate. Most business leaders dread this prospect, although some – such as the vacuum-cleaner entrepreneur Sir James Dyson – agree with May's pre-election claim that 'no deal is better than a bad deal'.[42] They see such an outcome as an opportunity to embrace cheap imports from the rest of the world, and they believe that competition will act as a spur to greater efficiency even if some fail.

The pro-Brexit minister presently responsible for exiting the EU, David Davis, has said that Britain is ready for no deal, even if it is not the most desirable outcome. For a deal to be secured, several contentious issues still need to be resolved, including the size of the divorce bill, the fate of EU nationals living in the UK and of British citizens living in the EU, and the delicate matter of the border between Northern Ireland and the Republic of Ireland. Theresa May signalled her willingness to compromise on some of these issues in a major speech in Florence in October 2017, but the biggest EU players, Germany and France, were still not satisfied with the size of the proposed financial settlement.[43]

The government's difficulties in delivering Brexit are not limited to managing negotiations with the EU, however; they are supplemented, indeed exacerbated, by parliamentary considerations. On the one hand, MPs will be extremely busy over the coming years as they pass Brexit-related legislation. There will be plenty of opportunities to delay or obstruct these laws. On the other hand, most MPs, including Tories, were Remainers and would prefer a soft Brexit. The numbers are thus generally against any government pursuing a hard Brexit or flirting with a 'no deal' outcome. Furthermore, there is an electoral incentive for the other Westminster parties, with the exception of the DUP, to undermine the government. A drawn-out process of government defeats and amendments may be imminent. The Conservatives will be keen to avoid a repeat of the delay and strife that accompanied Parliament's ratification of the Maastricht Treaty in the early 1990s.[44] Far from resolving the issue, as David Cameron wished, the outcome of the referendum has created new conflicts. The Tories are still 'banging on' about Europe.

Finally, the Conservatives' pledge to 'take back control' of the UK's borders in the general election campaign may create tensions with their new partners in the DUP.[45] This party's position on Brexit is complex. It supported Brexit in the referendum but is concerned about the impact of leaving the EU on agricultural subsidies. The DUP is also opposed to a hard border with its southern neigh-bour because of its likely impact on the Northern Irish economy. It is far from clear how the Conservatives can reconcile their pledge to the UK electorate with the concerns of the DUP. It is clear, however, that pushing all the Brexit legisla-tion through Parliament will almost certainly be a gruelling experience.

The other parties

For the time being the mammoth issues of austerity and Brexit are pressing issues for the Conservatives. It is they who will have to take immediate respon-sibility for them. But their actions will not take place in a vacuum; they will have regard to the behaviour of the other parties, beginning with Her Majesty's Official Opposition.

For the left of the Labour Party, the 2017 general election was both a vindi-cation and a cause for celebration. Both the campaign and the result radically altered Jeremy Corbyn's standing in the party. For the first two years of his lead-ership he teetered on the edge of one leadership challenge after another. After Labour's surprisingly good performance in the election, however, he was virtu-ally unassailable. For many centrist Labour MPs, on the other hand, the election results were dreadful. The 9.5 point increase in the party's vote share and net gain of 30 seats laid bare their claim that Labour could not win under Corbyn. Some Labour MPs would have preferred to have seen the party lose ground, providing them with an opportunity to mount a successful leadership challenge. Instead, many were forced to admit that Corbyn had fought an effective cam-paign, and were obliged to demonstrate support for him. The left was now firmly entrenched in the party hierarchy. Corbyn also succeeded in making it more likely that another leader from the left would replace him by lowering the threshold for any aspiring leader: 10 per cent of MPs and MEPs are now needed to nominate a candidate in any future leadership election. As Thomas Quinn points out in Chapter 2, the lower number of parliamentary nominations required by candidates and the composition of the Labour membership means that the next leader will almost certainly be of a similar stripe to Corbyn. Until then, the idea of prime minister Corbyn is no longer a preposterous idea but a serious possibility.

Under Corbyn the Labour Party has also pivoted on the issue of austerity. Two decades ago, Tony Blair and Gordon Brown strove to transform Labour's reputation for economic mismanagement and for pursuing 'tax and spend' pol-icies. Ed Miliband's 2015 manifesto, though considerably less austere than the Conservative's, continued to accept spending cuts. The 2017 Labour mani-festo made some big spending promises and also pledged to increase taxes on corporations and on the incomes of the top 5 per cent of earners. In the euphoria that followed the 2017 election, it was forgotten that confusion reigned over whether Labour had promised to repay all existing student loans. Although moderates in the party remain cautious about making un-costed spending commitments, Labour is still less divided on austerity than the Conservatives, if only because it is always easier to argue for extra spending from the opposition benches.

The issue of Brexit is a far larger challenge for the Labour Party than austerity since its supporters are hugely divided on the issue. In 2017 the party managed to present two mutually exclusive visions of Brexit: it accepted withdrawal to the delight of many of its working-class, less educated, northern and older voters; and it advocated a softer Brexit to the delight of many of its middle-class, educated, southern and younger supporters. There are common interests between these two groups, such as addressing the housing crisis and underfunding in the NHS, but there are also diverging interests over the role of immigration in the economy and Britain's place in the world. Corbyn is widely suspected of being at heart a 'Lexiteer' – a left-wing advocate of withdrawal from the EU – and of viewing the EU as a neoliberal club designed to suppress workers' wages. In the referendum campaign he publicly but unenthusiastically campaigned to remain in the EU. This ambiguity was electorally helpful in 2017, with working-class Leave voters sticking with Labour, and younger Remain voters in wealthier areas also turning to the party. Whether these disparate groups of voters can be held together remains an open question. The wider party, including its many new pro-Corbyn members, are mostly Remainers, which is likely to put pressure on the party to push for a soft Brexit. In turn, Labour will be vulnerable to accusations that it is 'soft' on immigration.

Of the other British political parties, few, other than the DUP, had much to celebrate after the election. The Liberal Democrats had hoped to see a surge in support from Remain voters, as John Curtice describes in Chapter 3, but this did not materialise. The party made only marginal gains, adding just four seats to its 2015 tally of eight and losing Sheffield Hallam, its former leader Nick Clegg's seat. Such is the party's predicament that Clegg later urged voters to join Labour or the Conservatives to stop Brexit from happening.[46] After Tim Farron stepped down as leader, the Liberal Democrats elected Sir Vince Cable in his place. Cable, a former business secretary in the coalition government, regained the Twickenham seat he had lost in 2015. Cable is a well-known and popular figure, not least because of his performances on the BBC television programme *Strictly Come Dancing*. He will certainly need quick feet if he is to resurrect the party's fortunes.

UKIP, the party that achieved the third highest vote share in 2015 – 12.6 per cent – had an even worse 2017 general election than the Liberal Democrats. As Paul Whiteley, Matthew Goodwin and Harold Clarke describe in Chapter 4, the party won just 1.9 per cent of the vote and was left with no seats at Westminster and seemingly little opportunity to resurrect its fortunes. Thanks to Brexit, the UK will not participate in the 2019 European Parliament elections, something that would have given UKIP a platform. The party has had five different leaders (including two acting leaders) since Nigel Farage stepped down in the wake of the 2016 EU referendum and remains riven with infighting. Given that UKIP's purpose was to secure Britain's exit from the EU it is hard to imagine that it will achieve significant levels of popular support again. Any delays in the Brexit process may give the party and its latest leader a chance to reach out to former Leave voters. Otherwise, UKIP faces the prospect of becoming a marginal and potentially more radical party.

For the Scottish Nationalists, 2017 was the first electoral setback in a decade: they lost 21 of the 56 seats won in 2015. As Robert Johns describes in Chapter 5, the issue of the union is now the key electoral divide in Scotland. This divide helped the Conservatives – the principal champion of unionism and now the main rival to the SNP – to increase from one to 13 their MPs north of the border. The SNP's leader and Scotland's first minister, Nicola Sturgeon, remains popular, but the SNP is facing increasing scrutiny and criticism. Having made the transition from a party of protest to a party of government, it now finds itself subject to 'the costs of ruling'. If the SNP can continue to project itself as the successful defender of the Scottish interest, it will prosper. The Conservatives' deal with the DUP, not to mention the economic consequences of Brexit, may also provide it with a grievance to exploit.

The party system

The British party system is now both more changeable and difficult to predict than it has been since the early twentieth century, when the creation of the Labour Party challenged the existing two-party system.[47] The irony, of course, is that the 2017 election appeared to put recent history into reverse. After 40 years of increasing fragmentation, Britain appeared to make a bold leap back to two-party politics.[48]

For most of the period after the Second World War, politics in the UK could be largely explained with a simple two-party narrative.[49] The Conservative and Labour parties were the institutions that defined politics. The electoral pendulum swung between them on a pretty much uniform national swing. There was little regional variation, with the exception of Northern Ireland, and there was a close relationship between class identity and party support: approximately two-thirds of working-class voters supported Labour and around two-thirds of middle-class voters supported the Conservatives.[50] These social cleavages were associated with different values and were institutionalised in trade unions and other social organisations such as the churches. This class-equals-party model of British politics began eroding in the 1970s as society became increasingly differentiated by other factors, including housing tenure, sector of employment, region and lifestyle.[51] The rise of nationalist parties in Scotland, and to a lesser extent in Wales, disrupted the national pattern. The Liberal Democrats gained ground as the two major parties either vacated the centre or failed to deliver in

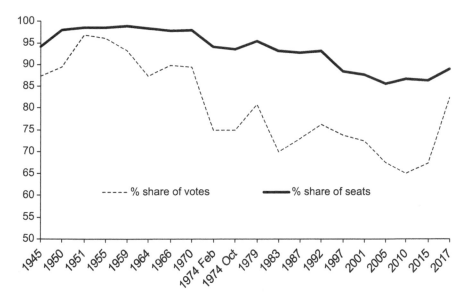

Figure 9.2 Conservative and Labour combined vote and seat share, 1945–2017
Source: House of Commons.

office.[52] Between February 1974 and 2010, the British party system arguably resembled a two-and-a-half party system with the Liberal Democrats gaining between 14 and 23 per cent of the vote, though this translated into a far smaller proportion of the seats in the Commons.

In 2015, the SNP's resounding success in Scotland and UKIP's high vote share led some people to ask whether the UK had finally become a multi-party system. Although the combined Conservative and Labour vote share of 67.3 per cent was comparable to the 65.1 per cent they obtained in 2015, the Liberal Democrats' demise and the surge in support for the SNP and UKIP suggested a radical departure from usual patterns. The 2017 election, however, saw yet another change. The SNP's share of the vote plummeted from 50 to 37 per cent in Scotland, and UKIP was virtually obliterated everywhere. The combined Conservative and Labour vote share increased to 82.4 per cent, the highest two-party vote since 1970 (see Figure 9.2). And, in 519 out of the 650 individual contests, the Conservative and Labour candidates were ranked in the top two places.[53]

It is far too early to proclaim the return of a stable two-party system, however. For a start, the two-party vote share is still below the levels of the 1950s. Second, Scotland, Northern Ireland and, to a lesser extent, Wales retain highly distinctive party systems. The devolved institutions and their more proportional voting systems will ensure that parties such as Plaid Cymru, as well as the SNP, continue to enjoy a permanent base outside of Westminster. The circumstances of the 2017 general election were also uniquely favourable to the two largest parties: the Liberal Democrats were still reeling from their participation in the coalition, and UKIP had lost its purpose after securing a vote for Brexit.

Above all, the electoral system corralled many voters in 2017, often unwillingly, into supporting one or other of the two major parties. British party politics in the immediate post-war period were underpinned by both class and partisan alignment. As John Bartle shows in Chapter 8, class differences all but disappeared in 2017. To be sure, this was partly due to Brexit, but class dealignment was evident well before that election, and there are few grounds for believing that it will return to the levels seen in the 1960s.[54] Emotional attachments to parties are also both less prevalent and far weaker than before. Voters are simply more willing to shop around and switch their loyalties than they were in the immediate post-war period.

As the EU referendum revealed, British voters are now divided not just along economic lines but by social values and by attitudes to immigration and the wider world. These divisions, moreover, often cut across traditional left–right divides. There is a profound sociological and geographical basis to these new fissures. People living in economically declining post-industrial areas exhibit markedly different attitudes to those living in prosperous areas with high-skill employers such as tech companies and universities.[55] In the 2017 election, participation was higher in Remain-leaning constituencies and those with greater numbers of young people, ethnic minorities and graduates in the population. In these circumstances, it is extremely difficult for either of the two major parties to offer 'catch-all' programmes.

A related challenge facing the parties is how to address the growing generational divide in British politics. Soaring house prices, particularly in the South East of England, have excluded many young people from entering the property market. According to the Office for National Statistics, 67 per cent of 25–34-year-olds were homeowners in 1991, yet by 2014 this figure had dropped to just 36 per cent.[56] Meanwhile, younger people, especially graduates, are increasingly burdened by debt. A generation ago, many students could expect to receive a maintenance grant to cover half their living costs and a small student loan to cover the rest. Their university tuition fees would also be paid for by the state, leaving them with only a few thousand pounds of debt at the end of their studies. Two generations ago, students' grants covered all their living costs and some even reported sending money from their grant home to mum. Much has changed since the initial introduction of tuition fees in England in 1998, and their dramatic increase in 2012. According to the Institute for Fiscal Studies, average student debt today is well over £50,000.[57]

The behaviour of younger voters – defined as those aged 18 to 40 years – was an important factor in the 2017 general election, just as the behaviour of older voters was decisive in the vote to leave the EU in the 2016 referendum.[58]

While – contrary to the initial polling evidence – the youngest members of this group were no more likely to vote than in 2015, those aged 24–40 did turn out in larger numbers. To be sure, these voters were still less likely to vote than older voters – but, when they did, they tended to vote Labour.[59] This development has challenged the political orthodoxy. It can no longer be assumed that the best strategy is to focus on the grey vote. The Conservatives in particular must respond to this challenge before a generation of young voters are lost to them and before their older voters literally die off.

To repeat a point already made, the sociological basis to the various divides in British politics makes it extremely difficult for either of the two political parties to design effective vote-winning programmes. The success of the two major parties has always depended on building coalitions of different voters. But their coalitions are coming under ever more strain. The Conservatives are divided not only on social issues but on the future of the economy post-Brexit. Their successful hoovering up of UKIP voters has alienated significant factions of their own voters, including many of their wealthy, more cosmopolitan, supporters. Labour may be less divided by social values but is certainly divided over Brexit. Its uneasy coalition of middle-class and more traditional working-class voters are being pulled in different directions.

After the EU referendum there was much speculation and some activity around the possible formation of a break-away party from Labour as part of a realignment of the centre. Despite the chatter, nothing materialised. The electoral system remains a daunting hurdle for any new party. Above all, the fate of the ultimately unsuccessful Social Democratic Party in the 1980s provides a lesson about the costs of division in a plurality voting system.[60] For centrists whose goal is to be in government, creating a new third party is not an attractive offer. Meanwhile, proponents of a new 'progressive alliance' of left-wing parties – Labour, the Liberal Democrats, the Greens and so on – also face the same problems facing the Labour Party.[61] They still need to find ways of accommodating Brexiters and Remainers and of reaching out to older and younger voters.

It may turn out that the 2017 election was a 'critical election' in which voters realigned themselves into two blocks in support of one of the major parties.[62] It is more likely, however, that the unique confluence of events in 2017 – specifically the ongoing weakness of the Liberal Democrats, the collapse of UKIP and Labour's ambiguous approach to Brexit – artificially inflated the two-party vote. It might easily decline at the next election with a different configuration of party positions, and further exogenous shocks, because it is not sustained by deeply held party identities. The first-past-the-post electoral system tends to incentivise two-party voting, at least regionally, but UKIP demonstrated the rapid effect a new party can have in a system where party loyalties are diminished. There is no reason to think that smaller parties may not continue to have similar impacts in the future. What comes next for the party system is anyone's guess.

Notes

1   'Statement from Downing Street', 18 April 2017, available at: http://press. conservatives.com/post/159746418610/theresa-may-statement-from-downing-street-18th, last accessed 20 October 2017.

2   'Statement from Downing Street'.

3   Paul Webb, *The Modern British Party System* (London: Sage, 2000).

4   See for example Philip E. Tetlock, *Expert Political Judgment: How Good is It? How Can We Know?* (Princeton: Princeton University Press, 2017).

5   See Howard R. Penniman (ed.), *Britain at the Polls: The Parliamentary Elections of 1974* (Washington, DC: American Enterprise Institute, 1975).

6   When they do vote – and only when there is a tie – the Speaker and Deputy Speakers are expected by convention to cast their vote in support of the status quo.

7   This is derived as follows: first, the seven Sinn Féin MPs, the Speaker and the three Deputies are subtracted from 650, giving a total of 639. This number is then divided in half, which equals 319.5. Or, in other words, 320 MPs will always be able to out-vote the remaining 319.

8   For the closest thing to a constitutional guide, see Cabinet Office, *The Cabinet Manual: A Guide to Laws, Conventions and Rules on the Operation of Government* (London: Cabinet Office, 2011), pp. 14–15.

9   Philip Norton, 'The politics of coalition', in Nicholas Allen and John Bartle (eds), *Britain at the Polls 2010* (London: Sage, 2011), pp. 242–265.

10 HM Government, *The Coalition: Our Programme for Government* (London: Cabinet Office, 2010).

11 Thomas Quinn, Judith Bara and John Bartle, 'The UK coalition agreement of 2010: Who won?', *Journal of Elections, Public Opinion and Parties*, 21 (2011), 293–312.

12 Jonathan Tonge, Maire Braniff, Thomas Hennessy, James W. McAuley and Sophie Whiting, *The Democratic Unionist Party: From Protest to Power* (Oxford: Oxford University Press, 2014).

13 Jonathan Tonge, *Northern Ireland: Conflict and Change* (London: Routledge, 2001).

14 The Tories, unusually for a UK party but in keeping with their own unionist values, have fielded their own candidates in recent Northern Irish elections, though they attract derisory levels of support.

15 Tonge *et al.*, *The Democratic Unionist Party*.

16 Jonathan Kirkup, *The Lib-Lab Pact: A Parliamentary Agreement* (Basingstoke: Palgrave Macmillan, 2016).

17 See Prime Minister's Office, *Confidence and Supply Agreement between the Conservative and Unionist Party and the Democratic Unionist Party* (London: Prime Minister's Office, 2017).

18 See David Butler and Dennis Kavanagh, *The British General Election of 1997* (Basingstoke: Palgrave Macmillan, 1997).

19 On the link between polling day and government formation, see Anthony King, *The British Constitution* (Oxford: Oxford University Press, 2007), pp. 58–60.

20 Prime Minister's Office, *Confidence and Supply Agreement*.

21 Heather Stewart, 'Tory-DUP £1bn payment needs parliament's approval after Gina Miller challenge', *Guardian*, 11 September 2017.

22	This quote is taken from 'The Downing Street Declaration', which was issued on 15 December 1993 by John Major, then British prime minister, and Albert Reynolds, then Taoiseach (Irish prime minister), on behalf of the British and Irish governments.

23	Rajeev Syal and Peter Walker, 'John Major: Tory-DUP deal risks jeopardising Northern Ireland peace', *Guardian*, 13 June 2017.

24	Peter Hain, 'A deal with the DUP will be painful for Theresa May, and put peace at risk', *Guardian*, 12 June 2017.

25	As in Chapter 5, the use of a capital 'N' and 'U' when referring to 'Nationalists' and 'Unionists' in this chapter is quite intentional. In this case, Nationalism and Unionists refers specifically to those parties in Northern Ireland who campaign either for the reunification of Ireland and an end to British sovereignty, or for the continued division of the island and retention of British sovereignty.

26	Michael Moran, Sukhdev Johal and Karel Williams, 'The financial crisis and its consequences', in Nicholas J. Allen and John Bartle (eds), *Britain at the Polls 2010* (London: Sage Publications, 2011), pp. 89–119.

27	Alistair Darling, *Back from the Brink: 1000 Days at Number 11* (London: Atlantic Books, 2012).

28	Institute for Fiscal Studies, *Filling the Hole: How do the Three Main UK Parties Plan to Repair the Public Finances?* (London: Institute for Fiscal Studies, 2010).

29	For a full discussion see Moran *et al.*, 'The financial crisis and its consequences'.

30	Tom Clark and Nicholas Watt, 'Confidence in economy at lowest since 2008 crash – poll', *Guardian*, 21 November 2011.

31	Patrick Butler, 'Report reveals scale of food bank use in the UK', *Guardian*, 29 May 2017.

32	Labour Party, *For the Many, Not the Few: The Labour Party Manifesto 2017* (London: Labour Party, 2017).

33	Polly Toynbee, 'This is Corbyn's moment: He's rescued Britain from the chains of austerity', *Guardian*, 12 June 2017.

34	Henry McDonald and Jessica Elgot, 'DUP promises to use pact with Conservatives to tone down austerity', *Guardian*, 16 June 2017.

35	Rajeev Syal and Anushka Anthana, 'Public sector pay cap: May "recognises sacrifices of workers"', *Guardian*, 4 September 2017.

36	Tom Peck, 'Philip Hammond hints at end to austerity as he admits public are "weary" of cuts', *Independent*, 3 July 2017.

37	See Figure 1.1 on p. 10 of the present volume.

38	The Lisbon Treaty contains provisions to extend the two-year period. Article 50.3 reads: 'The Treaties shall cease to apply to the State in question from the date of entry into force of the withdrawal agreement or, failing that, two years after the notification referred to in paragraph 2, unless the European Council, in agreement with the Member State concerned, unanimously decides to extend this period.'

39	Anthony Wells, 'Majority favour pushing on with Brexit – but many are tempted by a softer path', YouGov, 15 June 2017, available at: https://yougov.co.uk/news/2017/06/15/majority-favour-pushing-brexit-many-are-tempted-so/, last accessed 5 November 2017.

40	Christopher Hope, 'Canada's trade deal with the EU will form the basis for Britain's Brexit deal', *Daily Telegraph*, 17 September 2017.

41　Sebastian Payne, 'Theresa May marks the end of "no deal is better than a bad deal"', *Financial Times*, 22 September 2017.

42　Toby Meyjes, 'Sir James Dyson says Brexit with no deal will hurt Europe more than Britain', *Metro*, 14 September 2017.

43　Payne, 'Theresa May marks the end of "no deal is better than a bad deal"'.

44　See Hugo Young, *This Blessed Plot: Britain and Europe from Churchill to Blair* (Basingstoke: Macmillan, 1998).

45　Simon Jenkins, 'Without Irish unification, a hard Brexit is impossible', *Guardian*, 4 August 2017.

46　Rajeev Syal, 'Nick Clegg urges voters to join Labour or Tories to keep UK in EU', *Guardian*, 5 October 2017.

47　Paul Adelman, *The Decline of the Liberal Party, 1910–1931* (London: Longman, 1995); Ross McKibbin, *The Evolution of the Labour Party, 1910–1924* (Oxford: Oxford University Press, 1974); Martin Pugh, *The Making of British Politics, 1867–1939* (Oxford: Blackwell, 1982); Alan R. Ball, *British Political Parties: The Making of a Modern Party System* (London: Macmillan, 1981).

48　John Elledge, 'Why are we back in a two-party system?' *New Statesman*, 6 July 2017; Andreas Whittam Smith, 'After three decades of splintering, two-party politics is back – sort of', *Independent*, 9 June 2017.

49　Webb, *The Modern British Party System*.

50　David Butler and Donald Stokes, *Political Change in Britain: The Evolution of Electoral Preference* (London: Macmillan, 1974).

51　Ivor Crewe, Bo Sarlvik and James Alt, 'Partisan dealignment in Britain, 1964–74', *British Journal of Political Science*, 7 (1977), 129–190.

52　Jack H. Nagel and Christopher Wlezien, 'Centre-party strength and major party divergence in Britain, 1945–2005', *British Journal of Political Science*, 40 (2011), 279–304.

53　See Table 8.6 on p. 185 of the present volume.

54　Crewe *et al.*, 'Partisan dealignment'.

55　Will Jennings and Gerry Stoker, 'Tilting towards the cosmopolitan axis? Political change in England and the 2017 general election', *Political Quarterly*, 88 (2018), 359–369.

56　Office for National Statistics, 'UK perspectives 2016: Housing and home ownership in the UK', 25 May 2016, available at: https://visual.ons.gov.uk/uk-perspectives-2016-housing-and-home-ownership-in-the-uk/, last accessed 5 November 2017.

57　Chris Belfield, Jack Britton, Lorraine Dearden and Laura van der Erve, 'Briefing Note (BN211): Higher Education funding in England: Past, present and options for the future', Institute for Fiscal Studies, 5 July 2017, available at: www.ifs.org.uk/publications/9334, last accessed 5 November 2017.

58　See Oliver Heath and Matthew Goodwin, 'The 2017 general election, Brexit and the return to two-party politics: An aggregate-level analysis of the result', *Political Quarterly*, 88 (2016), 345–358.

59　See Chris Prosser, Ed Fieldhouse, Jane Green, Jonathan Mellon and Geoff Evans, 'The myth of the 2017 youthquake election', available at: www.britishelectionstudy.com/bes-impact/the-myth-of-the-2017-youthquake-election/#.WnMdJk1LGUk, last accessed 1 February 2018.

60 Ivor Crewe and Anthony King, *SDP: The Birth, Life and Death of the Social Democratic Party* (Oxford: Oxford University Press, 1995).

61 Peter Walker, 'Labour's block on Tory-limiting alliance a "betrayal", says Lucas', *Guardian*, 2 May 2017.

62 Pippa Norris and Geoffrey Evans, 'Introduction: Understanding electoral change', in Geoffrey Evans and Pippa Norris (eds), *Critical Elections: British Parties and Voters in Long-term Perspective* (London: Sage Publications, 1999), pp. xix–xl, at p. xxxi.

Appendix: Results of British general elections, 1945–2017

Election	Turnout	Percentage of popular vote						Seats in the House of Commons					Government majority
		Con	Lab	Lib	Nats	Other	Swing	Con	Lab	Lib	Nats	Other	
1945	83.9	39.7	47.7	9.0	0.2	3.4	-12.2	210	393	12	0	25	147
1950	82.6	43.3	46.1	9.1	0.1	1.4	2.6	298	315	9	0	3	6
1951	76.8	48.0	48.8	2.6	0.1	0.6	1.0	321	295	6	0	3	16
1955	78.7	49.6	46.4	2.7	0.2	1.1	2.0	345	277	6	0	2	59
1959	77.1	49.4	43.8	5.9	0.4	0.6	1.2	365	258	6	0	1	99
1964	75.8	43.3	44.1	11.2	0.5	0.9	-3.2	304	317	9	0	0	5
1966	72.0	41.9	47.9	8.5	0.7	1.0	-2.6	253	364	12	0	1	97
1970	78.8	46.4	43.0	7.5	1.7	1.5	4.7	330	288	6	1	5	31
1974 Feb	72.8	37.8	37.2	19.3	2.6	3.2	-1.4	297	301	14	9	14	None
1974 Oct	76.0	35.7	39.3	18.3	3.4	3.3	-2.1	277	319	13	14	12	4
1979	72.7	43.9	36.9	13.8	2.0	3.4	5.3	339	269	11	4	12	44
1983	75.3	42.4	27.6	25.4	1.5	3.1	3.9	397	209	23	4	17	144
1987	77.7	42.2	30.8	22.6	1.7	2.7	-1.7	376	229	22	6	17	101
1992	71.4	41.9	34.4	17.8	2.3	3.5	-2.0	336	271	20	7	17	21
1997	59.4	30.7	43.2	16.8	2.5	6.8	-10.0	165	418	46	10	20	178
2001	61.4	31.6	40.7	18.3	1.8	7.7	1.8	166	412	52	9	20	166

2005	65.1	32.4	35.2	22.0	2.2	8.2	3.1	198	355	62	9	22	65
2010	66.2	36.1	29.0	23.0	2.2	9.7	5.0	306	258	57	9	20	77
2015	68.8	36.8	30.4	7.9	5.3	19.6	-0.4	330	232	8	59	21	11
2017	72.8	42.3	40.0	7.4	3.6	6.6	-2.1	317	262	12	39	20	None

Source. House of Commons Library Briefing Paper CBP7529, *UK Election Statistics: 1918–2017*. 'Lib' refers to the Liberal Party (1945–79), the Liberal–SDP Alliance (1983–87) and the Liberal Democrats (1992–2017). 'Nats' refers to the SNP and Plaid Cymru. 'Swing' refers to the Butler swing and compares the results of each election with the results of the previous election. It is calculated as the average of the Conservatives' percentage gain and Labour's percentage loss compared to the previous election. A positive sign denotes a swing to the Conservatives, a negative sign denotes a swing to Labour. The Labour Party formed a minority government after the February 1974 election, just as the Conservatives did in 2017. The Conservatives and the Liberal Democrats formed a coalition government after the 2010 election. The Speaker is excluded when calculating the size of the government majority.

Index